HIGH INCOME CONSULTING

How to Build and Market
Your Professional Practice

Tom Lambert

NICHOLAS BREALEY
PUBLISHING

LONDON

First published by
Nicholas Brealey Publishing Limited in 1993
156 Cloudesley Road
London N1 0EA

© Tom Lambert 1993
The right of Tom Lambert to be identified as the
author of this work has been asserted in accordance
with the Copyright, Designs and Patents Act 1988.

ISBN 1 85788 0307
ISBN 1 85788 0358 Pbk

British Library Cataloguing in Publication Data
A catalogue record for this book is available from
the British Library.

DTP by Book Production Services, Norfolk
Printed and bound in Finland by
Werner Söderström Oy

Contents

iv

High Income Consulting
CHAPTER FLOW CHART

EXECUTIVE SUMMARY

INTRODUCTION
* Build and maintain profitable practice
* Reader profile
* How to use book

PART ONE - BUILDING THE PRACTICE

CHAPTER 1 #
* Assessing the opportunity

CHAPTER 2 #
* Establishing Your Practice

CHAPTER 3
* The Consultancy Process

CHAPTER 4
* Networking for Synergy

CHAPTER 5
* Business-winning Proposals

CHAPTER 6
* Profitable Fee Setting

CHAPTER 7
* The Consultancy Contract

\# Experienced readers may wish to skim
these two chapters which are aimed mainly
at the needs of newcomers to the profession

PART TWO - MARKETING THE PRACTICE

CHAPTER 8
* Tactical Marketing
* Building Reputation and Image

CHAPTER 9
* Marketing with a Brochure

CHAPTER 10
* Advertising for Professionals

CHAPTER 11
* Winning Referrals

CHAPTER 12
* Personal Selling for Professionals

PART THREE - ADVANCED SKILLS

CHAPTER 13
* Consultant roles and responsibility

CHAPTER 14
* Intervention strategies

CHAPTER 15
* Consultancy standards

CHAPTER 16
* Recognising and Avoiding Problems

APPENDICES
and
CONSULTANT TOOLKIT

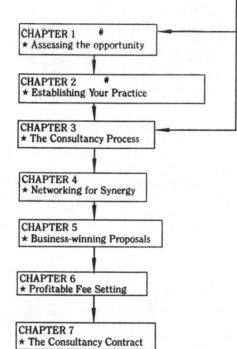
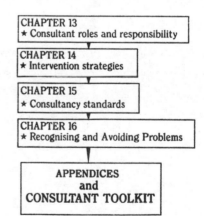
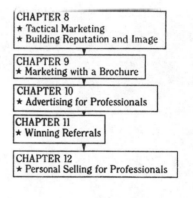
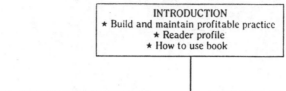

Introduction

This book is written with a straightforward purpose. It aims to help its readers to build and sustain very profitable high quality professional practices capable of providing excellent levels of secure income virtually regardless of the state of the economy. Aimed at the experienced professional as much as the newcomer, it is based on exhaustive research on what is actually done by the top earners on both sides of the Atlantic.

It is tempting to assert that the top earners are the best consultants. Tempting, but by no means necessarily true. Many of the highest earners show talents and skill far above the norm, but others would be little better than run of the mill were it not for their remarkable capacity to attract business and make money. Meanwhile an even larger number of first rate practitioners can do little more than get by. This book is designed to enable the capable but less successful to use their skills to optimise their personal incomes.

It is not, however just about making money. Consultancy is an ethical profession or it is nothing. It is a profession which has been growing at a cumulative twenty per cent per year and shows every sign of continuing to do so. To maintain and deserve that growing business opportunity it must aspire to the highest standards of professionalism and take seriously the activities of those practices which let standards slip in the interests of maximising short term earnings. Equally guilty are those major consultancies which send into client premises poorly trained, naive, though undoubtedly intelligent graduates to learn at the expense of the client and the small practices and 'one man bands' which accept assignments for which they are unqualified and under-resourced.

The recession has driven a major shift in the balance of business. More is going to the small firm in the interests of economy. An increasing number of individuals are being forced into offering their services as free-lance consultants into a growing market at a time when jobs are scarce. This is all to the good. The profession needs new ideas and recent practical experience. This book will help good new consultants to be successful new consultants.

The major consultancies have 'delayered' expensive staff and show no signs of changing their policy toward the use of the inexpensive, but commercially naive recent graduate. In this volatile combination of circumstances how can we best ensure that the quality of service rises to the level which our clients pay for?

I am convinced that the only long-term solution will be accreditation. Accreditation is more than mere qualification in that it is granted by a qualified third party and can be withdrawn if the standards and ethics of the profession are not fully adhered to by the certificated consultant. It should, however, be more than that. It should be firmly based on an internationally agreed Common Body of Professional Knowledge which relates directly to the practical needs of providing added value solutions to real world clients. Above all it should not become an excuse for those who currently enjoy a dominant share of a lucrative market to seek to exclude competition and create a closed shop. The market must remain free and open to all, but users of services must be given some clear and unambiguous indication that their chosen consultant is committed to and capable of delivering pre-determined outcomes. This book makes a brief, but serious contribution to that debate.

Finally, I hope that this book will help to serve the needs of the buyer of consultancy services. It is almost axiomatic that the buyer is investing in something which is in the nature of a mystery wrapped in an enigma, to misquote Churchill. Consultants are brought in when the knowledge pool of the organisation is inadequate for present purposes. In such a situation it is difficult to assess in advance whether the chosen outsider is right for the job.

By developing an understanding of how the best and the most successful strategies are combined in practice the working manager can extrapolate his own strategy for maximising the chances of success.

How will this book work? It will achieve results by providing you with a personal and comfortable strategy to attract clients. It will ensure that you can maximise your legitimate income and avoid giving your services away without payment. In short, it will turn good professionals into successful professionals. So please grab your pencil and start work.

For whom will the book work? It will serve members of any profession where the building and maintenance of business is dependent on the reputation and image of the people involved. It will work for those newly entering the profession and for those who, after years of experience, are still open to new ideas. Above all, it will work for those who are able to evaluate ideas, discard those which conflict with their aims or personality, and apply what remains with dedication, imagination and consistency. Please regard the contents of this book as if you were being offered a menu. All of the dishes have been tasted by your fellow professionals and have proved excellent. Select those which are most appropriate to your taste and they will enable you to achieve your goals.

The examples in this book are taken from the profession of management consultancy. That is where the writer's experience lies. The concepts have been shown to be applicable across the professions - all that is demanded is that the reader who is an accountant, lawyer or psychologist, doctor, architect or veterinarian constantly ask and answer four simple questions:

- How does this relate to my specific situation?
- What can I use from this to build my practice and profit?
- To what degree is it consistent with my preferred behaviour and desired image?
- What can I do right now to exploit my new knowledge?

I am writing this during a recession, a period when a record number of good businesses have turned out to be rather less good than hoped or expected.

Consultancy remains good business, along with many of the professions. In spite of the economic situation, indeed because of it, the demand for consultancy and other professional services continues to grow. Very few businesses are recession-proof, but selling your services to provide professional advice and support can blossom even in a slump. But with success comes increased competition. There is a bigger cake, but more who are fighting for a slice. The opportunity is there, but we need an edge to be able to exploit it. This introduction considers the opportunity, and the rest of the book will explain how to exploit it profitably and professionally.

Many potential clients have reduced their staffing levels far beyond trimming the fat, and they will need help to exploit any new business opportunities because the few people that they have left are over-stretched and sometimes under-qualified. It is fact that the most able people tend to be the most mobile. Firms have not only lost numbers, they have often lost their best people (indeed, they may have recently lost you)! Those who have gone are often the people who, when the chips were down, could always manage the extra effort which makes the difference between success and failure. Those with talent and self-confidence are often among the first to leave when separation is voluntary or when internal politics rule the organisational culture.

Now, for many companies, the slightest problem or opportunity means that the extra skill, knowledge or manpower that is needed is no longer available 'in-house'. It must be bought in.

The balance of business is also changing. Some professional practices are having a tough time during recession. The fat organisations with enormous overheads find life increasingly difficult as revenues fail to keep pace with costs. In my specialist field of management consultancy, major firms which have depended in the past on size and a famous name and who have used inexperienced people 'on a long leash' are now finding things uncharacteristically difficult.

The small practice, however, can flourish in recession, particularly the specialist small outfit with an intelligent appreciation of the market and a commitment to quality and exceptional value at sensible cost. In 1991 the growth of business for small practices was estimated to be 28.3% (approximately double the best scenario increase for the large practices).

By no means all large practices find the going tough. Arthur Anderson achieved an increase in revenues in 1991 of better than 29%. Large practice or small, with effective marketing and real added client value there is still the potential for great success.

But the shift toward using the small practice is strong and there is no reason to believe that, given a high standard of service, this trend will not accelerate. Small is becoming more than beautiful. In professional services small is economic for the user and very profitable for the practitioner.

Major management and economic thinkers share the view that information is the commodity of the future. Drucker, Handy and others stress the future value and scarcity of the knowledge worker. Whole nations are basing their commercial and economic growth on a total dependence on information. Knowledge workers will be hard to find and expensive to retain.

Organisations are increasingly discovering that beyond a core of essential day to day skills, the economic approach is to buy in expertise when and only when it is required. The resource which will be the key to success will be held not inside the corporation, but in the brains and experience of external advisors. The first tentative signs of real recovery will open floodgates of demand for high quality services. When the signs become apparent, those who have taken appropriate steps to be ready and to be known will be in a position to be selective with a growing number of prospective clients requesting them to serve. They will do business on their own terms.

No recession lasts for ever. When recovery ceases to be the vague hope of politicians and becomes a reality, there will be fortunes to be made. Those who will be best placed to exploit the coming opportunities will be the few or the many who have steadfastly worked to build their reputation and status without cutting either corners or prices.

This book is dedicated respectfully to tomorrow's fortune makers.

PART ONE :
BUILDING YOUR PRACTICE

1 To Be or Not to Be

Many people who have lost their job in a period when new ones are hard to find very sensibly consider some form of consultancy as a means of putting bread on the table. Considering consultancy is fine, but rushing into it without sufficient information to make an informed decision is less so. Let us look at some of the factors that should be considered.

Income

High incomes are perfectly possible, even likely, if the profession is approached in the right way, but are by no means certain even for the most able. The late Howard Shenson, who was for years the unchallenged authority on the subject, used to say that there are two kinds of consultant: 'Good consultants and successful consultants. Sadly there are many more good ones than there are successful ones.'

If you want to make yourself really depressed, consider that since by no means all successful consultants are good, there must be a hell of a lot of excellent people just about getting by.

Recent research, completed during the deepest, longest lasting recession in living memory, gives a useful indication of how well the newcomer to the profession may expect to do in the first year or so. If you read this book and put its ideas into practice you will do better than the average newcomer.

New practices – first year revenues
N=221

Revenue Higher than Plan	38%
Revenue Equal to Plan	22%
Revenue Less than Plan	26%
NO PLAN	14%
Profit Higher than Plan	28%
Profit Equal to Plan	28%
Profit Less than Plan	30%
NO PLAN	14%

I am appalled that apparently more than one in 10 people entering a profession in which they expect to have others pay for and follow their advice lacked the basic business knowledge to formulate even a simple business plan. Are these sort of statistics trustworthy, or do they distort the true picture?

There is an increasing tendency for large companies with imposed headcount restrictions to reduce their permanent staff and then to 'outsource'. Not surprisingly, those who have recently left are the best qualified to carry out the work, and come Monday morning, some who were bade a fond farewell on Friday are back at their old desks as self-employed 'consultants'.

Good luck to them, but it may distort the research a little. Revenues for some are artificially high in the first year because, as part of a separation package, they have been offered ongoing freelance work with their old employer, and have reduced the need to build new clients from scratch.

Worse results for profit than for revenue are in substantial part due to the new consultant's inability to put a proper price on his services. There is also an element of underestimation of overhead. (We will deal with both these potential minefields as the book unfolds).

We have no way of assessing whether the plans of those new to the profession erred on the high or low side. To take revenue and profit figures in isolation is therefore potentially misleading. What counts is the number who derived sufficient income to confidently stay in the game. So what percentage of new entrants cease operation during the first year?

First, what looks like bad news. Approximately 20% of those

who offer their services as consultants go out of business at or before the end of their first year.

The good news is that almost 15% do so because they have been offered employment as a result of contacts which they have made while marketing themselves to prospective clients. A further 3% cease trading some time after they evaluate their first year results. So a total of around 8% of new entrants find the going too tough by the end of the first year. (It is certain, therefore that even among those who are incapable of producing a plan for their own business, at least some survive to fight another day. In a deep recession that says something about the opportunity). In summary, some 92% either choose to continue on their own or are offered job opportunities.

Consultancy is very much a field of birds of passage. Most experienced consultants, myself included, move in and out of private practice as other offers are made. Sometimes the move is into bigger practices who want to strengthen or develop their team. Often such appointments are limited in duration or ongoing satisfaction, and the professional may return to private practice enriched, in both senses, by the experience.

Other considerations

Running his or her own practice usually involves the former executive in the novel experience of working alone. In the early stages most of us have to do everything alone. Strategic planning, typing, developing materials, answering the telephone, marketing, filing, writing articles, making tea, selling services, doing the books - the list is endless and each responsibility ours alone.

Anyone who has spent much of their business life protected by secretaries and supported by staff may find the going tough and lonely.

If you are used to endless opportunities for bouncing ideas off colleagues in stimulating meetings before taking a decision, you can have real problems with no-one to talk to but the cat. In my early days my telephone bill was inflated less by my committed search for business opportunities than it was by the need to hear another voice. I would call anyone on any pretext just to kid myself that I still had colleagues to talk to.

If I suggest that your wife, husband or lover may be of little help, I intend no impertinence. Your marriage partner is not necessarily your business partner. You need to talk 'shop', they have their own things to do and their own schedule to keep. You cannot call them to a meeting whenever it suits you, and even if they try very hard to fill the void, there is an excellent chance that since you are, by definition, an expert they will have little understanding of what you are talking about. Worse, they will not share your old employees' belief that it pays to agree with the boss. If I ask for my wife's opinion that is what she gives me, and I have been known not to like it.

So you have to be ready to work alone, take perhaps uncharacteristic risks, do all the menial tasks and almost certainly work seven days a week most weeks without apparently getting paid for it. If you can do all of that and deal constructively with rejection, frustration and stress you will make a consultant. If you can also offer the market valued, flexible and infinitely transferable skills, you will make a good consultant. If you can market your skills effectively, you will make a successful consultant and probably become a rich one.

You have been warned about some of the drawbacks, but the rewards are worth considering in a little more detail.

Will you or won't you?

Income can be high. Job variety can be exciting.

Job satisfaction can be incredible. The key to business decision making, however, always comes down in the last resort to the balance of opportunities against risk.

Consultancy is a multi billion pound business which has been consistently growing at 20% plus a year for a decade, and in spite of some gloomy prognostications it looks as if it will continue to do so for the forseeable future. Present difficulties mean that the balance of market share is tilting toward the small firm and that is probably to your advantage.

The reputation of consultants and consultancy is not uniformly high, but if you can offer real added value and quality interventions your chances of success may be enhanced by the shortcomings of others. Some are working hard to raise professional standards, and this book will help you to join them.

There are risks, but this is one of the few professions where you can do well with virtually nothing more by way of assets than the pinky-grey jelly in your skull. You do not need fancy offices, expensive equipment and luxury transport to succeed. They are good to have, but you can do without them. It will be tough at times, but initiative and creativity will take you a long way.

If you get depressed in the early stages when bills come in with regularity, but cheques are noticeable by their absence, you may wish to remember a story told by Walt Disney. Walt's brother was company accountant, and whenever he sent for Walt that was a sure indication of trouble. 'Fantasia', the follow up to 'Snow White', was failing to draw the huge audiences predicted after an unprecedented investment. The studio was in hock. As Walt entered his brother's office he was greeted with:

> 'Walt, do you know we're in debt to the tune of twenty five million dollars?'

> 'Wow that's great. I can remember when no-one would lend us twenty five hundred.'

Unlike the film studio, your risk is almost entirely controllable. The opportunities are as big as our imagination. But imagination alone is not enough.

Specialist or generalist?

It is essential that you position yourself clearly to avoid confusing your potential clientele. There is a healthy and often well-founded distrust of the 'Jack of all trades', so decisions have to be made. Will you offer yourself as a specialist or a generalist?

As a specialist you may choose to practise in one discipline or in a single industry. Many have built successful careers marketing into a single commercial sector. More of my professional life than I would wish has been committed to the automotive industry. That is where I am known, and that is where it used to be particularly easy to attract assignments. If you tie yourself to an industry, however, you may be particularly vulnerable to sector downturns in business.

The automotive industry was a happy hunting ground for specialist consultants until 1989, but when the downturn of 1990 became the slump of 1991, which in turn became the disaster of 1992, many projects which had been started were cancelled before they were completed. Consultants who continued to specialise fought for the small amount of business still available as budgets were slashed. As budgets were cut prices were slashed to match. Those who had either not foreseen trouble, or worse, having foreseen it ignored the signs and refused to approach other sectors, found themselves in serious difficulty.

But this is by no means unavoidable. Skilled marketing and an ability to identify and respond to the emerging needs of an industry, even one in decline, can pay off handsomely. One consultant I know has specialised throughout his professional life in an industry which many have written off as being in terminal decline. With very little competition for what others see as meagre business, he has done very well. He is now recognised as the industry guru, and attracts good business from the few but now rapidly growing companies which dominate the sector.

You may choose to market yourself as a specialist in a single discipline. You could for example sell yourself as the expert in administering and analysing the results of just one psychometric test. Many do, and find that it has the advantage of ease of marketing which comes with having a product which can be promoted and sold as a simple package. It also carries the potential disadvantage that if the market turns against your product, you are left with literally nothing of value to offer. By being flexible in your planning and adaptable in your approach, you can overcome the difficulty and extend the life of your product by constantly looking for new applications.

A bigger and more serious problem of narrow specialism is best encapsulated by Abraham Maslow's saying that: 'If the only tool that you have is a hammer, you tend to treat everything as a nail'. Force-fitting the client's problems to whatever you are peddling is an example of the 'snake oil' approach which has done enormous disservice to the consultancy profession and to the clients it serves. If you look critically at the real top earners, the Peters, the Blanchards, the Robbins' and the like, it is hard to resist the conclusion that they have a single product, flexibly applied and cleverly promoted.

You may decide that you are a generalist. That means you have a range of skills which are infinitely transferable across industrial and situational boundaries. Fine, but think about it for a moment. Clients, remember, are simple people. They believe that an individual only has sufficient time to be a real expert in a limited field. What credibility will you or I have if we enter the market place saying: 'I can do just about anything. Hire me?'

Confidence in even the most plausible renaissance man is flimsy. Widget manufacturers really do believe that there are key differences between green widgets and yellow widgets which only a dyed-in-the-wool green or yellow widget expert can understand. They are almost certainly wrong, but it is they who do the hiring.

If you decide that you are truly a generalist, you may have to hide many of your lights under huge bushels and present yourself to each client as a narrow specialist in the area of greatest immediate need, introducing other skills as emerging situations dictate. In short, when it comes to marketing, promote yourself as a specialist and a niche market. Have a hundred specialisms and a hundred niches if you will, just offer them separately and sensitively to each prospective client.

In general, a specialist tends to be able to charge somewhat higher fees - and if you are hell bent on becoming famous (and I trust that you are) you will achieve success most easily by consistently hammering away in, or about, a single field.

Operational or advisory?

When I was young and easy under the apple boughs, there was only one kind of consultant. A consultant was, as Bob Townsend describes, one who borrows your watch, tells you the time and then pockets your watch with the fee. Perhaps it is my age, but they are remembered as the good days when consultants advised and others did the work.

Today 90% of consultants are operational. Not only do they recommend, they roll up their sleeves and play a major role in implementation. Without the ability of consultants to get things done, many highly desirable plans would moulder for lack of resources or skills to put them into effect.

If like myself and Mrs Thatcher you believe that advisers advise and others 'do', you need to make a commitment to rise to the top of your profession. Only there today can you hope to avoid the need to get stuck in. Take heart. Those at the top of the profession earn the level of daily fee which makes up for having fewer opportunities to work. If you choose to limit your market to those who can implement your ideas without your further help, you are reducing it to a very small market indeed, so you must be sure that it is profitable.

Those who like the idea of seeing the job through to completion have two advantages. The time per assignment is obviously longer and earning potential higher in the longer term, and with the de-skilling of industry and commerce which has taken place in the 'eighties' and through the 'nineties' to date, opportunities for work are greater.

Personality traits and success

If you intend to be a successful consultant you must make up your mind to be directive, assertive and controlling. You will be dealing with clients who have only one justification for hiring you. There is an old business maxim that 'power flows from he who knows' and as a consultant that is who you are. You need to consider at an early stage how comfortable you will be when exercising your power.

The client, not surprisingly, looks for signs of your credibility from the first meeting. Their confidence in hiring you will be largely determined not by your expertise - the client probably has no basis for judging that - but by your demeanour. Are you prepared to look, think and act the part of a successful professional all of the time? If not, this may be the wrong profession for you.

A number of studies conducted in the United States and in the United Kingdom identifying personality profiles which are indicative of success in consultancy careers have shown remarkably similar results. The following is a condensed version of the information currently available.

Most of the studies are published and in the public domain, others have been carried out for specific clients by the author. You may find it interesting to compare your beliefs and values with those which are indicated by the research. Be clear, however, that the research neither shows that only those with the following traits are successful, nor that all who demonstrate these traits succeed regardless. The traits however have been found, all other things being equal, to be reliable indicators of success potential.

Vocation
Effective consultants are strongly committed to the significance and purpose of the profession and the industries in which they work. Consultants with this trait demonstrate considerable pride in the outcomes to which their efforts lead. They are eager to show that their interventions make a significant difference to the lives of clients and colleagues through the further development of systems, solutions, product support and services. Above all, concentration is on personal contribution rather than dependence on others outside the immediate team.

Growth
The consultant is expected to score high against this trait both in his own development and in attracting and supporting talented others with whom to work. The focus is on using the strengths of others, particularly the client and his immediate team, to optimise profit opportunities. A significant negative indicator is if a consultant makes any statements which point to the strengths of others as being a threat either to his or her position or self-perception.

Affiliation
The ability to build rapport with associates and show empathy is, in the successful consultant, specifically directed at the attainment of objectives and is not aimed at the development of a cosy warmth within the team. Affiliation is not a process of seeking to be loved

by all. The effective consultant always shows concern for people, but is able sensitively and strongly to put a case even where the truth as he sees it may lead to a degree of unpopularity.

Focus
The development of specific rather than general objectives typifies the effective consultant. He should show a clear ability to maintain direction in the face of difficulty. A typical profile of one who is strong on focus invariably includes role models, and the consultant is keen to learn from their success.

Power
The quintessential trait of the successful consultant is the sensitive use of power to get things done within the framework of the client organisational culture. This is the use of power in the institutional, rather than the personal sense, and clear goal direction, based on the agreed needs of the client dictates how and where power is applied. An inappropriate use of power is when the consultant relies on personal status and authority to get things done which do not attract the commitment of the client.

Subordinate traits

The following, although important, are recognised as being highly variable within individuals. Ideally the team, consultant-consultant, or consultant-client, should be balanced to ensure that each trait is represented and applied appropriately.

Enthusiasm
The ability of the client to maintain improvements is frequently a function of the consultant's enthusiasm and confidence that the resulting tasks can be achieved.

Organisation
Although there are examples of unorganised consultants who succeed in completing brilliant interventions on behalf of their clients, such people are usually highly specialised, technical experts. The effective consultant usually demonstrates an orderly and organised approach.

Achievement
Contrary to popular mythology the effective consultant is an expert team player rather than a prima donna. A drive for achievement is

normally moderate and directed toward client or team success by the most effective consultants.

When taken to excessive lengths, the desire for personal achievement gets in the way of developing the client toward autonomy, and leads the consultant to seek and engineer ongoing dependence.

Stamina

The effective consultant works when necessary at a high tempo and with considerable endurance. The tenacious pursuit of goals over a long period is more a characteristic of effective management than consultancy. Typically, the consultant prefers high levels of activity for shorter periods.

Analysis

The ability to extract key factors in a situation and use them strategically in the future typifies many consultants.When taken to excess, this trait denies real analysis by leading the consultant to react to insufficient evidence which suggests, but does not prove, a similarity to a previous experience. Many clients perceive a tendency to superficial analysis leading to an assumption that two situations which are in fact different are really the same as a major weakness of consultants.

Creativity

Only where a consultant is able to balance the ability to learn from the past and resist change for change's sake with a detailed analytic approach is the ideal client serving combination found.

Sadly, most psychological studies indicate that no correlation appears to exist between true analytic skill and creativity. Consultants tested to date appear to have an unbalanced tendency to favour one, rather than a desirable approach incorporating both. This frequently leads to force-fitting the client problem to an established solution, or the promotion of novelty where tested and proven approaches are more appropriate.

Professionalism

In spite of the horrors some have perpetrated in its name, consultancy is a profession, and it must be a proud one. It is a profession in which individual reputation and image are the key to success. Professionalism in everything that we do is vital.

I will have much to say on the subject as this book progresses, but for now let me discipline myself to one area. If you are new to the profession you will have a very reasonable wish to get 'bread on the table' from the earliest possible moment. This is a very understandable aim, but there are dangers in accepting any assignment, or any client, just because they are there and you are hungry.

You will not, I assume, accept any assignment that you are not qualified to complete. This means that it is your responsibility to get to know your colleagues in the industry. When you are not the right person for the job, you owe it to the client to introduce the specialist who is. If you take on work which you are unable to do to the standards required, you will almost certainly get away with it in the sense that your fee will be paid and you will not be sued for malpractice. You will, of course, be unlikely to be assigned again by that client, but you may take the view, as many do, that there are plenty more where that came from. That view is as short-sighted as it is unethical.

Your reputation is your stock in trade. If you fail to perform effectively it will be destroyed, and without reputation you will cease to attract business. Worst, and most insidious, you will confirm the low opinion which some hold of consultants, and you will have placed your own personal brick in the wall of mistrust and low expectation which can so easily constrain the market in which we all have to operate. If enough of us do that, we will all eventually go down.

One day, soon I hope, consultancy will be a fully certificated profession. Until then we are all dependent for our future on the professionalism of those, like you and me, who can without any restraint at present, enter the market and call ourselves 'consultants'.

I am making numerous assumptions on your behalf. For example I assume that you would not accept an assignment which, if you carried it out as requested, would damage rather than support your client.

I have a valued client, let us call him Tony. Now Tony has one major shortcoming; he is a very easygoing and pleasant person. As is not unusual with nice people, there are times when others seek to take advantage. When working for Tony, it is important that any consultant is unusually sensitive to the need not to usurp his position with his employees. I had been working with Tony and his team conducting some strategic planning and team building workshops. As frequently happens when the consultant has control of process and is inputting a wide range of skills, his personal status within the group rises rapidly, sometimes to the detriment of the formal leader.

Having in my early days inadvertently pulled the rug out from under the occasional boss, I now always try to be particularly careful to bolster the leader in the eyes of his group. Groups enjoy novelty, and if they see an informed and accessible consultant who seems to be full of ideas they are often tempted to try to push him into the leadership role. The facilitator must reject the overtures of the group to take over leadership, and must build the status of the formal leader in the eyes of his group. Failure to build the relative status of the formal leader can create the danger that an informal leader will emerge and try his luck in a power struggle.

To avoid this I have developed approaches which are aimed at highlighting the formal leader's control not only over his own team, but over me, 'the hired hand'. A small, but significant strategem that I have found useful is to arrange covertly with the leader that, at a signal from me, he will interrupt me, apparently in full flow and redirect me to an area or process that he (and I, as it happens) want to address.

As I said, Tony is a nice person and found it impossible publicly to assert himself over me, even at my instigation. His response to my suggestion was always some variant on: 'No. I am very happy with what you are doing, Tom. I'll leave it to you.'

A similar response was elicited by most of my other strategems and I found myself, by default increasingly perceived by the group as the 'real leader'.

Eventually I had my opportunity. It was essential that a key leadership task be undertaken, and Tony asked me to do it for him. I refused. I coached him quickly and carefully in how to do it himself and walked away, losing in the process a couple of days work that I could ill afford at that time. The coaching session had been short, less than half an hour far and I could hardly invoice a, few minutes work, so I kicked myself as I walked back to my car.

The next morning I anxiously searched my mail for any positive response which could lead to an early assignment. There was a note from Tony which simply said 'thanks', attached to a cheque for a full two days of consultancy. Multiplying the time taken by the value of the cheque, it was the best rate of pay I had ever received. As an emotional lift and reinforcement that the professional approach is always the right one, it was priceless.

The undesirable client

Sometimes it pays to reject clients who do not meet the requirements of building your status and reputation.

Your choice of client has an effect on your perceived status. That is why most of us mention, without betraying professional confidence, our blue chip clients at every opportunity.

In the early stages it is difficult to be choosey about the clients for whom you are prepared to work, but please consider the following.

You need clients who:

Pay their bills
Many don't, and are known for not doing so. It does as little for your reputation as for your bank balance if you are seen to be working for those who have a reputation for not paying. You look either desperate or daft, and neither builds your professional image.

Are ethical
Most clients are ethical, but those few who are not can destroy your reputation by association. If you have any doubts, steer clear.

Enhance your image
It is not only the blue chip global enterprises which can enhance your reputation when you are seen to be working for them. In any industry there are opinion leaders and companies and individuals who have the respect of their peers. Seek them out and look to serve them. It will repay your effort.

Have goals you can accomplish
Nothing succeeds like success. Be careful that a liking for challenge does not lead you to risk failure too often. You may be paid for your best efforts and not by results, but you will find that you are re-hired strictly on the basis of your track record.

Will appreciate what you do
Referral business is the most economical, most profitable business. To get referrals you need to be proactive – we will discuss precisely how later. To win referrals you need something to work on, and what you work on is a client who is delighted with what you have achieved together and is happy to tell the world.

Summary and action plan

• Consultancy is good business in good times and bad.

• The market is expected to grow at a compound rate of about 20%.

• The balance of trade is shifting to the advantage of the small firm at least in the short term.

• Building your personal reputation and status is the primary goal.

• Consultancy, as well as offering excellent income prospects in its own right can be a stepping stone back into the world of paid employment for those who prefer that world.

• The one man band needs to consider his ability to do everything himself and withstand frustration and loneliness.

• Most newcomers stick it out and are more or less successful.

• Good consultants outnumber successful consultants. The purpose of this book is to help you to become or remain a successful consultant.

• To be successful you need to be clear about what it is you offer. Particularly what you offer that others do not.

• The successful consultant builds her credibility through assertive behaviour and by being selective in the choice of clients.

Before reading further, please take a few moments to consider:

•What are the full range of skills and knowledge which you can offer to the market place?

_____
_____
_____
_____
_____
_____

• Are you a generalist, or a specialist?

_____

• Who specifically is likely to buy your skills and knowledge?

_____
_____
_____
_____
_____

• How can you most quickly, cheaply and effectively contact potential buyers of your services?

_____
_____
_____
_____
_____

• What are the unique features that you can offer?

_____
_____
_____
_____
_____
_____

• Is there a fashionable concept of the moment that you understand really well? (TQM, JIT, investors in people, NVQ's, downsizing, rightsizing, outplacement, environmental auditing). _I have purposely not explained any of the jargon or alphabet spaghetti. If you are not familiar with any of it, find out what it is. It could be a business opportunity._

_____
_____
_____
_____

If there is, do you have, or can you come up with a new angle to it?

_____
_____
_____
_____
_____

•**And, most importantly, what will you really feel comfortable and happy doing?**

_____
_____
_____
_____
_____
_____
_____
_____
_____
_____
_____

Answer the above as fully as you can at present, but wait a little before you start to put together a detailed marketing plan. Take a pencil and write down your answers. Have a piece of paper handy to jot down all of your other ideas. They are important - certainly important enough to demand that you stop reading and think for a while about your future.

Limit yourself for the moment to being sure that you know what you have to offer. Be sure that you believe there is a market for your skills. Most important of all, give some thought to what suits your personal style and preferences. Look for that which is likely to reward you not just economically, but in terms of the quality of your life. If consultancy or another profession which is built on personal reputation and status meets the bill for you, this book will help you to build your success.

More work for you

I warned you in the Introduction that this is a workbook, and you are the worker. Now that you have done some careful thinking, I am going to ask you to commit your thoughts more formally to paper as the basis of your business plan. Most of you will be familiar with a tool called SWOT analysis, and so this is the methodthat I would like you to use. But 'use' is the essential word, so I have redesigned an old tool to ensure use rather than mere completion. A brief word of explanation is called for:

Strengths
Rather than simply list your strengths (and please include everything that you can think of - that is important), I want you to

consider from the beginning how your strengths relate to potential success in your chosen profession. Against each strength make a decision whether you have something that people will buy. If you are not sure, think about it until you are. Ask friends, family and colleagues. Use any creative techniques that you know to find a way to turn your strengths into earning opportunities. Underline or highlight those for which you see market opportunities. From today every attribute you have for which there is a market is your stock in trade. Don't sell yourself short. Work at it.

Having established your strengths, consider those which you can present as USP's (unique selling propositions). Anything for which there is a market and which is unique to you has an enormous value. And never forget: Anything which is not necessarily unique to you, but which   you promote when your competition simply takes it for granted, will look like a USP to the market.

Weaknesses

Look at your weaknesses from the perspective of the market. Only if a weakness affects your ability to attract and serve clients should it be included. Prioritise the weaknesses by using a scale of 1 - 5 in terms of:

Seriousness: Failure to address this weakness will have a severe adverse effect on your ability to attract and retain business.

Growth: Failure to do something to deal with this now will lead to it getting worse over time, therefore action is urgently needed.

On a clear understanding of the difference between importance and mere urgency, commit yourself right now to do something to overcome or ameliorate the one, two or perhaps three major problems. Never try to address more than a couple of problems at a time unless they are inter-related or easy to handle. Concentrate your attention on your strengths. Go back to them after looking at your weaknesses. Add to them and consider how much you have going for you. Commit yourself to read the rest of the book as an exercise in how to apply your strengths to make money and provide value.

Opportunities

'When opportunity knocks you're always at home' - Victor Kyam

From today you are an entrepreneur, whatever your role has been in the past. Opportunities are your lifeblood. List everything that you can think of. Read with the intention of identifying further opportunities and add them as you see them. Watch television with the same goals. Carry a small notebook or a personal dictating machine so that opportunities are recorded and not forgotten.

To decide which to address first, highlight those that you are qualified to exploit and from them filter out the least profitable and most difficult to get to grips with, leaving yourself with those that you propose to address at once. Only answer with a 'no' in the final column where the opportunity conflicts with your intended image and reputation or with your strong values, beliefs or personal feelings.

Threats

Threats come in two major forms - those which are avoidable with prior planning, and those which are not. For those which can be avoided, decide what can be done, write it down and do it in good time. For those which cannot be avoided by proaction on your part, identify the earliest indicator that things are going wrong and specify what you will do when you become aware of the coming danger. That is the difference between contingent and avoidance planning and without both the best of plans are vulnerable.

When you have done all of the above:

DEFINE YOUR MISSION
Now that you have completed the SWOT analysis - what Beckhardt calls the 'here and now' - I would like you to consider your future. Take the approach that nothing is impossible and answer for yourself the question;

'If I knew that I could not fail, what would I attempt?'

PRECISELY WHAT IDEAL BUSINESS AM I IN TODAY? (Who will be my immediate clients? What services will I offer?)

PERSONAL AND PROFESSIONAL STRENGTHS

DESCRIPTION OF STRENGTH	Marketable ?		Possible USP?		ACTION
	Yes	No	Yes	No	

Figure 1.1

PERSONAL AND PROFESSIONAL WEAKNESSES

DESCRIPTION OF WEAKNESS (AND EVIDENCE THAT IT WILL AFFECT CLIENT SERVICES)	PRIORITY			ACTION
	S	U	G	

To Prioritise: Score 0 (Low) to 5 (High)

For: Seriousness = Effect on ability to give client service
     Urgency = Degree to which weakness affects ability to meet needs of current Business Plan
     Growth = Tendency of problem to worsen if not addressed.

Figure 1.1(2)

OPPORTUNITY ANALYSIS

DESCRIPTION OF OPPORTUNITIES	Qualified to Exploit ?		Exploit?		
	Yes	No	Now	Future	No

Figure 1.3

THREAT ANALYSIS

WHAT COULD GO WRONG	AVOIDANCE PLAN	CONTINGENT PLAN

Figure 1.1 (3)

WHERE DO I WANT TO BE IN FIVE YEARS TIME? (Who will be my clients? What will be my revenues and profits? What will I be doing? Where will I be doing it? With whom, if anyone? What will be my personal reputation and status?)

_____
_____
_____
_____
_____
_____
_____
_____
_____
_____

WHAT WILL SET ME APART FROM THE HERD - NOW AND IN THE FUTURE? WHY SHOULD PEOPLE HIRE ME RATHER THAN THE OTHERS?

_____
_____
_____
_____
_____
_____
_____

WHAT ARE THE KEY VALUES AND PRINCIPLES WHICH WILL DRIVE MY BUSINESS NO MATTER WHAT?

_____
_____
_____
_____
_____
_____

'A man who has nothing that he would die for has little to live for' -
Martin Luther King

Additional notes
From what you have written develop a mission statement for your new business. To help you a sample is at the end of this chapter.
   Lastly write yourself some OBJECTIVES which are SMART.

SAMPLE MISSION STATEMENT
FOR TRAINING AND CONSULTANCY

QUALITY DRIVEN CONSULTANCY AND TRAINING

We provide superior consultancy and training because we believe in truly providing services designed to meet the client's researched needs, rather than standard packages. We design interventions which reflect the best validated current research so we are constantly mindful of our own development needs.

Our fee structure reflects the need to be able to provide sufficient time and resources to ensure the achievement of pre-determined measurable outcomes.

By ensuring that the client is made aware of government and other funding opportunities where they exist we maximise client choice, although we are not prepared to accept assignments under any current DTI scheme.

We refuse any assignment for which we are not fully qualified, but will assist the client to find qualified and competent consultancy elsewhere, rather than leave them to the mercy of the less ethical members of the profession.

We believe in the need to build an ongoing client relationship through providing added value in the form of additional information and coaching. In this way we help the client to make accelerated progress toward self-reliance.

Uniquely, we can offer consultants who are qualified in the field of management consultancy as well academic and business disciplines.

Figure 1.2

Specific: They express exactly what you intend to achieve.

Measurable: Put figures to things whenever you can, not just profits and revenues, but numbers of clients, standards of quality. Don't forget that 'All' or '100%' is a figure appropriate to many objectives.

Achieveable: Aim high, but don't saddle yourself with failure by going for the impossible dream. Identify the very best that you think that you can do and then stretch yourself just enough to make the extra effort fun and worthwhile.

Realistic: Test your objectives against your resources. The mission is intended to bring out your dream. This should ensure progress toward the attainment of your dream by moving in the right direction with what you have right now. Tomorrow you will get the other resources you need. Getting those resources is a proper objective.

Timely: Make it clear to yourself when you intend to achieve your key results, including critical sub objectives en route.

_____

_____

_____

_____

_____

_____

_____

_____

_____

_____

_____

_____

_____

_____

_____

_____

All checked for	SPECIFICITY	YES_____
	MEASURABILITY	YES_____
	ACHIEVABILITY	YES_____
	REALISM	YES_____
All	TIMED realistically?	YES_____

Where now?

The following Chapter will provide some brief notes on how to establish your practice. Subsequent Chapters detail how to run your practice and a range of no cost, low cost approaches to marketing which have been proven as the most effective by high earners on both sides of the Atlantic. Remember, they are put forward for your consideration much as a menu would be offered. Pick out those you feel comfortable and effective doing. Concentration needs to be on doing the things that 'feel' right with commitment, energy, dedication and a sense of fun. And remember:

> _'If you are not doing it for money or fun, what the hell are you doing it for?'_ - Bob Townsend

2 Beginners Only

This short Chapter is written to help those who are totally new to the concept of establishing and developing a business, and It should only be skim read by the established practitioner. That way I may avoid the danger of teaching some wily old grandmas the art and practice of egg sucking. There is, however, a potential drawback to this decision. Strange things are happening in the legal jungle, and since this Chapter is the appropriate place to discuss them, it may be that some who would benefit from a glimpse of even the most cloudy crystal ball may miss something of future significance.

I take some comfort from the assumption that if what I suspect may happen does happen, it will make sufficient noise for everyone to be aware of it - except its first victim. If you don't trust my assumptions, or you feel that lightning would not strike without first picking you out as a victim, put your mind at rest. Scan quickly the material hereunder headed 'liability' and leave the rest of the Chapter to those for whom it is intended.

For the real beginner I want to sketch in a few generalisations about starting a business. Please remember that they are generalisations. It is impossible for me to guess your precise circumstances, and nothing in this Chapter should be allowed to dissuade you from seeking professional advice from your accountant or lawyer.

Forms of business

Limited liability
For the majority of those who are proposing to found a professional practice there is little to be gained from establishing a limited liability company. The usual advantages of limiting your liabilities are unlikely to provide significant benefits to a management consultant. Consultancy is an activity which requires little or no investment beyond that of transport, a small computer, and time for your personal development. Most of your stock in trade resides, as I have mentioned before, between your ears.

Registering as a limited liability company would require you to submit your accounts to Companies House, and in a busy life it may be irksome to meet the time requirements. The penalties for failing to submit your accounts in time have recently been increased, and that alone is putting some people off the idea. The duties of a director have also been tightened in the last couple of years, and although a cursory glance at the newspapers would do much on most days to confirm some in the belief that they ought to be tightened further.

There are almost certainly some potential clients who would feel more comfortable dealing with companies who are entitled to put 'Ltd' after their name, but they are few. Unless you know that a company which you can happily and profitably serve is one of that small number, and you are determined to have their business at all costs, I see no value in the additional hassle.

For those who prefer to take the limited liability path in spite of what I have said, it could not be easier. For about £200 you will be able to buy a company 'off the shelf', and by registering a name change and the change of activity you will quickly be in business. There are other costs, such as the company seal, which may be considered, but your accountant will be happy to guide you through the details. My advice remains not to bother, but you are only paying for it, you do not have to follow it.

Partnership
This is where Mr Punch's advice to those about to get married comes back into its own: 'Don't'. Please think carefully about entering into a partnership, even with your wife. Joint and several liability could land her in Carey Street, and everything that you own jointly would be at risk.

There is a legal precedent which suggests that your wife cannot be held responsible for your business debts if she has no role in the business. If the house is in your joint names, you are advised to avoid having your wife sign away her half to guarantee your overdraft. As long as she gives no such undertaking and plays no role in the business, her half of the house remains her half, and is not accessible to you or your creditors. In practice this means that if the chips were really down the courts would probably protect her occupancy and ownership, which will keep a roof over your head.

Under no circumstances would I recommend you to form a partnership with anyone other than your wife. Even if you meet an angel hot-foot from heaven, (if she's from heaven, how come the 'hot feet'?), don't even consider a partnership. Liability for your partner's debts is unlimited, and 'unlimited' means what it says. In different circumstances, partners in a major consultancy practice are facing claims of more than $100 million as I write, so unlimited liability where others' debts are involved is not to be considered.

Sole proprietorship

The least glamorous sounding approach to forming a business is by far the least complicated. You will be fully responsible for your debts, but only for those which you personally negotiate, and you are free to trade without any major restrictions. To all intents you are free to start after about half an hour of friendly chat with your accountant.

Sources of capital

With assets limited to your skills and experience do not look to venture capital companies, they are unlikely to find your venture worthy of their capital. A simple business plan and a positive discussion with your bank manager backed by ongoing communication makes absolute sense, and is probably all the financial backing you will ever need. If you have been 'on the dole', and you are entitled to the enterprise allowance, claim it. You are going to find that a majority of your clients are not too proud to accept Government money, and some will expect you to get it for them, so don't be stiff-necked. If you are entitled to it, you are entitled. Talk to your Training and Enterprise Council, they will give you accurate and helpful advice.

Value Added Tax

While we are talking about people who are helpful, contrary to current myths and legends my experience is that the staff at the VAT office are courteous and helpful at all times. I would suggest that unless your accountant has good reason to advise otherwise, you register for VAT from the start. That will enable you to claim any VAT which you pay for start up purchases, and if you are worried about slow payers and cash flow problems, your local office will help you by arranging that you pay on a 'cash accounting' basis for your first quarter of a million in revenues.

Licences

Generally, management consulting is not a licensed profession in this country as it is becoming elsewhere. The situation may change, but for now anyone may call himself a management consultant and may practice the profession without restraint.

Liability

This is the brief paragraph that I suggest every practitioner should glance at and consider. There are in our law three types of public liability.

General liability
This requires all citizens to behave as 'prudent persons'. If I choose to allow my roof to get into a state of disrepair which leads to a tile falling on your head, I am liable. All you have to do is show that I have been negligent and you are entitled to compensation.

Professional liability
Specific to our business lives, we are required to work diligently in the interests of our clients. If we can be shown to have acted negligently, or we have committed an act of malpractice, the client has only to convince a court of our misdeeds, and compensation is again due. Some professionals take out considerable insurance cover against having to pay damages, and you would be well advised to investigate whether you ought to seek professional indemnity insurance. The chances are that you will get similar advice to that which I have received over the years – that you do not need it. But check it out anyway – if you give very specific advice it may be worth having insurance cover.

Product liability
For the best of reasons, product liability is different in character from both of the above.

Imagine that you manufacture a car. Imagine further that you have designed that car in such a way that the fuel tank is dangerously close to the rear panel. In the event of a rear end collision the tank is very likely to rupture. Any spark resulting from the coming together of metal bodies will almost certainly turn at least one of the cars into a fireball. Driver and passenger are likely to be incinerated. Your company is well into production of the mobile death trap when the worst happens. A minor rear end shunt on your test track leads to a major fire and the burning to death of two employees. You are shocked and horrified. You order an internal enquiry. The report which you receive clearly indicates the danger. You ought to have the car re-designed and the fuel tank moved. Will you?

As it happens you have three additional pieces of information:

- The last re-design of a vehicle which had already entered production cost $20million dollars, and was just a change of door handles, far less costly than re-siting a fuel tank.
- Your actuarial experts tell you that the type of crash which would lead to the blaze happens to this class of car infrequently and would add to the number of fatalities just one additional death per thousand units sold.
- Less than 50% of this year's customers will buy your products next time, so burning one in one thousand will have little direct effect on customer retention .

You have the report. Lock it away and it will be almost impossible for anyone to prove negligence.

I am sure that if you were in that position you would withdraw the cars from sale and redesign the positioning of the tank. Sadly, although your right-feeling attitude is one that you can be proud of, similar views and behaviour have not been shown by experience to be universal among businessmen. As a result product liability laws were enacted to be different in two key ways.

1. Negligence does not have to be proved, it is enough for the plaintiff to show that they have suffered harm, physical, financial or emotional, to win their case.

2. The defendant (the business) is required to prove innocence. In short the company supplying the goods is guilty unless they can prove themselves to be innocent.

In recent judgments it seems that judges have taken the view that services are covered as well as goods, and if services, why not professional services? If this is the proper interpretation of the law, the time may well come when a consultant, whose client has suffered harm after an intervention, may seek damages without the need to prove consultant negligence or malpractice. If that day dawns in an increasingly litigious society, we will all need insurance cover and lots of it.

Business cards and letterheads

A worthwhile investment is that of buying a well-designed letterhead and having it printed on good quality paper. Your letterhead says much about you and can affect the chances of your letters being read.

Business cards should be plain and of good quality. There is an argument for the card to carry only your name and where and how you can be contacted with no indication of what you do for a living. The argument goes thus:

You hand me your card.
I glance at it and ask: 'What do you do?'
You reply: 'I'm a consultant, what do you do?'
'I'm in civil engineering. What do you consult about?'
'Civil engineering. Let's talk.'
Cheeky, but I am assured by those prepared to do it that it works.

Conversely, my card says 'Marketing and Management Development' which, vague as it is, is enough to enable some prospective clients to think: 'I don't want any of that!' I keep them that way to use as a minor case study on my seminars as an example of how not to do it.

Working from home

It is becoming increasingly common for people to work from their homes, and as it becomes common it becomes acceptable. Gone are the days when no-one would take you seriously unless you had a showy office in the right part of town. Unless you intend to offer some sort of therapy, and intend to see your clients there, the spare bedroom or even the garage or garden shed can make a suitable office. If you do not want to use your home address for security reasons, or to stop salesmen cold calling, do not be tempted to use a PO Box Number: it makes potential clients nervy if they think that they will not be able to find you. If you must, use an accommodation address, but for my money, if you work from home you can use your normal address without problems.

If you want to make your home address sound grand, just give your house a posh-sounding name. Poets' names sound good: 'Keats House' or 'Coleridge House' for example. I'm a little worried about 'Dunroamin'!

Try to have your telephone answered during business hours by a human being. I know it is difficult, but a lot of people still dislike talking to answering machines. That said an answering machine is a must, even the best regulated households cannot guarantee to always be able to answer the phone all of the time. If nothing else happens, the occasional call of nature becomes more pressing than a telephone which may not call at all.

I do not regard a fax or car phone as essential, but don't let my attitudes cloud your judgment. Install both when you recognise the need and have the means. Add a computer with a decent integrated business software package, and you will want for nothing else.

Getting your business off the ground

You need to ensure that as many people as possible who may either need your services, or refer you to others, know that you are in business. The primary task of your first days is to spread that knowledge. It is infinitely preferable to have potential clients hammering on your door before you are totally ready to serve them than it is to have your 'store' superbly organised and beautifully laid out, but no potential buyers aware that you are open for sales. The entrepreneur markets first and organises afterwards. Since there is usually a delay between announcement and the arrival of clients, this is not a high risk approach, even for the perfectionist.

As a minimum:
- Write a short (one page) announcement that you are open for business and describing what you do. Make it as newsworthy as you can.
  - Do you have an interesting or exciting background?
  - Are you already well known in some local circles?
  - Is the service which you offer aimed at something which is currently newsworthy? (For example, the environment, helping the redundant or long-term unemployed, or surviving in a recession).

Read the press and tie-in if you can to repeated stories.
- Send your announcement to every local and regional newspaper, radio station, business magazine, professional body, chamber of commerce, Training and Enterprise Council, Department of Employment Office, careers counsellor, business colleagues and friends. Anyone, in short who may refer others to you.
- Make sure that your announcement makes it clear how you may be contacted for further information.

- If you have some less than widely known facts which relate to your activity, include them – especially if you have conducted some form of market survey which throws a new light on the state of local industry and commerce.

- Write a news release in addition to your announcement and send that to all newspapers and radio stations separately. Do the little which you can in the early days to create the impression that your name keeps being seen, everywhere they look.

- Consider the possible use of posters. If you have a computer and a simple DTP package, posters are easy and cheap to produce. Place them in Small Business Support Group Offices, Enterprise Agencies, employment offices and libraries.

- Telephone or visit everyone you can think of who may send prospective clients your way.

- Look proactively for ways that you can align what you do to the work of others to start networking from the earliest possible moment. The more like-minded individuals on the look-out for business opportunities the better. Don't expect others to cut you in on their hard won existing business, but look for as many ways as possible to build future business together.

- Offer yourself as a speaker to every local group which you can find which attracts those who may become your clients. Most Chambers of Commerce are happy to invite new businesses to give a five minute overview of what they offer at their regular lunch time meetings, so you do not have to be prepared to give a substantial talk.
  If invited to talk at one of these sessions a concise rundown of the benefits of using your services is infinitely preferable to a detailed description of the features. Tell people convincingly and pleasantly that you can help them to achieve their goals and they will take the trouble to ask you how.

The 21-day 'up and running' formula

Days 1, 2, 3, 4, and 5
Step One: Find and talk to a good accountant
Decide on the form of the business
Register for VAT

Step Two: Develop an outline business plan
        Mission
        Objectives
        SWOT
        Strategic alternatives and strategies
        Tactics
        Budgets, revenues and CASH FLOWS
        Concrete and human resources
        Potential problem planning

Step Three: Make friends with your bank manager
        Open business account

Days 6, 7, 8, and 10

Step Four: Develop marketing/promotional strategy in
        detail

Step Five: Design and order stationery, business cards

Step Six: Order ESSENTIAL equipment
        Ansaphone
        Desk
        Computer/typewriter/word processor
        Files and filing space

Step Seven: Draft press releases, advertisements and
        poster copy as appropriate.
        Check media information in BRAD or Willings
        Press Guide
        (While in library get to know staff,
         resources and layout of reference section)
        Prioritise sending of press releases in line
        with editorial closing dates

Step Eight: Begin to list all possible prospective
        clients and sources of referral

Days 11, 12, 13, 14 and 15

Step Nine: Make preliminary contacts and appointments

Step Ten: Receive equipment and stationery
        Print, or have printed promotional materials
        (Carefully proofread all materials in draft)

Begin planned distribution

Days 16, 17, 18, 19, and 20

Step Eleven: Begin visits to best prospects

Step Twelve: Develop no cost/low cost market strategy
(Read Chapter Eight)

Day 21 - Go for it. Good Luck!

The above is by no means exhaustive, but it will give the absolute newcomer a starting point which will be fleshed out as this book is read. For the experienced professional whose business needs a quick fillip there may well be the source of some quick and easy ideas even in so simple a guide.

PRACTICE BUILDING
THE SHORTER PATH TO PROFITABILITY

PATH ONE - GATHER THE FACTS

★ What is the general economic, social and legislative situation?

★ What specifically has changed, or is changing?

★ Do I see opportunities to exploit my specialist skills and knowledge?

★ Are there any potential problems for my clients?

★ **What are my competitors concentrating on?**

★ What is causing people to buy from them?

★ What are their relative strengths?

★ What can I offer to combat them?

★ What are their relative weaknesses?

★ What can I offer to exploit them?

★ What UNIQUE offer can I make?

Figure 2.1

GATHER THE FACTS

★ What are the major client problems and opportunities at present?

★ What opportunities could my skills and knowledge help them to exploit?

★ What can I offer to resolve their problems?

★ Are there sectors I ought to be addressing?

★ How do I reach them?

    - What do they read, listen to, view?

★ **GIVEN ALL OF THE ABOVE, HOW CAN I AVOID LOOKING LIKE A "ME TOO!" BUSINESS?**

★ What makes me different?

        ★ Skills and Knowledge

        ★ Company culture , values and beliefs

        ★ Details of my offering

Figure 2.1(1)

POSITION YOUR BUSINESS

Will you create the image of:

       ★ A local company serving local business?

       ★ An International Consultancy Practice?

       ★ A highly specialised practice?

       ★ A practice of wide - ranging skills and services?

       ★ A One Man Band where what you see is what you get?

       ★ The highest standards of Client Care?

       ★ Rolls Royce service at Ford prices?

       ★ Price Leader?

OR? e.g. DTI Specialist, Expert on Government Grants, Unusual personality?

Figure 2.1(2)

3 Consultancy at Work

The process of consultancy has 10 steps which may take a matter of hours, days, weeks or months to perform.

Research indicates that as a rule of thumb the lead time in winning a contract correlates positively with the value of the contract. The bigger and better the assignment, the longer the lead time.

Consultants need to consider this when directing their attention to specific business opportunities. The lead time taken to land the contract tends to equate to an average of about 12% of the contract value. One day selling equals eight days sold.

If, as a matter of strategy, you set your sights on large contracts you need to consider carefully how your activities will be financed up to the happy moment when the cheques start to roll in. Many who are new to consultancy find it politic to go for relatively small local contracts which will put bread on the table quickly in the early stages, and having established themselves and their finances seek larger contracts at a later date.

The stages of consultancy

Marketing and public relations
Target your marketing efforts on the sectors and clients that you hope to exploit in the early days, but take some thought to building your reputation nationally and internationally if that is where your future lies. Remember that if you choose to specialise in a limited

THE CONSULTING PROCESS

Consultant   Delighted Client

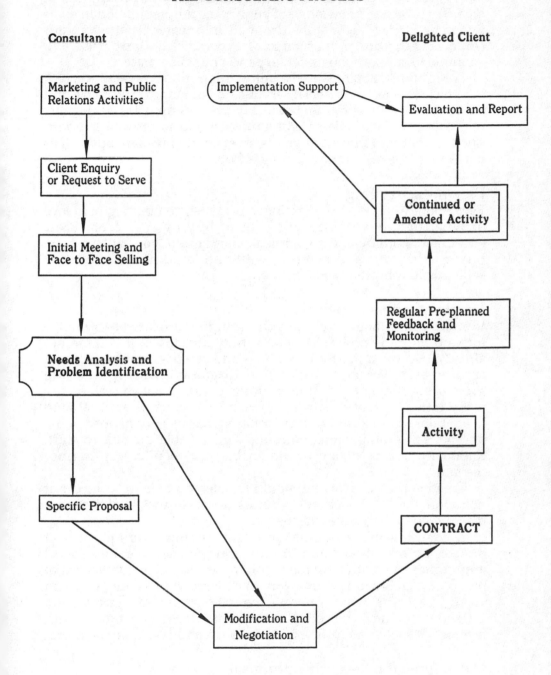

Figure 3.1

market sector you will become vulnerable to any downturn in that area. Try to widen knowledge of your name and reputation in ever-widening circles like a stone dropped into water. That way your contacts with your primary area of experience and expertise will continue to support you as you expand your client base.

For example, business in the automotive sector can lead to work in vehicle leasing, to financial services, to banking, to insurance and so on. As you become increasingly well known through your marketing activities clients will approach you to provide support. The fact that they approach you is an encouraging sign, but it does not obviate the need for marketing efforts.

Face-to-face selling
Psychological research increasingly provides compelling evidence of what people who are thinking of buying seek from their encounters with potential suppliers. Concentrate your attention on buyer behaviour and meeting well-validated needs, and then selling holds absolutely no terrors.

Problem or needs analysis
In most consultancy situations the solution is relatively straight-forward once the problem has been fully diagnosed. If you are not already, become a master of rational and creative problem solving approaches. Never forget that problem diagnosis is what you sell, and avoid being tempted to do it for nothing to show what you can do.

By rational problem solving I mean that which is applicable to 'deviations from norm', in short where what usually happens now doesn't. For example, one morning your reliable car fails to start. Rational problem solving would enable you, step by step to trace the fault.

Creative problem solving would enable you to leave your car at home for the AA to fix, but would get you to that vital morning meeting on time by other means.

A comprehensive rational problem solving technique is that developed by Kepner and Tregoe. One of the most successful approaches to creative problem solving is synectics. I believe that no consultant should be unaware of at least some of the 'problem solving packages' which can save many hours of undirected labour. I assume that any marketing consultant is fully conversant with techniques such as morphological analysis, and I need say no more.

Development of a specific proposal
Too many very good consultants give their services away without charge. I shall have a great deal more to say about this in due course. For the present let me suggest that the good consultant

always produces a proposal, even if the client does not ask for one or want to see one. By doing so the planning and costing of the assignment are much eased.

Modification and negotiation

The client may experience severe shock when the cost becomes clear. This is not an indication of the rapaciousness of consultants. It is simply the result of clients making inappropriate comparisons. By producing an effective proposal you will be well on the way to getting your client to increase his budget to hire you.

Contract

The Department of Trade and Industry consultancy initiatives are a far from splendid example of what may happen as a result of failure to agree a properly designed contract. Far too many clients are failing to pay their share for the very simple reason that they had a different view of what they would get for their money than that held by the Department, the managing agents and the consultants. Please commit yourself to use contracts, but make them relevant to the job and the client. Later I will tell you how.

Provision of service

When you do the job remember that this is a profession of trust and total quality. Your responsibility is to delight your client, but to do so at a profit. That way you will still be around to delight them again and again.

Report and evaluation

I am not a fan of long and impressive reports but I am a fanatic about predetermined meaningful outcomes. Whatever the appropriate style of report at the end of an assignment, it should always include three things:

- This is what we set out to do
- This is what we achieved
- This is what the client will now do to exploit fully
  that achievement

If such information can be conveyed on the back of an envelope or by word of mouth then that will suffice as long as it leads unfailingly to an empowered client taking the right action. If you need a weighty report for that outcome, then so be it - but beware of the type of person who likes such reports for their own sake.

What consultants ought to do

Let us look at what you do for your client, regardless of your specialism.

Do consultants 'borrow the client's watch, tell him the time, and pocket the watch with the fee'? Apart from the final accusation of light fingeredness the answer is 'yes,' but they do it in a way which gives added value immensely greater than any apparently inflated fee. The only source of meaningful information about a client's business lies in and around that business.

The consultant's contribution is to analyse the mass of information, bring a wider and less parochial perspective to bear, and leave the client with a richer range of useful choices than were previously apparent and greater power to exploit them. If that is what you mean by 'stealing his watch' Mr Townsend, you are right. What is more, I lift it with pride and return it cleaned and keeping better time than before.

In detail, borrowing the client's watch and telling them the time means that you do the following:

Build rapport

Consultant and client have to work together creatively and productively if they want to do a great deal better than just rub along. When you or I go into an organisation we have a specific client who hires us and has our absolute loyalty and support. The day that we are unable to provide that loyalty is the day that we must back out of the assignment. That means that there are no circumstances in which it is acceptable to go behind our client's back, either to the board or to his or her secretary. In a position of trust there is no such thing as 'wrong but acceptable'.

You must share your client's dreams. Those may change under your influence as the assignment matures, but at any time, making present dreams a reality is your goal.

Analyse information

The consultant analyses thoroughly the business situation, regardless of his specialism or background. To provide off the shelf solutions without analysis is wrong, and so is developing departmental solutions which damage the rest of the business. A business is a complete entity; you either bring to bear sufficient nous to analyse the whole, or if you lack the competence, you bring in others to help - or you walk.

Analysis must be dispassionate and objective, but it must be underpinned by a mandatory and passionate commitment to the interest of the client and his organisation. The consultant must enrich his depth of knowledge about the client organisation with the most current and effective best practice, and the best validated research.

Develop alternatives
The creation of choice is often the most important contribution of the consultant. Choices are presented without bias and with the weight of supporting evidence clearly explained.

Recommend options
Someone (do you remember who?) said; 'advisers advise, ministers decide'. Clients also decide, and unless that decision is unethical or illegal, consultants contribute to making it work. The effective consultant presents his recommendations as forcibly as the evidence warrants, and then supports the client in whatever he decides.

Motivate action
Recommendations which lie unimplemented are of no value to the client or to the reputation of the consultant. Recommendations which are badly implemented damage both. The consultant must ensure that his recommendations can be carried out with available resources and with the active commitment of all involved. Team building in the broadest sense is a part of every assignment.

Ensure growth
The consultant should leave every assignment with a client who is more skilled, more knowledgeable, more independent and more self-reliant than when the contract began. If that sounds to you like the death knell of your future income, fear not. Skillful, confident, effective clients grow, and as they grow they provide bigger and better contract opportunities for the consultants they have learned to trust. Conversely, 80% of clients in the Shenson survey about client fears quoted below indicated that they would have strong reservations about employing a consultant again because they feared ongoing dependency would result. That says something about our profession, and I for one don't like the sound of it.

Ethics and values
As a certified (Oh how I wish Americans would learn to say 'certificated') consultant to management, I have signed an ethical undertaking and a code of practice which has the same effect on me as the Hippocratic oath to a medical practitioner. I have no wish to impose my values, my job being to offer practical advice, but I believe that there are practical benefits to be gained from working to a strict code.

A practical approach which I stole from somewhere long ago might be a sound basis for those about to establish their own ethical and practice values. The consultant should recommend only that for which there is a sound business purpose, will at least pay for itself in an acceptable time, and which can be explained in simple language to those who must make it work.

Teams within teams

Although the consultant must become loyal to a single client, he must also become involved with the client organisation's team. The central idea that the consultant's recommendation serves no purpose until it is successfully put to work means that all consultants, regardless of their discipline, need to have an operational understanding of team building strategies.

One of the most practical and influential approaches of recent years is that developed by Dr R Meredith Belbin. A brief overview of the concept follows, but I would strongly urge all professionals to study Belbin's book, 'Management teams - why they succeed or fail' with care. Belbin's research suggests that successful teams are a blend of people bringing together different personal styles to the effective completion of any task. No style has greater value than any other, although given a specific task one or more may make a uniquely important contribution because of the nature of the job in hand or the stage which it is at.

Given the wide range of activities which any team needs to address, it is probable that the key weakness in unsuccessful teams is the lack of someone with the appropriate team style allocated to the right task at the right time. Thus,a team of great creativity and intellectual brilliance may come up with a range of superb ideas, any one of which would be a winner were it put into effect. But if the team lacks solid dependable people capable of beavering to get the job done, no plan reaches fruition, and the team fails because it is seduced by novelty and the boredom threshold is low. Worse, since an unsuccessful team eventually tends to seek the causes of failure in terms of the faulty contribution of its own members, even the flow of ideas may cease, and the group may descend to pointless infighting.

As a consultant you enter your client's team when assigned. Although you must be careful to maintain your objectivity in analysing the situation and making recommendations, your role remains that of a team member throughout the assignment. You need therefore to consider carefully the appropriate team member behaviour at every stage of your work, and the effective consultant is prepared to find ways of plugging the gaps in the client team. At

Belbin's Team Roles
Figure 3.2

Role Description	Team Style	Key Strength	Key Weakness
Chairman	Calm and Confident Goal driven	Open Minded Self Confident	Limited Creativity Limited Intellect
Company Worker	Well Organised Committed	Hard Working Sees Job Through	Inflexible Limited Imagination
Team Worker	Socially Oriented Promotes Team Needs	Self Effacing Sensitive to Others	Indecisive Under Pressure
Shaper	Challenges and Tests Ideas	Dynamic Analytic	Often Highly Strung Irritable
Plant	Unorthodox Thinker	Imaginative Individualistic	Sometimes Impracticable
Resource Investigator	Makes Contacts Drives Progress	Extrovert Responds to Challenge	Grasshopper Mind Careless of Detail
Monitor Evaluator	Practical Hardheaded	Judgement Prudence	Lacks Inspiration
Completer Finisher	Capacity to Follow Through	Conscientiousness	Reluctant to Let Go

the implementation stage this need becomes paramount to ensure economic progress. You will do much to ensure that your ideas are carried out competently by thinking constructively about the team which must implement them.

If the consultant can do no more than identify the essential team roles, develop others in assuming those roles, or take the responsibility himself, and help to manage the social and task effects of team operation, his contribution to the ongoing effectiveness of the client organisation will be immense.

The consultant should always be mindful that the organisation is an integrated system. It is almost impossible to take an action in one part of the business which will have no effect, for good or ill, elsewhere. In my opinion it is a prerequisite of professional practice that the consultant takes all opportunities to expand knowledge of areas beyond the confines of his narrow specialism. I doubt the ability of any consultant to be fully effective without a working knowledge of:

• The way people behave in organisations;
• The marketing concept;
• Finance and the role of profit;
• Management information systems.

This is not to say that every consultant should become a total polymath where business is concerned, but it does suggest that both self-development and working with fellow professionals is essential to us all.

Undertaking self-assessment

This is not a complex psychometric test. It is a simple self-assessment to enable the professional advisor to management to plan his ongoing self development on the basis of current and validated research findings.

To use it, read through the statements and decide which are true of you;

• All of the time;
• Most of the time;
• Some of the time;
• Rarely or never true of you.

Mark the applicable description with a cross.

Ideally, use the second copy of the inventory to have a trusted client or colleague complete a second assessment of your professional behaviour. Compare and discuss, if appropriate, the two results focusing on any differences of perception.

Identify where you choose to change to more effective behaviour by drawing a circle around not more than four crosses.Transfer the key behaviours to the change planning sheet in the form of objectives and write a simple strategy statement for each to indicate the specific actions which you commit yourself to take - starting today.

Do not seek to change more than three or four behaviours at a time. Concentrate on those which you regard as most important and most easy for you to change right now.

Most importantly:
Commit yourself to reward every improvement which you achieve, no matter how small. In spite of the relative decline in academic support for behaviourist approaches, no more effective means of re-inforcing desired behaviour than that of relating it directly to pleasure has yet emerged.

Undertaking Peer Assessment

The person giving you this assessment form is expressing great trust in your openness and ability to act constructively.Please read each statement and assess on behalf of your colleague how true it is of him/her.

Is it:
• Always true;
• Usually true (more often true than not);
• Sometimes true (less often true than not);
• Never true in your experience.

Please indicate your assessment for each item by placing a cross in the appropriate column.

Your colleague intends to make practical use of your input, so please approach the task seriously and be prepared to discuss your assessment constructively.

Thank you

Figure 3.3 Consultancy skills inventory

			True of me	
General skills	Always	Usually	Sometimes	Never
I think before I speak	—	—	X	—
I am comfortable with my education	X	—	—	—
I am comfortable with my experience	—	X	—	—
I understand my motives for wanting to work in a helping profession	X	—	—	—
I read group behaviour accurately	—	X	—	—
I can separate personal issues from work	—	X	—	—
I listen effectively	—	X	—	—
I appreciate the impact of my behaviour on others	X	—	—	—
I understand my need to compete with others	—	X	—	—
I can deal with conflict and anger	—	X	—	—
I can build an atmosphere of trust and openness	X	—	—	—
I work on the basis of a clear theory	—	—	X	—
I can use relevant theory as the basis of effective practice	—	X	—	—

Consultancy skills inventory 2

Problem solving skills	Always	Usually	Sometimes	True of me Never
I state problems and objectives clearly	—	X	—	—
I recognise the difference between rational and creative problems	—	—	X	—
I have skills in rational and creative techniques	—	—	—	X
I am skilled at summarizing	—	X	—	—
I sell my ideas effectively	X	—	—	—
I can keep people on track	X	—	—	—
I challenge ineffective approaches	X	—	—	—
I recognise key similarities	—	X	—	—
I recognise key differences	—	X	—	—
I am able to ask others for help	—	X	—	—
I can evaluate critically and effectively	X	—	—	—
I can contribute a range of proven techniques	—	—	X	—

Implementing skills

	Always	Usually	Sometimes	Never
I am strong at attending to detail	—	X	—	—
I can help people make best use of their skills and resources	X	—	—	—
I take responsibility	X	—	—	—
I am flexible	X	—	—	—
I can build and maintain morale	X	—	—	—
I can control my anxiety while performing any task	—	X	—	—

Consultancy skills inventory 3

Implementing skills	Always	Usually	Sometimes	True of me Never
I can intervene without threat to my clients	—	X	—	—
I can recognise my own defensiveness	—	X	—	—
I seek feedback on my performance	—	X	—	—
I can admit to errors and mistakes	X	—	—	—
I use my mistakes as a basis for learning	X	—	—	—
I learn from my strengths	X	—	—	—
Evaluation skills				
I can accurately assess my own contribution	—	—	X	—
I can acknowledge both failure and success	—	X	—	—
I feel comfortable with clients reviewing my work	X	—	—	—
I can deal with unexpected changes	—	X	—	—
I can devise forms, inventories etc. to aid evaluation of my work	X	—	—	—
I can let go when the task is complete	X	—	—	—
I follow up effectively	X	—	—	—
I refuse to blame failure on 'client resistance'	—	—	X	—

Please remember that the 'I' in this instrument is the colleague who asked you to complete this on his/her behalf, not you.

Consultancy skills inventory

General solving skills	Always	Usually	True of me Sometimes	Never
I think before I speak	—	—	—	—
I am comfortable with my education	—	—	—	—
I am comfortable with my experience	—	—	—	—
I understand my motives for wanting to work in a helping profession	—	—	—	—
I read group behaviour accurately	—	—	—	—
I can separate personal issues from work	—	—	—	—
I listen effectively	—	—	—	—
I appreciate the impact of my behaviour on others	—	—	—	—
I understand my need to compete with others	—	—	—	—
I can deal with conflict and anger	—	—	—	—
I can build an atmosphere of trust and openness	—	—	—	—
I work on the basis of a clear theory	—	—	—	—
I can use relevant theory as the basis of effective practice	—	—	—	—

Consultancy skills inventory 2

Problem solving skills	Always	Usually	Sometimes	*True of me* Never
I state problems and objectives clearly	—	—	—	—
I recognise the difference between rational and creative problems	—	—	—	—
I have skills in rational and creative techniques	—	—	—	—
I am skilled at summarizing	—	—	—	—
I sell my ideas effectively	—	—	—	—
I can keep people on track	—	—	—	—
I challenge ineffective approaches	—	—	—	—
I recognise key similarities	—	—	—	—
I recognise key differences	—	—	—	—
I am able to ask others for help	—	—	—	—
I can evaluate critically and effectively	—	—	—	—
I can contribute a range of proven techniques	—	—	—	—
Implementing skills				
I am strong at attending to detail	—	—	—	—
I can help people make best use of their skills and resources	—	—	—	—
I take responsibility	—	—	—	—
I am flexible	—	—	—	—
I can build and maintain morale	—	—	—	—
I can control my anxiety while performing any task	—	—	—	—

Consultancy skills inventory 3

				True of me
Implementing skills	Always	Usually	Sometimes	Never
I can intervene without threat to my clients	—	—	—	—
I can recognise my own defensiveness	—	—	—	—
I seek feedback on my performance	—	—	—	—
I can admit to errors and mistakes	—	—	—	—
I use my mistakes as a basis for learning	—	—	—	—
I learn from my strengths	—	—	—	—
Evaluation skills				
I can accurately assess my own contribution	—	—	—	—
I can acknowledge both failure and success	—	—	—	—
I feel comfortable with clients reviewing my work	—	—	—	—
I can deal with unexpected changes	—	—	—	—
I can devise forms, inventories etc. to aid evaluation of my work	—	—	—	—
I can let go when the task is complete	—	—	—	—
I follow up effectively	—	—	—	—
I refuse to blame failure on 'client resistance'	—	—	—	—

Change planning sheet

The behaviour I choose to change is:

think before I speak

My objective with regard to this behaviour is:

Thinking more rationally + detached emotionally

My strategy for changing my behaviour is:

- Counting to 3 before I respond or speak

- Phrasing thoughts in my head before I say them.

- Speak to David + practice phrases that give me thinking time.

I see an ideal opportunity for changing my behaviour when:

Speaking to Bob —

(Activity or situation)

My major reward when I am satified totally with the change will be:

Buy a set of headphones

Interim rewards for progress will be:

- Positive "thought-talk" to myself

Change planning sheet

The behaviour I choose to change is:

_____
_____
_____

My objective with regard to this behaviour is:

_____
_____
_____
_____

My strategy for changing my behaviour is:

_____
_____
_____
_____
_____
_____
_____

I see an ideal opportunity for changing my behaviour when:

_____
_____
_____
_____

(Activity or situation)

My major reward when I am satified totally with the change will be:

_____
_____
_____

Interim rewards for progress will be:

_____
_____
_____
_____

Change planning sheet

The behaviour I choose to change is:

_____

_____

_____

My objective with regard to this behaviour is:

_____

_____

_____

_____

_____

My strategy for changing my behaviour is:

_____

_____

_____

_____

_____

_____

_____

I see an ideal opportunity for changing my behaviour when:

_____

_____

_____

_____

(Activity or situation)

My major reward when I am satified totally with the change will be:

_____

_____

_____

Interim rewards for progress will be:

_____

_____

_____

_____

Change planning sheet

The behaviour I choose to change is:

_____
_____
_____

My objective with regard to this behaviour is:

_____
_____
_____
_____

My strategy for changing my behaviour is:

_____
_____
_____
_____
_____
_____
_____

I see an ideal opportunity for changing my behaviour when:

_____
_____
_____
_____

(Activity or situation)

My major reward when I am satified totally with the change will be:

_____
_____
_____

Interim rewards for progress will be:

_____
_____
_____
_____

4 Networking for Synergy

There is probably no more irritating waste of time to the dedicated consultant than networking as it is practised today. What happens is that a group of independents, usually with different specialisms, come together with the honest aim of developing mutual business. When I find a client whose needs are better aligned to your skills than mine, I introduce you.

You, it is to be hoped, contract to perform the assignment, and pay me a percentage of the total fee, usually about 10%, for passing you the lead. In the fullness of time, it is expected that you will provide me with business leads on the same terms. We will both be busy, fat and happy.

It sounds great. So why does it not work? It fails for a number of reasons, the first of which is human greed.

Most people who have attempted to establish networks have concluded, sooner or later, that the provision of hot leads is a one way street. You introduce me to clients, but there are no reciprocal arrangements. Somehow I do not seem to come across others who need your skills. On the other hand I do seem to seek your advice with some regularity about 'little problems that I have come across in a major assignment'. These are never enough to require your attendance at the client's premises, but are significant enough to compel you to spend long periods advising me in response to my frequent telephone enquiries.

The trouble is that I have realised something which has yet to register with you, namely that the cost of marketing is substantially greater than the 10% you are paying me for handing the client to you. The arrangement becomes a case of what is yours is mine and what is mine is my own, regardless of the quality of service that my attempts to perform work I am ill-qualified to do may provide for the client. What is more, although the client will get less than optimal service, he will probably never know, and I may be able to keep him. If I let you in to do a better job, whose client is it then?

In these circumstances I really am enjoying the best of every possible world. I keep my clients carefully to myself, and am kept busy while devoting myself exclusively to the development of my own practice. I benefit from my own marketing activities and yours, and have you as an unpaid provider of resource which in many cases will enable me to 'satisfice' my way out of potential trouble. If I can multiply you by half a dozen or so, and if each is as generous and ingenuous as you, my one way street is a highway to riches - at least until you realise your problem.

We have a number of problems:

- My greed;
- Client ignorance of what could be achieved, and probable low expectation of result
- Mistrust, in that I suspect, and judging by my own behaviour I am entitled to suspect that you will 'elope with 'my client"
- My ability to ensure some degree of marketable professional development by taking advantage of your generosity. (With free resource thrown in)

The potential value of networking is immense. In the early days of a practice, when doors must be opened and the chances of hitting the opportunity window which relates ideally with your skills is minute, the ability to multiply your prospecting efforts could make a substantial difference to your capacity to feed your family until your growing reputation brings the clients to your door. So how do we resolve our problem?

Equitable networking

I suggest that networking arrangements would be better for a touch of formality. A simple letter of agreement which makes clear the reasonable expectations and the responsibilities of membership would reduce the possibility of misunderstanding. In the event of a member's specialist skills being required for less than a half day, remuneration on an agreed internal hourly rate should be paid. The circumstances under which such a special rate is payable should be included with the rate specified. Half days or more should be paid at the normal daily rate, and should be encouraged in the interests of quality.

On the subject of payment, the percentage paid to the 'finding consultant' should be considerably higher than 10%. A minimum of 25% is required,   allied to an understanding that the client remains that of the initiating consultant would enable you, having passed work to me, to visit your client at least one day in four of the contract, helping to ensure client satisfaction and recognising work opportunities for other members in the team. Above all it would obviate the untrue use of 'the client wouldn't like....' from the one member of the team who has client contact.

To be effective, a network must be a team operation, providing, if not an equal amount of work for all, at least a fair opportunity for each member to use his skills and knowledge to provide the highest quality service to the client. In a profession dependent for its survival on trust, client service ought to be our constant guiding principle.

It may be a sad reflection on our society that the most effective way to promote quality is through the distribution of cash, but that is the way the world works. (I commend the following thought to those consultants who specialise in BS 5750 or BS 7750. Those who believe that the client will be best motivated to take action by an appeal to his concern for quality or for the environment will be disappointed. Try showing, factually, how the client will be more profitable by pursuing these valuable social and commercial goals and you will win more business).

Networking is probably the only efficient way for the 'one man band' to attempt to exploit the wider market. It can be made to work as successful networks testify, but if you wish to build a network that is equitable, then get things agreed in detail from day one.

Networking agreement
The precise form and style of a network agreement will depend entirely on the way that the members wish their association to operate. It should, however, include as a minimum, the following:

- An undertaking from each member not to carry out work for which another member would be better qualified.
- An agreement on the fee rate to be quoted by members when acting on behalf of the network.
- The level of the 'finder's' fee.
- Which consultant, 'finder' or 'doer' will be responsible for invoicing. (Personally I favour the 'finder' invoicing his client

and assuming the role of 'project manager'.)
- Standard network terms and conditions of business to be binding on all members.
- The circumstances under which a third party MUST be introduced during an assignment.
- Rates at which third parties are re-imbursed for interventions of less than half a day.
- The timing of payment to members of cash receipts.(This is vital).
- Agreed quality control arrangements.
- Whether the client will be seen by the network as being the customer of 'finder' or 'doer'.
- Any agreed period during which those who leave the network agree not to make a direct selling approach to any client of the network.

Unless the above are fully thrashed out there will always be 'bones of contention' to fight over.

Networking is the key to effective solo or small firm consultancy, just as it is basic to the success of the largest practices. At least one major practice devotes 50% of its total marketing budget to internal networking - that is how important it is. To be successful it must be done properly. Try to ensure that you build rather than join a network if you believe that the rules under which the existing group operates are less than optimal. Take the lead in this as in all things. It is that important. Get it right first time – networking will be in the long-term interests of yourself, your colleagues and your clients.

Rules for effective networking

1 Ensure that the selling consultant has sufficient income from the job to ensure that she can afford to take a high-profile position with her client. (At least one quarter of the value of the contract).

2 Work only with people who are fully agreed on the ethics and process of consultancy.

3 Develop a written contract to avoid misunderstandings.

5 Business-winning Proposals and Other Ways of Getting Paid

What do you do if the client says: 'I like the sound of what you are telling me. To hell with any proposal. When can you start?'

What I do is to look in my diary and agree a start date, shake hands and leave. Then I go home and write a proposal anyway. Let me counsel you always to write a proposal, whether the client wants one or not. It is an essential tool for planning your intervention. When you have completed your proposal it will be clear to you exactly what you will do, when you will do it, why you are doing it, and how much it will cost.

As a planning tool, a well-constructed proposal is useful. As a marketing tool it is indispensable. If something in your business is indispensable you must have a labour-saving and effective approach to its production, but before we discuss that, let me tell you why it is so vital in marketing your business.

Forget for a moment any fancy definitions of marketing. Let's be both basic and selfish. What is your marketing effort for? It is to bring you profitable business. All the good stuff about 'creating, identifying and satisfying' only makes sense if it builds and maintains your business at a profit. The Bible says something about 'what shall it profit a man if he gain the whole world and lose his immortal soul?' The consultant's version ought to be 'what shall it profit me if I look a real smart alec, and give away my expertise for free?'

That is precisely what too many consultants do when they present a proposal. They make a present of their expertise in the form of a 'recipe' which tells the client, in ravishing detail, how to turn the assignment into a 'do it yourself job'. Worse, where the client is completely without principle, the detailed and comprehensive proposal finds its way into the hands of a competitor who is either cheaper, or an old buddy of your hoped-for client.

So we have three basic requirements of any proposal that we write:

1 It should be easy to write with the minimum investment of time.

2 It should avoid all danger of giving away your services for free.

3 It must be an effective marketing tool which will win you business, and preferably win you business on your own terms.

Sounds easy enough to meet those little requirements doesn't it? Let's have a look at how.

Writing the proposal

Put a simple thought into your mind, and cling to it through the process of proposal writing. Remember:

'The purpose of writing a proposal is to win business. It is not to explain my activities.'

Every time you find yourself tempted to explain, ask yourself:'If I resist the temptation at this point, will it lose me the business?' Unless the answer to that question is an absolute 'YES', explanation will be at best merely incidental local colour, and at worst may be all that the client needs to do the work internally, or to pass it to a favoured but less qualified friend.

Have a formula for your proposal and stick to it. That is the way to make production of the document time-efficient, and it will steer you clear of temptation.

A formula which has served me, and many thousands of others is;
1. Draw a Flow Chart of Activities
Your flow chart will say:
- What you propose to do
- The order in which things will be done
- The time each activity is forecast to take
- Any activities which are simultaneous or overlap

- Any optional activities which are desirable
  but not essential to the pre-determined
  outcome
- That the costs are justified because the
  activities are essential and the time
  carefully estimated.

Your flow chart will not say *how* **you will do anything.**
It is essential that you are clear on the difference between what is
done, and how it is done, so please bear with me while I make sure
that I have made the key distinction plain.
'What' might include:
- Complete feasibility study
- Identify training needs
- Conduct interviews
- Identify strategic alternatives
- Analyse statistics

'How' you do these things is precisely what you are paid for
knowing, and you do not give away your stock in trade for nothing
by providing details to your client at this stage.

Clients will, however ask 'how?'. Perhaps in spite of all our
efforts to cast you in the mould of the surgeon, the situation is not
the same. Given that some clients will behave in an this
uncooperative way and ask 'how' questions, what then is your
response?

I suggest that there are two viable strategies. If your relationship
with the client is such that plain speaking is valued above all else
you may choose to reply: 'How I do it is what I am paid for. As
soon as the contract is signed I will tell you that in detail.'
Alternatively, you may do what I do. I give them a more detailed
level of 'what', but I never tell them 'how'.

The conversation may go like this:
Client: 'That's interesting, how do you do that?'
Consultant: 'I interview your staff.'
Client: 'How?'
Consultant: 'I design a structured interview'.
Client: 'How do you do that?'
Consultant: 'I develop carefully designed questions which probe
the areas I need to analyse'.
Client: 'How do you know that you have the right questions?'
Consultant: 'I test them on a small sample'.........and so it goes on.
Eventually the client is satisfied because he believes that he now
understands how I work.
I am happy because I have a satisfied client, and I have given
nothing away.

Of course if I am in really in selling mode I might change to: 'Look you're obviously very interested in this aspect of the work. Why don't you try to find a little time to sit with me while I'm doing it, and I can fill you in on exactly what I am doing, and how it works. If we were to start on the first of next month, would you be free?' If he gets his diary out, I think I have an assignment.

2 Develop a benefit statement for each activity
- Show how each box on your flow chart represents benefits to the client
- Structure the list of benefits logically so that it is clear how each activity contributes to the achievement of the desired outcome
- Avoid indicating through unnecessary justification of a benefit 'how' it will be achieved.

3 Detail the reporting and consultation timetable
- Explain when you will meet with your client management and what form the communication of progress will take
- Show that management's ongoing input of ideas will be solicited through the assignment to ensure that your activities will be attuned to their possibly changing needs as the consultation progresses
- Tell them that all necessary information and training will be built in to enable the client staff to implement your recommendations.

4 Prepare a time line
Draw up a simple Gantt Chart which shows the dates when key activities start and are forecast to be completed.

5 Summarise costs

6 Add the ESSENTIAL extras
These may include:
Your terms and conditions of business
Your practice mission or value statement
CV's of the people involved, limited to what is relevant to this assignment.
Only add what is essential to help you to get the assignment. Always remember that big is by no means always beautiful. Any extraneous information which you add to a proposal to make it look 'impressive' may contain something which for a reason unknown to you causes the client to react negatively. This is a case where brevity is the soul of discretion - if I can mix proverbs with gay abandon.
If in doubt -leave it out.

What this form of proposal says about you

The flow chart shows that you understand the needs of the client in detail. Any fears which they may have about your competence are allayed. Together with the summary of benefits, the flow chart indicates the basis for your fees and shows through value that such fees are not excessive.

You have shown that there will be no lack of management control. Communication is central to your proposal, as is intelligent flexibility. Continued dependency will not be a problem because you have stated that the implementation by the client team will be fully facilitated.

Finally, the Gantt Chart demonstrates graphically that you plan to complete the work promptly and within the client's time frame.

Later you will read that research shows that client fears concerning the use of consultants are:

• Potential consultant incompetence
• Lack of management control
• Continued dependency
• High fees
• Inadequate consultant time
• Need for consultancy an admission of failure
• Fear of disclosure
• Improper diagnosis
• Lack of independence.

One simple document, kept to a practical minimum, does much to deal with them all. Only the consultant's possible dependence on a single product or style and the client's probable concerns over the communication of proprietry or sensitive data remain. Surely it can be argued that your proposal can and will demonstrate that you are flexible as well as capable. And since open and planned communication is central to your approach, a confident two way flow can quickly be justified.

Have I missed something? What about 'fear that the need for using consultancy may be seen as an indication of failure'? I contend that a professionally drafted proposal puts that to bed as well. Such a proposal provides your client with all the information needed to refute such a criticism.

Writing proposals has never been easier. These days it is easy to store your chosen format and generalised content on computer and save time by inserting the specific and tailored parts of the proposal quickly and easily.

Don't miss opportunities to 'recycle'. When your proposal fails to get you the business - and that will happen even in the best regulated of worlds - don't throw it away. Take out any client specific information. Write a letter which explains that you have been investigating issues and problems facing the industry and have sketched out a possible way to deal with some of the most pressing, and send letter and proposal to other key players in the same business sector. You may well find that your proposal wins you business after all.

How else can you win business and avoid giving away your services? Let us consider the tricks clients play.

Imagine (many readers will not have to!) the following situation. You have just completed an assignment. The work has gone well. Both you and your client are delighted with the outcome. Days or weeks elapse and you are busy with new work, or with finding it. One evening you get home to find a message from your satisfied client that he would appreciate a call. When you call, it is not the half-anticipated referral. Apparently one member of your client's team is having minor difficulties implementing your recommendations. Could you just call by tomorrow, and put him back on the right track? Of course you could, you are very pleased to have an opportunity to give exceptional service, in spite of your slight surprise that there is a problem after all the trouble taken to predict and prepare for all eventualities.

You travel somewhat out of your way and delay the start of an important meeting and to find on arrival that the problem has little or nothing to do with your work. It is just that they have a new idea which excites them, and they were keen to have a chance to 'bounce it off someone'.

You are still happy. It is good to know that your opinion is valued in other areas. A couple of weeks later, a similar call, a similar outcome. The new idea has some complex features, and 'what exactly was that planning technique you mentioned to Fred that time?'

Before long you find yourself conducting an impromptu workshop, and you really feel good. It's great to be appreciated, and you are being appreciated something like once a week. Of course you are not getting paid for it and it does interfere with other work. But what the hell, you are laying-up treasure in heaven! Or are you? Perhaps you have just signed up as an unpaid non-executive director, and if you continue to give such good service you may have a job for life. Unpaid of course.

Every professional worth his salt wants to give exceptional value. But there has to be a time when commercial pressures prevail. And there is worse to come. The more that people enjoy your services for free, the less they value them. Your sterling efforts become just part of their ordinary day to day existence – nothing special, just something that happens all the time. And if you believe that is the worst that can happen, think again. They may not value greatly what you are doing while you are doing it, but try to withdraw it, and see how ill and unfairly treated people can feel.

The answer is both very simple and very difficult. It is very simple, because when it becomes obvious that the client has a continuing need for your services you can regularise the situation by drawing up a retainer agreement. It is difficult, because seeing the opportunity before you are enmeshed requires considerable powers of precognition. It is more difficult because raising the suggestion of the retainer at an early stage may look like rapaciousness.

Experience suggests that the only way to avoid problems is, as usual, through good communication. Do the first follow-up. Do it with good grace and do it well, whatever it may be. Then when asked to do the second, make it clear that although happy to do the work, it is costing you the opportunity to sell your time and your time is all that you have to sell.

If the need for your services continues, you will have to invoice. Do the second task at least as well as the first, and immediately suggest a retainer agreement for the future.

Do it quickly enough and on the back of exceptional service, and you will have little difficulty in persuading your client that your continued availability is worth investing in. Do it late, or after being forced to either rush a job, or refuse to undertake it, and you will lose a client. What is worse, it is a sad reflection on human behaviour that through an excess of client care you can turn an ingrate into an enemy.

Retainer agreements

There are two basic styles of retainer. The first is where the client knows that your services will be required regularly for 'x' days per month for the forseeable future. This is sometimes called a 'time' retainer. If you attract this type of retainer, regard yourself as shrewd, or lucky, or both. You will be able to pre-book work, and you will not have to wait around to discover if you really are wanted or not. You will have a regular source of income for which all marketing costs have ceased. It is even simple to decide what to charge. Start with your normal daily fee rate, and if you feel generous, offer a small discount in recognition of the regularity of the income.

If, however, you feel that a discount is appropriate, always use it to obtain a quid quo pro. In this case it might be proper to suggest that payment be made on or before a given day each month. It would also be wise to establish that any discount which you are able to offer for regular work is not automatically transferable to other assignments for which your standard daily rate applies. Put any such agreement in writing, and if any retainers are substantial, check with your accountant to ensure that nothing that you are contemplating is likely to prejudice your status as self-employed for tax purposes.

The second style of retainer is a little more complex. Perhaps your client is unsure whether there will be a need for you to do anything in any particular month, but would like you to pencil in a set number of days each month when you will undertake to be available if required. Now you have a slight problem. The client is unlikely to want to pay your full fee each month if you are not needed to do any work. On the other hand, if you have reserved time for your client you cannot sell it to anyone else. This means that for each day you are not used a valuable opportunity is lost. Worse, you may occasionally find yourself having to turn down work, because you are ethically bound to hold yourself available.

An appropriate fee structure for an availability agreement is as follows. For being available, and for nothing else, you should charge 50% of your standard daily rate: if it turns out that in any given month you sit doing nothing for several days waiting to be called, you have some, albeit limited, income. If you do work for the client you need to be compensated both for the loss of opportunity when not used, and the outcome when you are. For days when you work you should, therefore, charge your full standard daily rate in addition to the 50% levied for being available. In summary, available but not used, 50%: available and used, 150%. If your client finds that the need for your services is more frequent and regular than was anticipated, you can always return to a 'time retainer', where your full income, or something close to it, is guaranteed.

Needs analysis: a cautionary tale

Don't provide analysis for free

When I was young, and more than a little green, I fell in, as luck would have it, with a client who would have described himself as 'shrewd', and whom others described as being anything between a cheap crook and an expensive one. Like all who are new to the business I was enthusiastic, anxious for work, and trusting.

It was suggested that I should complete, without payment, a training needs analysis for the company which my client served. I should then develop a training plan, and having sold it to the board of the client company, I should design and conduct, for a modest fee, those programmes for which I was qualified. It sounded like a promising start to my career which would bring in about half of my forecast income for the first year. It promised relatively early and regular income, and since I would be less than qualified to design and teach every programme, it would bring me into early contact with fellow professionals in non-competing complementary fields of expertise. I set about the task with vigour.

I completed the needs analysis, drew up the training plan, convinced the directors of the value of the programme, provided a wide range of samples of materials which I felt would be useful and even talked to manager and employee groups to encourage interest and attendance. I had no contract, but why should I care, I was dealing with nice people.

I woke up when I found that several of the programmes which I was highly qualified to present were to be given by another consultant and I, having done all the pre-work and having no contract, had no redress. As it happened, I eventually found out why the contract had been placed with the other firm. You see I, and most of my competitors, charged £500 a day at the time, while the firm which had 'won' the contract charged £750. An indication of higher quality? No, the programmes were almost universally condemned by participants as useless or worse. An example of snobbishness gone mad? No, the answer was simpler and more venal. The company which had won the contract at the high price had a very practical approach to getting business. They were not greedy. Content with the norm for those days of £500 per day, the remaining £250 was paid to the manager who placed the contract in recognition of his placing it with them.

I tell this cautionary tale for two reasons. First, it is true in every particular. Second, although an extreme example it is typical of a favourite ploy to get you to provide your professional services for nothing.

The promise of a major assignment when the preliminaries have demonstrated 'what you can do' is almost never kept. Whether you complete a problem diagnosis or a professional needs analysis, you have done the most difficult part of most assignments. After your excellent groundwork almost anyone, within or outside the client company, can take over. They may be cheaper, or there may be other reasons for handing the work to them. Do not take the risk. Always charge for needs analysis, diagnosis or feasibility studies, and charge at your full rate. You are providing professional services of a high order in work that is difficult and time-consuming. If you must, and only if you must, do a deal along the following lines:

Charge for the initial work at your full daily rate. If a substantial contract is placed with you for the completion of the assignment before payment of your first invoice is due, then you may waive all or part of your charges for the preliminary work.

The only circumstances which I can see which would justify such a step would be where the competition had been foolish enough to offer to do what I so stupidly did when I knew no better.

A little diversionary tactic

You are working for *Plant A* on an assignment for a company with more than one plant. One day your client tells you how satisfied they are with your work, and asks if you would go over to *Plant B* and look at a 'little problem' there.

At such a request bells should sound a warning in your skull and distress rockets should be firing between your ears. This is truly a double trouble situation.

If you are a professional, you have agreed an outcome at *Plant A* which will be achieved within an agreed time. That is what you will be measured against. Any distraction which takes you to *Plant B* chasing 'little problems' and their solutions puts your performance and your reputation at risk. Believe me, against that the fact that you will probably not be paid for the extra work is a minor irritant. Yet it seems a reasonable request from a valued client, so what do you do?

First, you take out your diary, and reminding the client of the agreed outcome and timeframe and the progress which you have made to date, you indicate when you will be free to attend to *Plant B's* 'little problem' without adversely affecting your ability to complete the current job to standard and to time. Next, you politely ask whether the extra expenditure has been authorised or whether it would help if you drafted an amendment to the contract. Having established a time when you can properly attend to the needs of *Plant B* and that you expect to be paid for your efforts, you can concentrate on *Plant A*, or only address *Plant B* if your client is prepared to change his priorities. If such a change in priorities is insisted on, visit *Plant B* as requested and immediately put into writing your recommendation for completion of the now enlarged contract.

Dispensing advice
Once you become a professional adviser, people will seek your advice. That is reasonable and desirable. What is less reasonable, and far less desirable, is that many will seek to obtain that advice without payment.

You will find that you are approached on social occasions, at parties or in the pub, by the kind of people who, were you the doctor, would remember the little pain that has been bothering them for weeks. What makes matters worse is that this is probably an indicator that you are a helpful person, at your happiest when passing on helpful tips or information. Try not to do it. Steer enquirers gently and firmly toward business hours and your office or theirs. Help them to value your services, and remember that 'owt tha gets for nowt in't worth what tha paid for't.'

In the Chapter on selling your services I refer to an interesting recent study which suggests that there are occasions when from your perspective the client is trying to get something for nothing, while from their point of view all they seek is value.

The study shows that around 15% of clients expect to be billed for the initial 'marketing' meeting, and spend much of that meeting trying to get information which represents value. At the same time the acute consultant, with no intention of charging for what is an exploratory meeting, fences skillfully to avoid giving anything away which might later earn fees.

The result of this miscommunication might be funny were it not that business can be lost and relationships can be mistrustful from the start. 'If in doubt communicate' is a lot better advice than 'if in doubt say nowt' in this case. If you have any indication that your client may expect to be billed for your initial meeting, explain that just as you always expect to be paid for work you do, you never expect to be paid for simply exploring the possibility of doing work. That way you can both relax and identify how you may most usefully serve.

That will lead to more business as surely as the use of a properly constructed proposal leads to more profitable and better business. And for the doubters - IT DOES.

THE ROUTE TO SUCCESS

Developing Business-winning Proposals

1. The Essentials

A detailed Flow Chart of ACTIVITIES - WHAT is to be done

A brief BENEFIT statement for each ACTIVITY - WHY it is to be done

A Gantt Chart or TIME LINE - WHEN it is to be done

TERMS and CONDITIONS of Business - HOW MUCH it will cost to do it

2 The Desirables

An overall BENEFIT SUMMARY

An EXECUTIVE SUMMARY

3 The Optional Extras

MISSION STATEMENT or VALUE STATEMENT of the practice

Relevant CV's of the consultants involved

Detailed explanation of CHARGES and TOTAL COST justification

A good proposal is limited to saying:

WHAT is to be done

WHY it should be done now

WHEN it will be done

ANYTHING which indicates HOW it will be done is an invitation to the client take the results of your expertise and offer those results as a recipe to the less able and less scrupulous who may do the work at lower cost.

Figure 5.2

EXECUTIVE SUMMARY

This proposal covers the design, development and conduct of a research and market driven training programme to replace QCT8.

The proposal is that it be developed by a team which includes each of the relevant disciplines and that intellectual ownership will be assigned to XYZ.

The programme will be developed from scratch in order to ensure its relevance to the XYZ business plan, and a brief but necessary analysis of specific client needs and readiness is proposed.

The emphasis will be on practical application of all learning, and the programme will support a strategy aimed at either exploitation of an existing and growing market sector, or the empowerment and support of mature employees in the development of autonomous but related service enterprises in line with the XYZ Japan model.

Sample proposal (1)

INTRODUCTION

It is a paradox of an emerging era in which information is increasingly the driving force in competitive advantage that technological advances continue to accelerate at a pace which creates downward pressures on prices and margins.

XYZ have a strategic advantage which goes beyond the market standing of their products . They have established a relationship with their customer - clients which enables them to exploit an opportunity which is supportive of, and consistent with their core business. The development of consultancy services within the strategy has been timely. With changing and growing expectations of the consultant now is an ideal time to reassess the market and respond to its realities.

Increasingly the narrow specialist approach which characterised consultancy is being replaced by a market-driven demand for a "holistic" style of intervention. Any change within the business is finally being understood to affect all operations, unequally, but importantly, and the expectation that the consultant will be able to take a top-down strategic view is growing. The consultant is expected to understand the vision, facilitate its achievement, and guide the client through the often complex chain reaction which operational decisions create. The need for information is paramount, but the development and effective use of information is increasingly requiring new process skills.

The market has developed a view of the type of consultant who will be able to bring to bear on any problem the comprehensive skills and knowledge which are required. Research on both sides of the Atlantic increasingly demonstrates that in a condition of less than perfect information the client responds to cues which are embedded in the specifics of the Consultancy Service's marketing approach.

This proposal, therefore is designed to centre on the key factors of current process which is infinitely transferable within the business, and client- centred marketing techniques which have a proven record of success.

The timeliness of XYZ's decision to review aspects of their Consultants Education Programme cannot be ignored. The market for consultancy is projected to continue to grow at better than 20% per annum domestically as we emerge from the current recession, and global opportunities: in developed markets, as yet undeveloped markets of the Pacific Basin and Eastern Europe are immense.

The team brought together to develop this proposal is uniquely synergistic. It combines experience in the professional development of consultants at all career stages with specialist IT and marketing consultancy skills. In addition it offers immediate access to research on both sides of the Atlantic "as it happens" and can provide truly state of the art inputs. A key requirement for an industry in which "state of the art" changes with almost incredible speed.

Sample proposal (2)

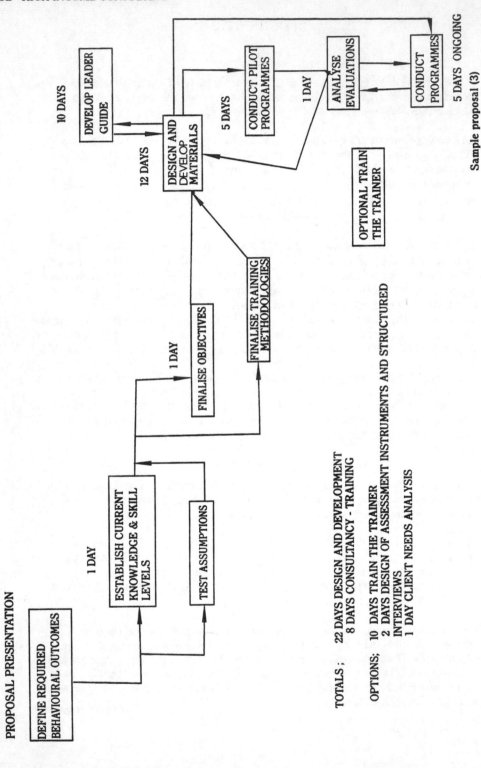

PROPOSAL PRESENTATION

DEFINE REQUIRED
BEHAVIOURAL OUTCOMES

1 DAY

ESTABLISH CURRENT
KNOWLEDGE & SKILL
LEVELS

TEST ASSUMPTIONS

1 DAY

FINALISE OBJECTIVES

FINALISE TRAINING
METHODOLOGIES

12 DAYS

DESIGN AND
DEVELOP
MATERIALS

DEVELOP LEADER
GUIDE

10 DAYS

5 DAYS

CONDUCT PILOT
PROGRAMMES

1 DAY

ANALYSE
EVALUATIONS

CONDUCT
PROGRAMMES

5 DAYS   ONGOING

OPTIONAL TRAIN
THE TRAINER

Sample proposal (3)

TOTALS ;   22 DAYS DESIGN AND DEVELOPMENT
            8 DAYS CONSULTANCY - TRAINING

OPTIONS;   10 DAYS TRAIN THE TRAINER
            2 DAYS DESIGN OF ASSESSMENT INSTRUMENTS AND STRUCTURED
                   INTERVIEWS
            1 DAY CLIENT NEEDS ANALYSIS

OBJECTIVES

On completion of the programme all participants will:

* ★ Understand, commit to and use appropriate personal marketing techniques which build status and reputation.
* ★ Analyse their own key strengths as consultants and seek opportunities to apply them.
* ★ Recognise opportunities for the profitable provision of Consultancy Services.
* ★ Build exceptional rapport with clients.
* ★ Use effective consultancy processes which are appropriate to the client problem, industry and culture.

CONTENT AND METHOD

The programme will be highly participative, intensive and practical. A wide range of methodologies specific to the needs of the materials and the participants will be employed.

Content will concentrate on key areas of effective marketing of consultancy, application and use of process and relevant self-analysis and development. Research into client expectations and concerns will be emphasised. Current aspects of psychology related to managing the client will be explained and practised.

PARTICIPANTS

It is assumed that the participants will be drawn from the same population as that for which QCT8 was designed.

DURATION

The proposal is for the design and development of a programme of five days duration with significant evening assignments. It is suggested that the programme remain fully residential.

FACULTY

To optimise outcomes and ensure necessary one-on-one support indicates the need for two programme facilitators to be present at all times.

Sample proposal (4)

DEVELOPMENT AND IMPLEMENTATION TIME - LINE

WEEKS COMMENCE WITH ACCEPTANCE OF PROPOSAL

WEEK ONE	WEEK TWO	WEEK THREE	WEEK FOUR	WEEK FIVE	WEEK SIX

ESTABLISH CURRENT SKILL LEVELS

FINALISE OBJECTIVES

AGREE OBJECTIVES

DESIGN AND DEVELOP MATERIALS

CONDUCT PILOT PROGRAMMES

ANALYSE EVALUATIONS

ADDITIONAL DEVELOPMENT AS INDICATED

DEVELOP LEADERS GUIDE MATERIALS

IMPLEMENT PROGRAMME

Sample proposal (5)

ACTIVITY SUMMARY

DEFINE BEHAVIOURAL OUTCOMES

To ensure effective transfer of learning specific, measurable, achievable and realistic outcomes need to be established.
For effective programme evaluation sample or whole population behaviours (pilot) would be subject to measurement and analysis. Current XYZ evaluations could be used concurrently.

ESTABLISH CURRENT SKILL AND KNOWLEDGE LEVELS

Research points to a range of successful strategies, some of which are dependent for their effect on the exercise or more basic skills. This brief analysis would enable the designers to target the needs of the participant population for optimal economic implementation.

FINALISE OBJECTIVES

A major saving of development time would result from detailed prior agreement with the client of the programme objectives, session by session. This proposal assumes such an agreement.

FINALISE METHODOLOGIES

Participative methodologies and recent research into "coaching" would combine to ensure the optimal transfer of learning. The XYZ learning culture, and the degree of progress toward the concept of a learning community would clarify the appropriateness of "state of the art" techniques. Although concepts are well proven, they are culture sensitive.

DESIGN AND DEVELOP MATERIALS

To limit development costs, it is proposed to use existing case study material, experiential exercises and psychological instruments where appropriate materials exist. This is how we have been able to reduce the estimate of development time by 50%.

Sample proposal (6)

DEVELOP LEADER GUIDE

To enable XYZ to operate the programme with absolute flexibility, and to ensure adequate cover if the design team were assigned to facilitate the programme on a short or long term basis, comprehensive leader materials and references would be available.

These would be produced in line with established XYZ formats if examples were provided.

CONDUCT PILOT PROGRAMME

IT IS PROPOSED THAT THE DESIGN TEAM CONDUCT AT LEAST THE INITIAL PROGRAMME TO TEST MATERIALS AND DELIVERY. IT IS CRITICAL TO THE PILOT THAT IN SELECTING PARTICIPANTS, THEY ARE TAKEN FROM A POPULATION OF REAL USERS WITH A NEED FOR THE PROGRAMME, AND NOT MADE UP OF AN ASSORTMENT OF THOSE WHO CAN MOST READILY BE SPARED ON THE DAY. SIMILARLY IT IS IMPORTANT THAT THE PROGRAMME IS NOT IDENTIFIIED TO PARTICIPANTS AS A PILOT. ATTENDANCE AT SUCH OFTEN CREATES A MIND-SET INIMICAL TO LEARNING.

ANALYSE EVALUATIONS

To be certain that the fully implemented programme meets the client need in full this activity must be carried out as a joint exercise between the designers and XYZ Training Professionals with a direct responsibility for the QCT series.

CONDUCT PROGRAMMES

The design team will be happy to provide fully trained facilitators approved by XYZ Education and Training Management to conduct the programmes, in partnership with XYZ professionals if appropriate.

Sample proposal (7)

BENEFIT SUMMARY

★ Effective marketing of consultancy services assured by proven, current status and business-building techniques.

★ Ongoing research ensures that updating will be immediate while design team are working on the programme.

★ Implementation assured by measurable outcomes and methodology.

★ Total ownership of programme by XYZ ensures flexibility in delivery

★ Economic and effective long-term facilitation through development of Leader Guide and optional Train the Trainer

★ Design team range of specialisms ensure that XYZ consultancy team will be developed with consistency in key areas of Marketing, Business Strategy, Strategic Applications of IT, and HR as required.

★ Methodology and facilitation approach are designed to ensure transfer of knowledge.

★ XYZ continued role as industry leader supported

★ XYZ strategy supported either through flexible application of programme, or through design to meet specified needs.

Sample proposal (8)

STANDARD TERMS AND CONDITIONS OF BUSINESS

Consultancy (including problem definition, needs analysis,
programme facilitation and field research)   £750 per diem

Programme Design and Desk Research   £600 per diem

Expenses

Travel: Road   40p per mile
          Rail   First Class at cost
          Air   Business Class at cost

Accommodation;

Hotel bills normally to client account or at Cost + 10% if invoiced
Meals when travelling at cost

NOTE: Days spent in travel on client business charged at 50% of daily consultancy rate

Programme materials supplied as single master set,, additional sets or bulk materials supplied
at cost + 10% if required.

Bought in materials (Psychometric Instruments, Harvard Case Studies etc.) supplied in single
copies, bulk requirements to client account or at cost +10%.

Invoices are raised at 14 day intervals on extended assignments.
Payment terms 14 days nett.

Sample proposal (9)

6 Setting and Divulging Your Fees

If you ever feel suicidal and want to destroy your reputation and career at a stroke, make it a habit to horsetrade over your fees.

Imagine the situation if you will. You are completing the verbal presentation of the finest proposal that you have ever put together. You have seen buying signals from your potential client such as you have never seen before. You decide to end with a flourish and a trial close, after which you intend to sit silent for the few seconds it will take for pens to be grabbed and contracts signed. You have everyone in the room on the edge of their seats with excitement as you summarise the key benefits, and you end with the words:

'And so you see, gentlemen, we will solve the problem and ensure that it will not return for only £30,000.'
You sit down, half expecting cheers of delight and tears of joy.
What you get is:
'Well, we like your proposal, but there is a snag. The budget for this job is £25,000. We sweated blood to get that. There's no hope of getting it increased.'
What do you do? I will tell you what the non-professional does. He gulps, perspires a little, thinks about the mortgage and says:
'OK. I'll do it for £25,000.'

Now he has problems, and we can afford to wish him luck with them.

- He probably doesn't know for certain whether there is profit in the assignment. (If he is bidding for a fixed price job he could be in real trouble if any unforseen snags arise).

- More important, if anything can be more important,he now has a client who thinks he was 'flying a kite' with his first price – a client who no longer trusts him and is only delaying turning down the proposal in order to satisfy his curiosity as to just how far the price could be driven down.

What then does the professional do when faced with the problem of the diminishing budget? First, he congratulates himself for his good sense in producing a professional proposal. Then he takes his flow chart of activities, and says to his client:

'Let us see how we can reduce the cost. We are agreed that all of these activities are essential. So let us look at those which can be done either by your team on their own, or by your people with limited support from me.'

He then goes with his client, box by box, through the chart, discussing the feasibility of having work done internally. If some jobs can be carried-out by the client team, that is fine: part of an assignment is better than either none at all, or a major job done for no profit.

What is more likely is that the client will want the consultant to do the work in its entirety just as proposed and will be willing to find the additional money. Try it, it seldom fails. But to be confident enough to make it work you have to be scientific about your fees.

Your fees must do three things:

---

1 They must provide you with a personal income appropriate to your skills, knowledge and experience.

2 They must meet ALL the costs of running your business.

3 They must provide a surplus, or profit which will enable you to invest in your business and allow it to grow in size, services and quality; and recompense you, the owner, for the risk which you are taking with your resources.

Let's start close to home with your personal income. Make a cool assessment of what your skills, knowledge and experience would bring you in the market place as an employee. Avoid any tendency to be modest. You are presumably good at what you do or you would not be offering yourself to clients. What is more, you have to build the client's confidence in using you and that means that you need to appear to be the kind of person who can command high earnings. Think for the moment only in terms of salary. Keep it simple.

Let me assume that you are worth £50,000 a year for the sake of example. You would expect to be paid, if you were in employment, for working days, high days and holidays. That is you would expect to be paid for 261 days each year. (You do not usually get paid for weekends and 365 less 104 Saturdays and Sundays comes to 261).

Divide £50,000 by 261 and you get £191.50 per day. That is your labour rate. With your daily labour rate established, we must turn our attention to your overheads, the cost of doing business. This is marginally more complicated, but not greatly so. Nonetheless, we will take it step by step.

Step One
Forecast the days you expect to be able to sell, on average, each month. Try not to be overly optimistic or you will fail to cover your costs fully. On the other hand, if you are unduly pessimistic you will make your forecast a self-fulfilling prophecy by establishing an unrealistically high daily rate.

My guesstimate of what you might reasonably aim for is 12 days each month. That is you will be billing clients for 12 days of the 20 that are available each month on average after fluctuations caused by holidays, variations in the business cycle and other activities which are not directly chargeable.

Step two
List and cost ALL your overheads.

Step three
Multiply each monthly cost by 12 and add to get an annual cost of being in business.

Step four
Divide the annual overhead total cost by the number of days which you expect to invoice to customers. On the basis of my guess, 12 days a month times 12 months comes to 144.

At this point you have established a daily overhead rate which you can add to you daily labour rate to give you a complete cost of being in business and of employing yourself. Before we go the last step, let us develop an example which will both clarify what we are doing and raise some important points about what to include. My example will be reasonably comprehensive. That is it will be, in the words of the insurance industry 'of wide scope'. Your categories and the figures which you put to each must be as specific and accurate as forecasting allows.

As a total aside ,my favourite definition of forecasting is one which I heard from David Myddleton: 'Forecasting is the art of stating what would have happened if what did happen didn't happen.'

Having got that off my chest, now for our example.

Overheads

Item	Monthly Cost £	Annual Cost £
Secretary	1000	12000[1]
Office Rent	250	3000[2]
Telephone	100	1200
Postage	65	780
Personnel Benefits	40	480[3]
Equipment	25	300
Stationery	12	144
Marketing		
Personnel (5 days)	958	11496[4]
Direct	500	6000
Practice Management (3 days)	575	6900
Dues and Subscriptions	12	144
Automotive	345	4140
Insurance	26	312
Accounting and Legal	225	2700
Miscellaneous	200	2400[5]
TOTALS	4333	51996

Notes

[1] If you charge any part of secretarial assistance directly to the client as an expense, you deduct that part from your overhead. The rule is 'The client always pays - but only once'.

2 A proper locally accurate office rent should be included even if you work from home. You may wish to compare your performance with others and you need to compare like with like and you may need to rent an office one day. When you do, you do not want to have to put up your fees. Clients notice such things.

3 You are entitled to whatever personnel benefits you would expect to enjoy if employed. (BUPA and or personal pension plan etc).

4 In case you have been wondering, this is where you cover the difference between billing clients for 144 days and paying your wages 261 days. The shortfall is eight days a month. The other three are charged under 'Practice Management'.

5 I hate to see 'Miscellaneous' in accounts, but it is useful for bringing together all the odds and other things such as meals when travelling and travel costs which cannot be directly charged to the client as expenses.

On completion of this exercise we have a daily overhead of £51996 which we divide by the days we expect to invoice which is 144. This gives us:

Labour rate	£191.50
Overhead	£361.00
TOTAL COST	£552.50

We are almost there. All that remains is to add our profit margin, but how much?

I can offer a rough guide based on experience. Most consultancies look to earn a profit of 15% to 25%, and coincidentally or not, it seems to be closer to 15% when interest rates are low, and nearer to 25% when rates are high. (If you are borrowing in order to trade, you will not forget to add the monthly interest paid into your overheads, will you?)

So let us go for the upper limit:

Cost of doing business	£552.50
Profit @ 25%	£138.125
TOTAL	£690.625

But £690.625 is an awkward figure to use, so we end up with:

Daily charge out or fee rate £700
And having worked it out properly we could, if we had to, justify it to the world as being the rate at which:

- We are properly paid for our labour
- Our expenses are met
- Our investment is rewarded with a fair level of profit.

You may be asked on rare occasions to break down your fee into its components. If you are the above will satisfy most clients with this proviso. Government employees tend to have a low regard for what they see as 'high salaries'; I would not wish to lead you into wrong-doing, but you would probably make a civil servant happier by reducing your labour rate and profit and increasing overhead to keep to the daily fee rate you have established.

Unveiling your fee

Getting or failing to win the business can depend on how your fee is presented to the client. One of the questions which I suggest that you must ask at the first client interview is:

'When you have used consultants before, what was the nature of the financial arrangement? Did they charge a simple daily rate? A fixed price? Or were they paid on results?'

The answer can be an important piece of marketing intelligence, let's analyse it.
Having established the type of financial arrangement you need to know how the client felt about it. Did it seem fair? Was it perceived as professional? Please note, I am not suggesting that you ask the above questions, but I am indicating the information that you need to have for your proposal, verbal or written. More open questions, such as: 'How did you like the arrangement?', intelligently probed will give you the information you need to present your price in a form which is most likely to appeal to the client.

Fixed fee including expenses

If your client shows a strong preference for entering into a fixed price contract and further wants it to include expenses, alarm bells ought to ring. A fixed price contract means that the consultant carries all of the risk. If the job is more complex than first appears, or if the client is more demanding of your time, you have a problem. No matter how long the job takes, you are only going to be paid the agreed amount. It is totally your responsibility to establish the precise nature and scope of the job, and to ensure that the contract specifies in detail what the client may expect for his money. Clearly the contract should also imply your willingness to take on additional work if the need arises, but it should state that such work will be charged at your normal daily rate. A fixed fee arrangement which is exclusive of expenses is better from your point of view only to the degree that if you are suddenly asked to fly to Japan as a totally unexpected part of the job, you will at least be refunded your travel and accommodation costs.

If you are forced to quote on a fixed fee basis, estimate the cost of every foreseeable contingency and include this in your quotation. Remember that you are being invited to carry an unknown risk. This entitles you to:

1   Minimise your risk as far as common sense will allow
2   Benefit from your own efficiency. If you succeed in completing the job in less time than was originally estimated, you, and not the client are entitled to the additional profit which that implies.

A fixed fee for the job implies that the value of the outcome is seen by the client as exceeding the cost.

Be like the engineer who tapped the machine with his hammer to get it going after breakdown. Be prepared to charge a penny for the blow and £999.99 for knowing where to strike.

Don't be paranoid, but be aware that in a fixed fee situation there is every inducement for the client to try to load the job and get your services for free. Your main aim must be to protect your interests while winning business.

Daily fee rate

This is almost the reverse situation, and is the one preferred by consultants. Here the client carries the risk. If the job is extended you simply keep on billing for time spent serving the client. A major reason why clients suspect that the consultant is hell-bent on building dependence is that most are happy to go on billing from here to Carey Street. If your client is happy with a standard *per diem* arrangement you are entitled to be happy too, but it is your responsibility to provide the client, through your proposal, with a realistic assessment of how long the job will take and the total likely cost.

You are not carrying the risk. If your efficiency is such that the job is completed early the client is entitled to benefit. Make sure, however, that if you are able to achieve the outcome in a shorter time than was initially estimated that the client knows what a bargain he has got and responds accordingly when asked for referrals.

A *per diem* rate is normally exclusive of expenses and so the client is carrying the risk there also. To minimise that risk, I offer the client the facility of making any hotel and travel bookings direct. This gives him control of the expenditure and enables him to take advantage of any discounts which his company normally enjoys. It also protects my cash flow, because when he books, he pays direct.

Performance contract

Recent research shows that approximately 12% of assignments in the United Kingdom are now carried out on a performance basis. That is where the consultant is paid a share of the savings or additional profits which are made as a result of the intervention. Twelve per cent may not seem a lot, but only two years earlier the number would have been in low single figures and limited to specialist interventions such as energy conservation. If it is true that we tend to follow the American model, it is important that all consultants and other professionals think carefully about how performance contracts work.The American level of assignments worked on this basis last year was estimated to have exceeded 70% of all work.

If you are invited to carry out work on a performance basis, the first thing which you need to consider is your personal attitude to such an arrangement. Are you to be paid for results, or is it your 'best efforts' and your knowledge that justify your fees? This is not a silly question. When the patient dies under the knife, the surgeon expects to be paid for exercising his skill to the utmost. You are entitled to the reach the same conclusion if you see yourself as a 'business surgeon'. You may, however, take the view that in the world of business everyone should ultimately be paid against results. If this is your view you will welcome the performance contract.

Guidelines for assessing a performance contract

- Is such a contract consistent with your image and values?

- Is the desired outcome feasible?

- Can the outcome be attained with the specific resources that you can bring to bear? Can you control the outcome?

- Is the value of the outcome sufficient so that your share of savings or profit will compensate you for the risk? (And the cash flow problems which may result from waiting for results.)

- Does a mutually acceptable and infallible process exist for measuring the outcome?

- Is the outcome clear and unambiguous?

- Will you enjoy sufficient income in the early stages of the assignment to enable you to resource it effectively?

- Have you a clear and binding contract?

Unless the answer to all of the above is positive, it would be unwise to enter into a performance contract, but it is an area of the market which will grow and it has obvious attractions to the client. You may have little alternative at some point in the future other than to reduce substantially your market opportunities or seek performance related payments. At least when that time comes you will not be taken by surprise. Take heart, the rewards can be enormous. A colleague of mine who works on a performance basis is currently involved in an assignment which, if successful, will pay him £2 million in a single and immediate payment. Of course if he fails he gets nothing other than agreed expenses, but he has taken on the job not in a flush of careless optimism, but as a result of a detailed analysis based on the above guidelines.

If you undertake more 'normal' performance contracts what can you expect to earn? Suppose that you are able to introduce into your client's business a process which will lead to substantial savings. You have thought it through and you are confident of the outcome. You may reasonably ask for:
- An upfront payment to meet your estimated expenses while working on the project.

- Reasonable payments 'on account' during the intervention.
- 30% of savings made in the first year.
- 25% of savings made in year two.
- 20% of savings in year three.

That can be a great deal of money and gives you the security of ongoing income over a period.

If the client complains about your fee

If during or at the end of an assignment the client complains about the level of your fee the chances are that, somewhere along the line, you have done a poor job of communicating.

To be confident that you have communicated effectively, ALWAYS:

- Agree specific and measurable outcomes for your work

- Work to a contract

- Explain precisely what your fees cover and what they do not

- Produce detailed, accurate and signed invoices at agreed intervals

- Keep your client informed of progress as it happens

- Advise your client of extra expense before incurring it

- Seek opportunities to boost the image of your client within his organisation during the assignment

- Create added value without giving your services for free by keeping your client informed of relevant external and internal information which you come across during the assignment

- Build a trusting relationship with your client by never doing anything in his company without his knowledge.

At the end of 1991 a major survey into fee levels was conducted. A summary of the results was as follows:

Mean daily rate	£720 p.d.
Range of fees charged	£100 - £3000
Normally distributed with 67.5% falling in the range:	£500 - £1000
Practice size	
Sole practioner	£500
Small practice (2 - 20 employees)	£700
Medium Practice (21 - 50 employees)	£850
Large Practice (more than 50 employees)	£975
Location of practice	
London	£825
South East	£750
South West and South Wales	£625
Midlands and East Anglia	£550
North and Scotland	£560
Average daily rate by specialism	
General management	£750
Human resource management	£825
Information technology	£725
Marketing	£600
Logistics and manufacturing	£525
Finance and administration	£500

The above are given for information only. No professional should pitch his fees at a level which does no more than reflect the market as a sample suggests that it is. A full assessment based on the interrelation between the value of what you have to offer, the cost to you of doing business and the volume of business which your best estimate indicates that you will enjoy is justified and necessary.

Business terms and conditions

Few consultants are ALWAYS able to do business in only one way. Most need to be flexible both in line with the client need and expectation and the job to be done. To give you a flavour of the mix, for this sample:

43% of jobs were done against fixed price + expenses

29% pure *per diem*

6% fixed price including expenses

12% performance contract

10% Some mixture of the above

Monthly invoicing appears to be the norm for more than two thirds of consultants while only 7% invoice fortnightly, weekly or in advance. This is something about which I shall have more to say.

Establishing your fee level

1. Annual Salary Requirement/261 = Daily Labour Rate

   Daily Labour Rate: £   p.d.

2. Estimate Number of Days to be Billed each Month:
   x12 = days per year. (Difference between this figure and 261 MUST be recouped as Overhead.)

3. Estimate Overheads:

ITEM	Monthly Cost	Yearly Cost
Totals		

Annual Overhead divided by estimated days billed = Daily Overhead Recovery Rate;

DORR = £ p.d.

4. Add DORR and Daily Labour Rate

5. Add PROFIT requirement

7   The Contract

No work of any significance - and at our daily rates all work is of significance - should be undertaken without a contract. Let me make myself clear from the start. A contract is not something on the basis of which you can successfully sue clients. To take your clients to court, whatever the provocation, is liable to damage you more than them. But a contract is more than useful, it is essential. It fulfills a key role in the process of communication which is vital to successful professional practice. Some of the uses of a contract may surprise you a little, so I shall explain those that I see as being the most important before I tell you how to draw up a contract and what it should always contain.

Uses of the contract

The basic use of a contract is self-evident: it states what you are bound to do and what you are entitled to receive. But it does a great deal more, and what it does says much for your professional status.

The fact that you always insist on a contract immediately identifies you as a serious professional. It adds to your status - and your ability to attract and retain business is based firmly on your status.

When a client is dealing with you for the first time, the use of a contract helps to remove both anxiety and euphoria and gives you both a firm foundation on which to build a relationship. Warren Bennis once said that business relationships are not founded on well-meaning exhortations to trust each other, but are based on doing things together and discovering that you can trust each other when there is a job to be done. By giving both parties to the agreement a sound indication of what is to be done together, the contract accelerates the process of building trust. The early period of uncertainty is clarified and that creates mutual confidence, while the sharing of information and knowledge develops rapport.

Imagine if you would a group of university students. Final examinations are approaching, and for some the cold realisation that the good times of the recent past may have to be paid for in the examination room is beginning to dawn. There is a sense of something greater than just urgency and expectation in the air, more a feeling of quiet desperation. Now suppose that a kindly professor approaches the group and suggests that he can help. He is prepared to conduct additional tutorials which will help them to identify and correct any weaknesses before they face the exam papers. Will they be grateful? Will they vow to attend any such sessions? You can bet on it. They give their verbal assurances that they will be there whenever the tutorials are conducted.

In due course our kindly professor announces that arrangements have been made. The tutorials will be held at his rooms at six in the morning each day for the three weeks prior to the examination. How many of those who so enthusiastically indicated their intention to take part will actually arrive? The experiment has been done and repeated, and the turnout averages a little over 10%. Very few will stay the course and attend at six each morning for the duration.

Now suppose that with another group the professor asks them to sign to say that they will attend at an equally anti-social time. How many will turn up, and how many will stay? The answer to the first question is somewhere between 70% and 85%, and of those who start the course better than 90% complete it in practice. The only changed variable is the requirement of a signature. That is why in American companies people are often asked to sign the corporate mission. Even knowing that the 'document' has no power in law makes no discernable difference. Most of us place great store in our signature. When we sign on the line, we take our obligations seriously. That makes the contract of value.

The contract also puts you, the professional, into a position of leadership. The fact that you are, from the beginning, dictating the conditions of business by insisting on and providing a contract creates the basis of influence on which you will have to build to ensure that your client gets optimal value from hiring you.

As a selling tool the contract has few equals. Most people who feel uncomfortable about selling manage to listen effectively, ask intelligent questions, present their solution and handle client objections without great difficulty. They do not win the contract mainly because the aspect of selling which causes them most concern is closing the sale. The fact that you have a contract eases that problem considerably. At the end of a discussion with a prospective client what could be more appropriate than to explain that you always work to a simple contract and that you would be happy to draw one up and have it ready for his checking and signature the next day?

If you have built the right relationship there is an excellent chance that the client will take out his diary and arrange a time for the next meeting. In these circumstances you know that it would be unwise to make any further selling effort. You are there. The sooner you can break off the meeting and leave the client to reinforce in his own mind his reasons for hiring you, the better. If, on the other hand, the client indicates that he is not ready to look at a contract yet, you know that you still have some selling to do.

That selling will be doubly easy for you because it is reasonable for you to explore where you have failed to satisfy him of the need for your services, and the end of the selling process is no longer the emotion-ridden act of reaching an agreement, but the less loaded situation of checking a contract.

Writing a contract

There are excellent books available on how to write contracts, some of the best of which include software, so I will not try to cover material which is readily available elsewhere. What I propose doing is to tell you:
• What constitutes a contract
• How to put together a contract
• How to get it checked economically
• What you should include as the minimum

What is a contract?
Let me warn you that I am not a lawyer, and what I say is no more than a layman's interpretation of what I have been told, and what I have read and done without problems arising. Since I admonish you to regard the contract as a matter of clear communication rather than a legal document, a layman's interpretation is appropriate and sufficient.

A contract is any agreement, verbal or written, explicit or implied, between individuals or legal entities such as businesses. Since a contract may be verbal and its terms may be implied, it is

reasonable to deduce that it does not have to be signed.
purposes, however, a contract must be written to full
communication function, and should be signed for .ie
psychological reasons outlined above.

No contract needs to be complex for our needs. The simpler you
make it, the better it will communicate. An ideal place to start is
with a simple letter of agreement drawn up in duplicate which both
parties sign.

Where possible follow the guideline of 'keep it simple and
straightforward' and construct a letter which includes the
following:

- What you will do and provide.
- What your client has agreed to provide to.
  enable you to do the work.
- How much, how and when you will be paid.
- Who owns the outcome(s) of your work.
- Circumstances under which the contract can be.
  assigned by either of you to third parties.

Let me explain the above, in case I have failed to make my meaning
crystal clear.

What you will do

This will be a brief outline of the service which you undertake to
supply. It may include specific agreed outputs and where
appropriate, dates for completion. It will not describe HOW the
work is to be done any more than the proposal would. This is your
undertaking to complete work. It is not a recipe.

What your client will provide

If your client has agreed to provide, say, secretarial assistance, or
data, or the output of previous work, your contract should specify
that input as clearly as possible. It should make clear that your
ability to fulfill your responsibility under the contract is contingent
upon you receiving the promised support as you require it.

How much and when you will be paid

Do not rely on your standard terms and conditions of business as
an assurance that you will be paid on time. Your client will have his
own, and those employees responsible for checking and passing
your invoices will work to their normal routine unless your client
instructs them otherwise. Only a contract is likely to have enough
emotional force to ensure that the instruction is passed on. If any
up-front payments are agreed, specify them and make it clear that

failure to make a payment when due will delay the project.

Who owns the outcome of your work

If you write a training course, or design a psychometric test, or conduct a major market survey as part of the assignment, it is important to know whether you are free to use those outputs on some future occasion. With training programmes in particular it is essential that you have worked out with your client whether his own staff can take over and conduct the training in your stead. If they can, the above paragraph about payment will show how you will continue to be compensated for your work.

Circumstances under which the contract can be assigned

As a general rule I advise that all agreements include a statement that they cannot be assigned to any third party without the consent in writing of both parties. This means that your client cannot, without your permission, hand your assignment to any other consultant or to a member of his staff once he has sufficient information on the 'how'. It also means that you cannot sub-contract to a colleague whom the client has not met and approved. That way you are both protected and the quality of the intervention is secured. If you want to be really legalistic you may wish to include a release clause to cover the contingency of either of you dying during the assignment.

- Cancellation fee: - Development fee

Drafting a 'proper contract'

There may be occasions when for the sake of appearances you need to produce a contract that has all the hallmarks of a 'proper' legal document, 'hereinafters', Latin phrases and all. If you do, resist the temptation to go running to your solicitor. To do that prematurely may be ineffective and will certainly be expensive. I am not suggesting that solicitors overcharge, but it is unlikely that you will be able to explain exactly what you require and against vague instructions a solicitor can only do his expensive best. That will probably mean several drafts are produced before you have the document you want and each draft must be paid for. Save some cash by producing the early drafts yourself.

Sit down with a pad and copies of old contracts. Write, cut and paste until you have something which seems to meet your needs. When you are satisfied with the outcome take the fruits of your endeavour to your solicitor, tell him why you need a more formal contract and ask him to answer two questions;

- 'Have I protected myself adequately with this document for the purpose which I have explained?'
- 'Is there anything else which in your opinion I should do?'

If your reasons for wanting a 'posh' contract are valid, the answers to the above will be well worth the solicitor's relatively modest fee and you will almost certainly end up with a better contract than many solicitors could produce from scratch with limited understanding of the need.

Much of what you will want in a contract will be in the form of a standard agreement. It is sensible, therefore to have a master copy which you can amend ready in your computer.

When you cannot provide the contract

There are two main situations where you cannot provide the contract, and it may be useful for me to comment briefly on both.

If your client is a major corporation there will be a rule that the employed legal officers always write any contract which executives sign. This is potentially a problem to you if the legal department has limited understanding of exactly what it is you are expected to do. Sometimes they write a paragraph which technically obliges you to perform something which is not in your power.

For example, you may have an assignment in which you are to assist your client to prepare for assessment for the quality standard BS5750. Since this is a matter of third party accreditation, you can at most only help to ensure that generally acceptable manuals and processes are in place – you cannot guarantee accreditation. If you are offered a contract which indicates that you will enable the client to achieve the standard, look carefully at the wording and get it changed to reflect what you are actually able to do, or you may find yourself working for very much longer than you anticipated for no additional fee. You can also bet that any legal department will tend to under-emphasise their own company's obligations and responsibilities.

Make sure that they are completely defined before you sign. Any variation in the corporation's standard terms and conditions which have been agreed may also be omitted, so check that the contract states fully what has been agreed about payments and ownership of outputs. Finally, make sure that your client is empowered to sign on behalf of the corporation, or if he is not, make sure that you at least touch base with the person who is. He may have concerns which could lead to delays.

A second situation is the more simple one where an

unsophisticated client tells you that they either do not need, or do not like contracts. My response in such a case, assuming that I have no concerns about doing business with the client, is to say that I will draw up simple terms of reference and let him have a copy.

The 'terms of reference' will, of course contain the same information as the contract. Terms of reference, for all its clumsiness as a phrase, is less threatening to some potential clients than the more 'legal' sounding 'contract'. Whether you have your client sign a copy after approval is a matter of judgment in these circumstances. From a legal point of view I am told that the signature is irrelevant if the letter is accepted, but you still have the psychological pressures of signatures to consider.

Collecting your cash

To collect money owing to you late is not as bad as not collecting it at all, but it is still bad and usually avoidable. Never forget that more companies are forced to stop trading because of cash flow problems than for any other reason, and make a firm resolve that your practice is not going to collapse for want of timely cash.

If you are a 'one man band' or a small practice it is easy for a client to believe that they could, at a pinch, do without your services more readily than you could do without their business. The market is unlikely to see what you do as being an absolute essential to their survival. Many will believe that you need them more than they need you, and so if anyone is going to have to wait for their money, clients may see themselves as doing least damage to their own business by making you wait.

This means that you have to be doubly vigilant and doubly resourceful.

When you are considering working for a client for the first time, insist on a formal contract and ensure that the client fully understands and agrees to the terms of payment which are specified. This way you can avoid many potential collection problems. If you work to a signed contract you have the advantage that people tend to remember more clearly what they have agreed. If you are, for whatever reason, working to an unsigned terms of reference style of document, go through it even more carefully with your client. Be as sure as you can be that it is understood.

Keep your client informed of every success as it happens during an assignment. A delighted client is more likely to ensure that you at least get paid on time. If you are working in a large organisation, find out who has the responsibility for checking and approving invoices. If the arrangements to pay you vary in any way from the company's standard arrangements make sure that all the relevant people know of your special arrangement. All major corporations have processes in place to 'walk an invoice through the system' and emerge at the other end with a signed cheque. Make an early opportunity to find out about them: be discreet, you don't want a client to think that you are excessively concerned.

You may have to ask how the system would ensure continuity of supply in the event of an accidental non-payment to a key supplier. Alternatively, you may need to know how a situation is dealt with where a key supplier is threatened by cash flow problems and it is in the company's interest to accelerate payment to keep the supplier in business. Whatever you have to do, do it. It is important.

Ensure that any progress payments which you are due to receive are paid on a specific date rather than something vague like 'the third week of the month', and ensure that every invoice which you issue carries the date when payment is due. The invoice should read 'payment due on 3 January 1993' and not some vague and usually ignored message such as 'payment terms 14 days nett.'

The date is meaningful on its own to the most cursory of glances. To make sense of '14 days' you need to look at the date of invoice. Most people just will not bother. While we are on the subject of invoices, sign yours. The fact that your invoice bears a signature differentiates it from the others from the moment it is drawn from the envelope. It implies that the charges have been checked and approved by someone in authority, and that gives credence to the invoice. It is wise to check thoroughly every invoice which you issue. Any inaccuracy is grasped joyfully as a reason to delay payment, as is any uncertainty as to what is being charged for. Make sure that your invoices specify the service in sufficient detail.

Limit your exposure where you can, and ask for advance payments to fund the resourcing of the project. It is often true that the early stages of an assignment involve the consultant in high expense. Ask your client to bear that expense: most will if requested, but few, if any, will volunteer. Try to avoid making payments to third parties on behalf of your client. Have the client book your hotel and your bill sent direct. It is no problem for the client– he will probably not pay the hotel any quicker than he would have paid you. The difference is that it is the hotel that waits.

If you have any serious doubt about the speed at which you are to be paid, withhold some vital information until the money that you are owed is in your bank. Never continue providing a service to a client when payments are overdue. You don't have to be obnoxious about it – just politely point out that your account has been overlooked and that you will be able to restart work as soon as your bank advises that payment has been received.

Any time that payment is slow, use it as an opportunity to evaluate the client and your the quality of your service to him. He made be withholding payment because he is unsure that he is getting value. Again, if in doubt communicate.

Summary

Your work
- Are you achieving agreed goals to schedule?
- Are you maintaining good communication with your client?
- Is your work moving in a direction which is unexpected and potentially threatening to your client?
- Have you allowed yourself to be diverted into any activities which are not central to your client needs?

Your client situation
- Is there any reason to believe that there may be a personality conflict growing between you and your client or within the client organisation?
- Is the client developing unrealistic expectations?
- Is the client fully appreciating the value of your services?
- Are there signs of new and critical problems in the client organisation?
- Have there been any signs of lack of interest in, or lack of commitment to your project by influential client management team members?
- Is there a danger that the client suspects that time which you necessarily spend off his premises is time spent off the job?

If there is any possible problem communicate guidelines for collecting the cash
- Work to a contract - always
- Keep your client informed and delighted
- Understand the client system of payment
- Agree and stick to specific payment dates
- Use actual payment dates on invoices
- Check invoices carefully for accuracy
- Detail services provided
- Sign your invoices
- Limit your exposure

Withhold key inputs when payment is due until the cash is in your bank. If payment is late - stop working.

PART TWO:
MARKETING YOUR PRACTICE

8   Tactical Marketing

Having spent much of my working life as an international marketing strategist, I am completely committed to the concept of strategic planning. But this Chapter is about tactics, not strategy, and my concern is with things for you to do no later than today or tomorrow to build your business. We must balance the longer perspective with ways of putting some bread on the table today.

The strategic implications remain – they underpin everything, but as far as this book is concerned they can be expressed in a few words.

Your professional practice will expand as your personal reputation and status grow. The time will come when your business growth opportunities increase at a rate far in excess of any accretion of fame. Some reading this page will reach that happy condition very quickly. For others, myself included, it takes a considerable amount of time and consistent effort.

You have an advantage over me. We can both learn from my mistakes, but I had to make them first.

Objectives

I always feel more comfortable in business situations if objectives are clearly stated and do not have to be deduced, so please bear with me for a few pages while I spell out where we are going.

On completion of this Chapter you will have selected one or

more low cost tactics which have been proven to build profitable business in the real world and are consistent with your personal style. You will also have committed yourself to put your chosen tactics into immediate effect by making your name known so that clients come to you for your services and, in the early stages of your professional career, are especially receptive when you go to them.

In short, the purpose of this Chapter is to make you just a little bit famous.

Background

Some interesting and consistent data has emerged from careful research over the last 16 years concerning the marketing tactics of the low earners in the profession.

1 They tend to do things which they hate like cold canvassing by personal call or telephone.
2 They spend considerable sums on mailings of expensive brochures.
3 They do very little of what the high earners do almost all of the time.
4. They say that what they do has very little effect on their business, other than to raise costs and personal stress.
5 They continue to do what they have always done, because, they say, they know nothing else to do.

Consider high earners. Some, a very small number, do certain of the things that the low earners do, but they do more. They are proactive in building their status and reputation, and it is from these latter activities that the bulk of their earnings come.

Image building and reputation

You are the product you sell and your product's brand image is entirely a function of how you are perceived. That is why your personal reputation and image are so important, and why we need now to look at the tactical approach in detail.

The lecture circuit

How do you feel about a diet of rubber chicken? That is how you are likely to be fed when you become a professional speaker. But it is still worth doing, because there are few opportunities to build your reputation at such little cost in money or in effort. In fact when you are in demand as a speaker, you may find that you need no other source of income.

There are more than 4,000 opportunities every week to give a talk somewhere in the British Isles. Secretaries are constantly on the lookout for people who have something to say. Those who can say it articulately with a little spice of humour are seen as being a gift from the gods

With so many opportunities to perform you can and must be selective. When you decide that it would be useful to talk to a particular audience you need to know if they have an association. Two directories from your local library will be of immense value. Both are published by CBD Research.

• The Directory of British Associations
• Councils, Committees and Boards

Both contain a goldmine of information, including the name of the appropriate contact, so you can write person to person and not have to worry about on whose desk your letter may finally arrive. When you write offering yourself as a speaker the information that they will need will be:

• Why you feel that what you have to say will be of interest to their members.
• The benefits to them of hearing your presentation.
• The unique things that you have to say. (More about this later, when I may appear to contradict myself).
• The length of your speech.
• Where you are prepared to travel.
• Special considerations including your fee and your expectations with regard to expenses.

Please be absolutely clear about the business of the fee. Professionals never speak for free, and you need to promote a hardnosed professional image at all times.

But suppose that you regard a certain group as being of such enormous potential value to you as a future source of business that you would be happy to speak to them if you had to pay! Am I saying that you would now pass up the opportunity for the sake of a few quid?

The answer is 'no'. You speak, – without payment if necessary – but you take the initiative. First you make clear to them the enormous fees which your talk normally commands. Second, you tell them how much you admire their organisation and how you share their goals. (Make sure that you know what their goals are by telephoning to enquire about membership, asking what the association is seeking to achieve). Third, make it clear you are so enamoured of their aims that your fee will be donated to their funds, and so you will not be issuing an invoice.

This harmless subterfuge will almost certainly ensure you a warm and favourable reception. The secretary will find it impossible to resist telling the chairman how he persuaded a highly paid speaker to appear for nowt. The chairman will find it equally hard to avoid mentioning in his introduction how the association has engineered such a coup. It is highly possible that the announcement of the meeting also carried this important piece of information. You will have an eager and enthusiastic audience.

Your objective is simple. You want to talk entertainingly for the agreed length of time so that you appear to be intelligent, articulate and well-informed about something that they find interesting and useful enough to give up an evening's drinking or time with the family to hear. That is less difficult than it sounds.

The secret is to tell them what they want to hear and confirm them in their beliefs. If you can do so by bringing to their attention some new findings which support their views, they will love you for it. But be careful not to be too highbrow about new information. Although you are the fount of all wisdom in your chosen area, you want to appear approachable so that those who have the greatest interest in your subject feel relaxed about talking to you after the meeting. This way you have an excellent chance of meeting the one person in eleven that research suggests will be looking for an opportunity to become your client.

As for the speech, that part is easy. Although many famous speakers have maintained highly successful and lucrative careers on the back of one speech, I suggest you have two. For normal evening or lunch time meetings one should be 25 and the other 40 minutes in length.

Without overemphasising the point, each speech should make it clear that you have gained your level of expertise through being a consultant. This simple and modest indication that you are prepared to accept fee earning assignments can be backed up by weaving into your talk examples of your consulting experiences and the data that you and you alone have available. You do not, of course, offer any information which could be construed as being of a client confidential nature, but if you can indicate the sharing of pre-publication information, so much the better.

Here are three rules for the content of the speech.

1 speech - 25 min
1 sp - 40 min.

- It should, in the interests of time management, be sufficiently general to be capable of being recycled to different audiences without onerous additional work.
- It must be sufficiently useful to be interesting, and it should not be so useful that it can have any worthwhile application without further recourse to you the expert.
- It is wise that it should, to a major degree, reinforce the views and experience of your audience. This appears to fly in the face of offering them something unique. But the research evidence is clear. Audiences like to believe that they are being offered information which is new, exciting and known to very few. What they like to hear, however, is something which will enable them to nod their heads approvingly and think:

'That's exactly what I've always thought. Nice to have it confirmed by an expert. I must get a word with him afterwards and tell him about my.......'

That is how clients are born.

You may find that you are so well received that you are building a paid speaking practice. If so, target your marketing and content on those who pay. Corporations pay handsomely for the right person, and national and international conferences often do too. National trade and professional associations usually offer something, but local branches seldom have a budget for anything more than that 'rubber chicken' dinner. After-dinner speakers can make an excellent living, and eat better.

Trade nights for distributors can be a very useful source of income. Car dealerships, for example have been known to pay (in 1991) £250 for an amusing, instructive thirty minutes which is supportive of what they are trying to achieve. It is not unknown for the speaker who is light-footed and able to resist the free drink to fit in more than one session in an evening.

Whenever you give a public talk, be sure that those who miss the opportunity to speak to you at the meeting know where to find you afterwards. This is not just a matter of handing out business cards. Create and distribute something of interest which they will keep, and to which they will refer. The more novel or useful the information, the longer life it will have.

My preference is for some useful data or formula, but an American colleague of mine hands out a little mathematical game which no-one ever seems to throw away. Some have even been known, years later, to call to be reminded of just how it works. Those calls frequently turn into assignments.

Remember that at a meeting many will be without briefcases,

so do not dish out copies of a glossy A4 brochure which they will clutch in increasingly moist hands as the evening progresses, waiting for an opportunity to dump it. Have your handout produced on A4 folded to fit into a breast pocket or handbag. Not only will there be more inclination to keep it, but when it re-emerges as pockets or handbags are cleared, (immediately, or days later according to the habits of the listener), it will serve as a potent reinforcer both of your message and of the skill with which you articulated it.

Be careful to ensure that your handout has your address and telephone number, and an invitation to people to contact you for further information, or to express their views. Always leave potential clients with a reason to want to contact you.

If you feel that the rubber chicken circuit is one that you would like to join, you can quickly be in business for the cost of a few stamps. If you like the idea, but doubt your skills, look in the telephone book and see if you have a local branch of Toastmasters. That way you could have fun and company while polishing your performance.

Directory listings

No-one other than a directory advertising space salesperson is likely to try to persuade you that many prospective clients seek professional help by sifting through a directory, but if only one does and you are not listed, your chances of that fee have just dropped from slim to zero.

Listing in telephone directories is straight forward. Thomson is free unless you choose to pay for a fancy entry, and although the same is true of British Telecom 'Yellow Pages', the entry is conditional on your having a business line. If you work from home and use your ordinary domestic telephone line, they do not want to know.

It is more important, because the potential for business opportunities is greater, to ensure that you have an entry in directories published by trade, professional or business associations for the convenience of their members. If you think that it would be useful for you to be known to the Antediluvian Society of Bottom Knockers, it makes sense to try to be listed in their directory. Of the thousands which are published, approximately half are happy to list you without payment as a direct service to their members. For the cost of a postage stamp you can make yourself accessible. The other half either make a small charge, or more commonly, restrict entry to those who have taken full or associate membership.

As I write, there is some speculation about the future of Training and Enterprise Councils, but while they exist make sure that they know that you are there and that you have skills which they and local business can use. Most by now have listings of locally based and national consultancies. You never know when such a list will be in the hands of a potential client at the opportune moment , so get listed while it is free.

Increasingly, the Training and Enterprise Councils are seeking to make money out of consultants by such schemes as 'Tecaware'. Under this scheme the consultant or trainer is required to pay a substantial sum to the TEC in order to be registered. If such registration offers a return in the form of assignments, then I see no harm in it. My experience to date, however, is that Training and Enterprise Councils are far from being the most effective salespeople in the world for consultancy, and schemes like Tecaware do little if anything more than give you the opportunity to sell their products for them. Since TEC 'products' have an amazingly short life, (I know of one TEC which claimed, with some pride, to have launched 70 products in one year) this may not be an appropriate way to launch or build your business.

Publish and be known

Publishing your own newsletter keeps your name in front of prospective clients. If a business regularly receives your newsletter it is perfectly possible that you are the only consultant they know by name. People like dealing with people they think they know. That is why 25,000 newsletters are currently published in the United States. Here the number is smaller, but growing rapidly: if this is an area where you have something worthwhile to contribute, now is the time to get in on the act.

Although the majority of newsletters are used as promotional material and are distributed free, some 40% are supplied on a subscription basis. If the content is right, prices can be high. Publishing a successful newsletter will promote your business at relatively low cost: if people will pay to read it you will also be provided with a source of income. So profitable has the market for newsletters become in the States that companies now exist which will write and distribute your publication for a fee. All that you have to do is to put your name to it and collect the excess income.

When you are tempted to mail a brochure to your prospects, it is worth your while to consider producing a newsletter instead. It may be a great deal less expensive: it will almost certainly be a great deal more effective.

An advantage of the newsletter as a form of promotion is that it insinuates a strong selling message without overt advertising. It says to the reader that here is someone who has valuable knowledge. What is more, it implies that the knowledge that you are imparting is not known to others. This raises you to the position of a guru. You may be well aware the information that you are providing is freely available to many others, but the situation is precisely analogous to marketing. If you and your competition share a strength, but you are the only one to tell the world about it, then in the world's eyes you are uniquely qualified. If you provide good, useful information in a newsletter, the world will see you as uniquely knowledgeable.

Newsletters are read. Let us imagine for a moment that you have invested in a glossy, beautifully produced, artistic brochure. Some £3,000 to £4,000 should produce something you can be proud of. You hire a mailing list and send out say, 3,000. How many will be read?

If by 'read' we accept anything better than eight seconds of attention, the research suggests an encouraging 10%, or 300. There is, however, a short window of opportunity during which the potential client is looking for consultancy support. If you hit it, fine - but what if you do not?

You cannot send out your brochure every month, as the expense would be prohibitive and the potential clients' boredom threshold would quickly be breached. So you are dependent, when the need for your type of service arises, on the busy businessman remembering your brochure and picking it out from the file.

Let us assess your prospects. Research indicates that the average businessman receives 90 to 110 pieces of 'junk mail' a week. Let us assume that your beautiful brochure arrived one month ago and further assume that it did its job and made an impression. One month and 400 mailing pieces later, what would you, on a common sense basis, give for its chances of being remembered?

But did it even reach the decision-maker? Half of the mail addressed to an executive is defined by somebody else as 'junk' and is thrown out by them. Anyone who has telephoned to talk to a decision-maker and has made the mistake of telling a secretary the reason for the call has experienced the response: 'Mr Brown would not be interested.......'

How much easier is it for the decision to be made concerning Mr Brown's lack of interest when dealing not with an articulate and persuasive person, but with a piece of paper, be it never so glossy? Of the 50% that reach the executive to whom they are addressed, research indicates that a further 50% are thrown away without a second glance. Of every 25 pieces left, 15 receive a quick glance and are then consigned to the waste paper basket.

Read 8 seconds The remaining 10% are treated with a little more respect, and receive some attention. That is not to say that they are read. The average attention given is eight seconds: given that by no means all executives are trained speed readers, it would appear that if some pieces are read in full, others will get little more than the cursory attention necessary to establish that there is no cheque attached.

Compare this with the fate of a newsletter. The newsletter is not perceived as 'advertising' but as information. It gets past the secretary. It then gets a brief glance from the executive and may or may not be read, depending on whether an item catches his attention. Assuming that it is not read there and then, what happens?

That depends on how easy you have made the newsletter for the recipient to treat it as a readily accessible resource. If you have taken the minor trouble of having it drilled or punched so that it will fit into a standard two or three hole binder, there is every chance that it will be filed that way and kept on a shelf, readily available and read. If not, it will be consigned to the interior of a filing cabinet from which, since it is no longer visible, it may never emerge, even in time of need.

Thus far the advantages of the newsletter may be summarised as follows:

• A newsletter brings your name frequently under the eyes of your prospects, building your perceived image.
• It enables you to embed subtle selling messages in factual text, giving them enhanced credibility. ' In a recent consultancy assignment for a major global conglomerate ......'
• It is far more likely to hit the executive's desk when that famous 'window of opportunity' is ajar.
• The newsletter is read.

If the content is of real interest and value, the recipient will actually look forward to its arrival as I used to look forward to my 'Beano' and 'Dandy' 100 years or so ago! If you are doubtful about whether or not you could charge a subscription, try this. Send out three issues gratis and make sure that they arrive on a specific day of the month. Write, but do not distribute the next edition. If your telephone rings with hordes of angry readers demanding to know why their newsletter is late, send out the current number with a subscription form attached.

There are other advantages. The newsletter plays a major role in winning referrals. The regularity with which image-building information about your activities is brought to the notice of clients past and present reinforces their confidence in their decision to hire your services and reduces the perceived risk in recommending you to others.

If you want to start small, limit your 'newsletter' to what the title implies. Send an occasional letter to contacts and clients with news of your recent achievements and the recognition which you have earned. People love to attach themselves to success. If you are good at what you do and achieve interesting and profitable results for your clients, find some means of telling the world.

Journalist for the day

If you publish a newsletter, use it as a means of getting to see people you would have difficulty meeting under normal circumstances. If you were to telephone the chairman of Megaconglom Inc, the world's supreme widget makers, you may find that he does not talk to consultants because he employs people to do that for him. He does, however, talk to journalists. A call in which you introduce yourself as the editor of your publication, and say that you are writing a piece on the widget industry and are seeking to interview the top three opinion leaders in the world of widgets is likely to get a positive response. You may even be given lunch. You must, however, act as a journalist and not as a consultant.

Conduct your interview. Draft your article and send a copy to the chairman for verification that he is happy that you quote him as indicated. After publication, send 20 copies and a brief 'thank you' note.

It is amazing that even people at the highest level still get a kick out of seeing their names in print. There is every chance that the chairman will mark a passage in each of the 20 copies that you have sent him, and distribute your newsletter for you to 20 important people. If some of those people are widget manufacturers that you somehow failed to interview, it is highly possible that they will contact you to explain that they are among the industry's brightest and best, and that they have a point of view which has not been adequately represented. If you do not know how to exploit this situation, you should have serious doubts about your future as an entrepreneur.

Getting your newsletter into circulation

Decide on the style, content and budget, and, with budget as the determining factor, either send the first edition to the 200 to 500 people whom you already know in business, or rent a mailing list, and widen your market.

To rent a mailing list you would be wise to use a broker. There are tens of thousands of mailing lists, some of them so precisely targeted that if you wish to mail to all newsagents who formerly worked in the circus and have lost one or more limbs and now live or work in coastal towns, you almost certainly can. What you almost certainly cannot do unaided is to find the appropriate list. A broker not only can, but must – his future business depends on it. What is more, you do not pay the broker for his services. The list supplier does that, and since the owner of the list will not pass on to you any discount as a result of saving the broker's fee, you have everything to gain and nothing to lose by using the services of a professional. Brokers are required to be registered under the Data Protection Act. The Act places responsibilities on the company which at least ensure that the registered firm is likely to use only reputable suppliers of lists.

Since compliance with the Act is not a cheap business, it is wise to think twice if offered unusually cheap lists. List costs vary, but the range £75 to £100 per thousand named recipients is a reasonable guide.

The rental of a list is for a single use. It is possible to buy lists, but it is wise to wait until you have tested the effect. If you cheat, you will find that the list supplier is very nice about it. He will not complain, he will not threaten, he will simply send you an invoice for each use. How will he know? Every list contains a few 'dummy' addresses which bring your mailing direct to the list owner. If you cheat he receives your mailing and responds accordingly.

Another reason for renting is that a list is only as good as it is up to date. Updating lists is difficult and expensive. I have a colleague who prefers to give others free use of his lists for life if they will undertake the cost and trouble of checking for him that no-one has died or moved on. While they are at it he usually has them carry out a survey for him. Surveys have a value all of their own (see Press Relations below). If you have a Newsletter, use it to survey your readers on a range of business and consultancy topics.

Professional meetings

The consultant must be prepared to get out and be seen in the business community. Your name must be the one that comes to mind when prospective clients are trying to identify a professional advisor. People are lazy: you will find that if your name is the one that the client knows, there is a better than even chance that when they invite you to visit and discuss their needs no other name will be in the frame.

Professional meetings are an excellent opportunity to be seen in a positive light if you approach them systematically. The important thing is to be noticed by those who can and will buy your services. It is better in general to attend meetings of institutes and associations which are not those of your profession. When you attend a meeting of the Institute of Management Consultants - and I hope that you will - the purpose is quite different from that of participating in, say, a meeting of the Institute of Directors.

Among your professional peers you may expect an excellent social and educational opportunity in which you can share information and ideas without needing to feel that you have to outperform the opposition. Let's face it, they are all opposition, and although their company may well be pleasant and even inspiring, the likelihood of any other consultant hiring you is limited.

With potential clients the objective, and therefore the role, is quite different. Now you are marketing yourself, which means that you need to be noticed. What is more important, you need to attract favourable attention, which means that you need to be noticed for the right reasons. You require a tactical plan.

Get there early. A prima donna entrance after the speaker has started is a display of appalling manners which impresses no-one, but there is a very practical reason to arrive in advance of proceedings. You need to select your seat.

Research indicates that people take most notice of those that they can see as well as hear. They also are most inclined to look at those whom they can see with least effort. You need, therefore, to sit near to the front of the room where you will be seen by the majority of the group without them having to turn and crane their necks. Research also indicates, though I am at a loss to say why, that the left hand side of the room as you face the platform is better for the purpose of being seen than the right.

Discipline yourself to speak briefly and cogently no more than twice during the meeting. Resist the temptation to speak for longer than the guest, make your point clearly and briefly, and sit down.

During the interval, or as the meeting breaks up and attendees socialise, take up a central position where people who would like to pursue the point that you made will find you easily. If there is a bar, try to get a drink in your hand quickly - it does not help to be seen as trying to cadge one. Be single minded, you are there to attract potential buyers of your services. Identify and shrug off the professional citizens and fellow consultants who are always in evidence, and attend to the potential clients.

I strongly recommend that you are selective in the meetings which you choose to attend. Find organisations which, in addition to providing opportunities to meet potential clients, have purposes which you genuinely share. Once a member, be active and participate fully in the activities. Join committees and make a real contribution. I find that active membership of the appropriate organisations gives me an additional benefit which is worth a great saving in time and money.

I belong to a society where my personal development is stimulated by constantly hearing first class speakers from disciplines different from, but related to, mine. At their meetings I am on a fast track learning curve at almost no cost while I market myself by seeking and expressing the tie-in between my major discipline and the proceedings of the society.

It is not difficult to do. Give it some thought.

Writing articles

Few things build the consultant's reputation and image more effectively or quickly than having his or her name frequently in print. We have looked at the advantages of writing your own publication, and can now assess briefly the benefits of promoting yourself, and therefore your practice, through appearing in the journals.

Let me make it clear that by 'journals' I do not mean those solemn publications which are an essential outlet for the serious academic and of immense value as a source of information to the professional consultant. Any of us who take our trade seriously should allocate time regularly to keep abreast of research and developments in our specialism, but as a means of developing business they are literally a dead loss. Write a brilliant paper for an academic journal and the most you can reasonably hope for by way of business is an invitation to present your findings at an obscure conference, at a distant location, at your own expense.

When I speak of journals, I mean the down-to-earth trade and business magazines which are read by business people. They are the people who will seek to secure your services if they find what you have to say is interesting. What is equally important, if they have read your articles in the press they will be slightly in awe of you when you meet, and as we shall see later, you will be able to build on that situation to do business on your own terms. Nothing is more important to the long-term profitability of your endeavour.

It is not useful to fire off articles right, left and centre virtually at random. You will achieve the best results if you take a planned approach. For example, you may choose to write on a topic of interest to a specific industry or business sector, particularly one in which you have identified an opportunity which is not being exploited. Alternatively, you may prefer to concentrate your attention on a specialism, for example sales training or human resource development. Whatever your strategy is, you need the following information.

• The journals and magazines serving your target audience.
• The type of articles that they normally print.
• Readership figures and demographics.
• The name of the editor.

For most of this information you have a reliable source in your local public library. 'British Rates and Data' (BRAD) is my preferred resource purely because I feel comfortable with its layout, but 'Willings Press Guide' has the same information. Even the smallest of libraries tend to have one or the other of these invaluable publications in the reference section.

For further information, including, a copy of the magazine, you can telephone the advertising department of your potential publisher and ask for a 'media pack'. If you are unfamiliar with the normal media pack of a quality daily or monthly you are in for a treat. Most have valuable demographic and other information, beautifully presented. So rich a vein of information does a good media pack offer - and most are very good - that I am almost tempted to suggest that no professional consultant should be without a comprehensive library of them. However, their cost to the publications concerned urges restraint.

Once you have decided where to place your work, you will want to know what layout and form is acceptable. If you want to do it by the book, then suitable titles exist in great numbers in your library. I have always found, however, that regardless of what the books advise in terms of everything from margin sizes to preferred punctuation, all that editors require is error-free, double spaced typed or word processed copy. I think it is wise to double space, because editors do edit. That is no bad thing - some of my more wordy offerings have emerged with a lot more punch after professional editing.

If your work is accepted, you may expect to have to wait about eight to 12 weeks before seeing it in print. If you are impatient and feel that faster acceptance of your opus is appropriate, just compare this to the two years or so which it can take to get your work into some academic journals.

Make sure that your article is accompanied by a brief biographical sketch of you, the author, and details of where you may be contacted. If you offer to send further information to your readers, you can be sure that the magazine will print your contact address or telephone number. No title wants to deal with thousands of potential requests.

Do not expect to earn a large income from your writing. Unless you specifically ask for a fee, the editor will assume that you are offering your work gratis. At the time of writing, £100 for a thousand words is as much as you can reasonably hope for.

Those who feel that they would like to make a worthwhile income from writing articles need to consider syndication. This is a specialist area, and you need a good agent who is a expert in the field. Until you have had a good deal of work published it is not easy to find one prepared to take you on. You need to write material which is in demand internationally so that that your work can be placed. Neither is easy, but the rewards can be great. You would be paid a small sum, perhaps £10 pounds each time your work appears, but it may appear perhaps 200 times across the world and that is a lot of money for 1,000 words.

A second and perhaps more practical way to make an income from your writing while you build your reputation is by becoming a columnist. If you could be the widget industry's Claire Rayner, having a regular problem page in the 'Widget Makers' Gazette', for example, you could rely on a small but regular income. You would rapidly build your reputation in the industry and, best of all, through receiving a constant stream of problems and queries you would have a better grasp than most of your competition of where the opportunities for consultancy lie.

Writing articles is of such value in developing your reputation that it is the one area where I suggest that you really ought to be happy to give your services free. Not only will it help to get you known, but reprints from a recognised publication have much more credibility than brochures, sales letters or advertisements.

One last advantage. If you are perceived by the press as a fellow writer, albeit an amateur, there is a strong likelihood that when they come to write about the field in which they know you have expertise they will come to you for your views. To write articles confers credibility, to be quoted confers fame.

Writing books

For most of us in consultancy there comes a time when writing and publishing a book becomes a passionate necessity. We have a lot to give, and by God, they're going to get it - in spite of the fact that we know that 87% of books lose money and only 10% started by readers are read to the end.

But what is wrong with having a dream? If you can write a best seller, your name and fortune are assured, but best sellers are a minute sample of the vast number of books written. The time taken to write a book could used to write dozens of articles, so are there any short cuts?

Four come to mind.

1 Always seek opportunities to recycle. If you have written something which was effective in shorter form, article, seminar handout, see whether it might be expanded to fill a chapter.

2 Write a workbook rather than a word book. You can save yourself a lot of toil by leaving much of the writing to be done by your reader and can still describe yourself as an author.

3 Edit an anthology. Get a group of your friends together and invite each to contribute a Chapter on 'TQM', 'Leadership' or whatever. Edit their efforts, top and tail with introduction and summary, and suddenly you are all authors. You will need a print run of about 12,500 to justify the first printing with a dozen of you sharing royalties, so why not be really cheeky and choose a dozen contributors with means and not without vanity. Invite each to buy a thousand copies of their book for back of the room sales at seminars, or to give to clients. Have a dozen dust jackets produced so that each is personalised with a bigger photograph of the individual author than the other authors surrounding it, and you are in business with minimum labour and possibly at a small profit.

4 Offer practical workshops on authorship. Sell places to those who are anxious to get their names in print: 'Ladies and gentlemen, the objectives of this seminar are simple. By the end of the week we will have produced a book ready for publication.'

You need to provide leadership, some knowledge, research materials and a colleague who is a dab hand on the word processor to become an editor and trainer with reasonable earnings potential from what could be a popular seminar.

Letters to the editor

The most time effective way to get into print is through writing letters to the editor. Avoid the 'I loved your article on motivation, please give us more' type. Find something you want to have a fight about.

Be truculent and aggressive. Spice what you have to say with irony and wit. Invite replies and a continuation of the fight.

Half the people who read what you have to say will write you off as an idiot, the other half will think that you are brilliant. Among both halves may be some who will hire your services - after further discussion. The time committed is minimal and your name appears frequently where your potential clients seek information.

If you want readers to contact you direct rather than through the correspondence columns, ensure that your address is printed by offering some relevant information to those who ask for it. The journal may occasionally be willing to forward requests for further information that arise from a major article. That gives them a measure of the market response. They are unlikely to accept the same inconvenience for a letter, so they will print your address, often with a reminder: 'write direct to Mr Green at ....and not to us'.

Giving seminars

In spite of the recession and the remarkable tendency of many Western firms to cut down on training when they need it most, the market for seminars is growing and will continue to grow

What is more, seminars can create clients in good numbers as well as producing a source of income. Research indicates that an average of 8% of seminar participants provide consultancy or internal training opportunities for the leader.

To enter the seminar market does not require you to spend months developing materials and programme outlines. Address the seminar business as a businessman rather than as a trainer. Find out what the market wants, and decide what you could do, off the cuff, to satisfy a market need. Design simple handouts or a minimal workbook, promote your seminar and go. If you genuinely have something worth saying, people will get great benefit and your initiative will prosper. If by chance you have got it wrong, you have invested, and therefore lost, very little.

When you have a seminar that works you have a number of choices. If you have a real blockbuster of a success you may choose to franchise your materials and allow others to provide you with a steady living by the sweat of their brows. Alternatively, you may keep your programme to yourself, refining and improving it to reach wider and wider markets.

If it is an amazing success you may sell it outright. To give you an idea of how profitable this route may be, a price for a real winner might be as much as five to 10 years' gross receipts. It is relatively difficult to get seminars which are aimed at the general public off the ground. Your problem lies in promotion: how do you reach that relatively small proportion of the total population that invest in seminars?

Usually it is necessary to advertise in the press, and press advertisements are costly. It may well be a worthwhile and cost effective exercise to promote and conduct your seminar locally at first. Although the receipts may not excite your bank manager, neither are the costs a worry. You can go national or international when you are confident that you have a market.

To appeal to the general public your seminar needs to tell them:
• How to make more money
• How to keep more of the money they make
• How to develop their hobby or interest
• How to enrich or empower their lives.

You can appeal to the corporate market where participants do not have to dip into their own reserves of cash with a much wider range of offerings. It is little exaggeration to say that as long as you conduct the programme in a comfortable hotel, preferably near to the golf course, with good food and excellent wine the content can be as uninteresting as you care to make it. You think that you will not get consultancy assignments from a boring programme? You are wrong. Give your participants a sufficiently good time and they will love you anyway. Some of the less reputable 'business schools' rely almost exclusively on regurgitating tired and doubtful old materials in swish settings, and they do pretty well for consultancy assignments as a break from the day job.

Please be assured that I am not advocating poor quality— my passionate commitment is to high quality outcomes from training and development. I only wish that others, including participants who regard any training as just a break from work, shared my views. I simply tell you what others are getting away with so that you may promote quality content with confidence.

Using the press

There is no promotion so effective or so satisfactory as 'free ink'. Any consultant should make it an absolute goal to become famous, even if only on a local basis.

To become famous you must become news. Most news is manufactured by someone with the necessary skills presenting it in such a way that it appeals to a news-hungry readership. What you do can be presented as news to the trade and technical press, who serve the same markets as you do.

Your activities and triumphs can sometimes be news to the national press, radio and television if you present them as news.

Conduct surveys

Publications adore the results of surveys, and it seems to matter very little if the findings surprise or simply restate the obvious in a way which adds fuel to a current controversy. If you conduct investigations of any kind ascertain whether you can, without breach of any commercial confidentiality, release something to the press.

Analyse the social, economic, political (be careful), cultural and technological climates as they relate to your clients and the markets they serve. Become known as one who always has something to say, and before long you will not have to write so many press releases because the press will begin to appproach you for comments.

To be published:

- Write your press release on a single sheet if possible.
- Leave adequate margins for editorial comment.
- Make sure it is clear where you may be contacted for further information.
- Include a specific release date after which your release may be used.
- Send it to the editor by name (check in BRAD).
- Attach a press quality photograph (this alone increases your chances of publication by at least 28%).
- Having sent it never badger the editor about publication.

If it is published, show your gratitude by sending useful information to the editor when you can.

Time management

In order to market consistently and do all of the other things which are necessary in practice management, and make a living, you will need to become an expert on time management.

This book would become inordinately long if I tried to include a treatise on how to control your time, so let me do no more than draw to your attention one point which you will not find in the standard texts. Whatever you do, ensure that you get the utmost mileage out of it. If you write a proposal for a brewer and fail to get the contract, see if you cannot recycle it. It probably shows that you have acquired a good understanding of the industry, so after editing to ensure that it contains nothing of a commercial confidential nature relating to your hoped-for client, send it to the chairmen of other breweries with a note implying that you have analysed some key problems facing the industry and have a contribution to make to their solution.

Make it a rule never to use anything only once and the gain in time and the increase in creativity can be dramatic. If you write a good and inspiring talk, can it be recycled as a seminar handout? Or expanded into an article? A chapter in your book?

Whenever you have a huge and important thing to do and there seems no available time to get really stuck in to it, remember the old saw about eating an elephant a little at a time. Ten minutes here, 20 minutes there means progress, and progress has a wonderful effect on motivation and confidence.

Finally, never confuse what is important with what is merely urgent. If you always do the important things you will find that the urgent wait comfortably until they become important, or they just fade blissfully away.

The tactics for marketing your practice discussed in this Chapter are those which have been shown by Shenson's research in the USA and mine in Europe to be those which the high earners in our profession have found most useful in building their image and reputation.

If you select and consistently use those which appeal to you, your practice will grow as more and more clients, knowing your name and assuming your reputation, invite you to do work for them. When you have to go out to market directly - and changing circumstances will ensure that from time to time you must - the time that you have expended on building your reputation will be repaid as prospective clients are just a little in awe of you.

The most important factor in considering which of the above you will apply is that of personal comfort. Do only those things which you feel comfortable doing and do them consistently. While writing this Chapter I have also written and despatched five articles. That is what I mean by consistent: you cannot afford to allow the 'major assignment', however important, to interfere with your marketing efforts.

Be sure to set aside some time every week to market yourself. It will pay dividends.

There's more......... and some of it is work for you, right now.

Indirect marketing

The following are no cost/low cost marketing tactics which are consistent with my preferences and talents:

_____

_____

_____

_____

_____

_____

_____

_____

_____

_____

_____

To get me started I will take the following steps tomorrow:

_____

_____

_____

_____

_____

_____

_____

_____

_____

_____

_____

_____

_____

_____

To maximise the opportunity I need the following personal development or information:

_____
_____
_____
_____
_____
_____
_____
_____
_____
_____
_____
_____
_____
_____

To resource the above I can:

_____
_____
_____
_____
_____
_____
_____
_____
_____
_____
_____
_____
_____
_____
_____
_____
_____
_____
_____
_____

Are you certain that your plans fully exploit:

- **Your personal and professional strengths?**

- **The market opportunities?**

If in doubt, please look back and check.

9 Making Your Brochure Work for You

If you ever feel the need to splash out to no good purpose, an easy way to unburden yourself of unwanted cash is to follow the example of many of your fellow consultants by designing and using a brochure.

This is how to prove that you have more money than sense. Go out and hire a graphic studio to design something beautiful and exciting, then find a copy writer to develop your dream message. Use a master printer to produce your masterpiece on an exquisite art paper and wrap it lovingly in the highest quality folder that your inexhaustible supply of money can buy. Have 5,000 printed and rush them to a direct mailing service with an order to mail them cold to a personally bought-in list that you have had no time to check.

After that you are in the ideal position to tell me, as so many of your fellow professionals do, that brochures serve no useful purpose other than to bankrupt the consultant. Produced and used like that, you and they are right. Fifteen years of talking to consultants who use their brochures that way indicates that the response to the mailing, in terms of business acquired, seldom pays for the stamps. Yet they go on doing it, and when asked why they respond that they 'don't know see what else to do'.

I do not want to see you go bankrupt, so let me suggest some alternatives. First, consider whether you need a brochure at all. When your practice is small it is possible to write a tailored document for each client telling them precisely, and in sufficient detail, what they need to know.

You will not hammer on the word processor keys until you

fully understand your client's problem, but that is all to the good. Understanding your client's problem may lead you to concentrate specifically on how your unique skills and knowledge will help to provide the cure. Your client may then feel that his problem is more important to you than your own aggrandisement, and he may be more inclined to ask you to accept a contract.

There are some who try to avoid the brochure altogether and working on the valid assumption that it is their skills, knowledge and experience that the client may buy, they market themselves with their CV. The assumption is valid, but in most cases the conclusion is not.

No matter how impressive your CV may be, it has certain disadvantages when used as a marketing tool.There is a psychological response to a CV which is difficult to overcome. To most people the CV accompanies an application for a job. It automatically puts the sender into a subservient, almost supplicatory position. Our image marketing approach has been aimed at raising the profile of the consultant to that of independent specialist who may be persuaded to accept an assignment. The sending of a CV can reverse the perceived relative status of consultant and client at a stroke.

What is worse, all business organisations have a well-defined procedure for dealing with CV's - they are invariably passed to the personnel department. I do not have to share Bob Townsend's view that the interests of the company would be best served if all members of the personnel operation were taken out and shot to suspect that the receipt by them of an unsolicited CV triggers a standard response. Many a consultant has received a letter which thanks him for his interest in the company, advises that no vacancy appropriate to his talents currently exists, but that his application will be retained and he will be contacted when such a vacancy occurs. I have to add that although I know many who have elicited such a response, I am still waiting to meet that happy person who has been advised of a subsequent vacancy.

I suspect that in many personnel departments the knee-jerk response to such a letter is so ingrained that any written communication is likely to evoke it. When I was asked by the chairman of a blue chip organisation to forward a letter I had sent to him offering my services to each of his 13 personnel directors, quoting his name, the first response I had was exactly of the type summarised above - and that was to a communication without a CV.

Do not use a CV for marketing purposes for one further and compelling reason. Even if it is retained by the person you wish to influence and its purpose is fully understood, it is a poor tool for the job in hand. The CV contains a great deal of information which is irrelevant to your offer. Some of that information may detract from that which is important, or give the potential client an opportunity to reject you because although extraneous, it indicates something that he is biased against.

I find it interesting that recruitment specialists, whose stock in trade is the CV, when asked what should be included often respond: 'As little as possible.'

Writing your brochure

When marketing with a CV is ineffective and writing individual information for each client becomes impractical, then it is time to write your brochure.

Strangely, you may need two. The point of the brochure is that it will either open doors for you from 'cold', or it will reinforce a good impression which you have already made. These are by no means the same job, and it is by no means certain that the same tool will do for both.

If you publish a newsletter, or write articles, they will open doors, but if you choose speaking engagements or seminars as the main thrust of your marketing activities a 'giveaway' which will be kept and referred to is a must. The less it looks like a standard brochure, the better.

If you have a specific area of expertise, try producing a small leaflet which provides useful information - 'How to raise capital in a nervous market' or 'The environment and motivation', or whatever. Be careful not to answer all the questions, and ensure that you invite and facilitate contact from those who need further advice or information. Some consultants go to the lengths of writing a small booklet, and others have one of their practical articles reproduced in pocket size format. I have used simple, self administered 'psychological' tests with substantial, but less than comprehensive interpretive data.

As long as people find what you provide useful, but not so useful that it obviates the need for your services, it will work for you. Some consultants offer such a piece free of charge to those who respond to an advertisement. But composing the brochure proper?

Start by listing what our American colleagues sometimes call your 'stellar moments'. Those major achievements which demonstrate the range and depth of your abilities.

Don't worry if some of the principal attainments were accomplished as an employee, rather than as a consultant. As Howard Shenson used to say: 'No-one gives a damn how you were paid.'

If the achievement was truly yours and it demonstrates the effective application of skill or knowledge which you would be happy to market today, get it down. Against each stellar moment write the objective which your work enabled the client or employer to achieve and the other benefits which were gained en route. Add a list of the special skills and knowledge that you brought to bear

Write up each stellar moment, its objective, benefits and skills as a short, 40 to 50 word 'case study' .... and then spice it up a little. You add the spice by going to your CV and using those accreditations, skills or abilities which you feel cannot be ignored, and make sense in the context of what you have written. For example:

'My researches during my MBA programme enabled me to be unusually effective in dealing with the essential culture changes.'

'My fluent Hungarian ensured that I could advise the chairman on the nuances as well as the content of the President's statement.'

Have your spiced case studies printed on quality, but not excessively expensive A4 card or paper, folded to fit into the pocket. But do not do this until you undertake the nine year old test.

Most who are drawn to consultancy boast a better than average vocabulary among their basic skills, That would be fine if it were not for the fact that what we have, we use.

Most material written by consultants, including mine, uses words and structures which are more abstruse than they need to be (how often do your intimate business acquaintances use the word 'abstruse'?) The result is ambiguity instead of clarity. If we pass our written work to a nine-year-old and test that what is understood is what we intended, we would improve our style greatly.

Where nine year olds are thin on the ground, we may have recourse to tools like the Fogg Readability Index or the Plain English Society's editing software 'Stylewriter'. But in the short term, nine year olds are cheaper!

A final test of your brochure can be made by taking your

draft to a local college marketing faculty. Ask the head of department if he or she would ask the students to review your brochure as a case study in marketing communication. Try to arrange to attend the session in which your work is discussed.

You may not enjoy what you hear, but it will be among the cheapest and most useful consultancy assignments that you will ever commission.

Using your brochure

Brochures mailed cold routinely attract less than eight seconds attention, as the research quoted above indicates. That is not to say it is impossible to hit the jackpot with a cold mailing - just as it is not impossible to win the treble chance. Achieving either however is less likely than being struck by lightning.

The purpose of the brochure is to build on the good impression which you have already made by feeding the prospective client with information which enables him to construct his own arguments in support of hiring you.

Its role is one of reinforcement. It confirms the message that you are a competent, creative, successful consultant who will provide exceptional services to those lucky enough to be your clients, and it endorses the client feeling that they were right to talk to you. After reading your brochure they will feel that their risk in hiring you will be minute.

Your brochure must offer something special to your client. By being heavy on fact and light on sales 'puff' it will win you business by letting the client become your salesman.

Your brochure should be treated by you and by those that receive it with respect. It should be handed to the prospect after your discussion as evidence that he will experience the benefits which you have explained in detail and that those benefits will lead to the achievement of his most important current objective.

Draw the attention of the potential client to one of the 'cases' most closely related to his situation. Give him time and silence in which to read it and wait in silence for his reaction. If he comments positively, ask for the contract and wait once again in silence for his response.

Silence is vital. If you brochure is properly designed and presented, it is the final and most potent selling tool, but it can only work by providing your client with information which will persuade him to hire your services. For the client to influence his own decision, he must have time:

- To relate what he reads to his needs
- To use the new information to reinforce the apparent desirability of what you have already offered.
- To remove any fears or concerns that he may have in hiring you.
- To project the benefits into his future to experience vicariously their enjoyment.

That takes considerable time and happens only in the absence of distractions. If you speak, tidy your papers or rise to leave, that will be sufficient distraction to enable the decision to be put to one side. The primary ability of the effective salesperson is to shut up and sit tight. I will have more to say on selling later, but for now commit yourself to the idea that silence can do much of your talking.

When you have completed your task, let us look at off the page selling:

Brochure development

PERSONAL OR PROFESSIONAL ACHIEVEMENT (Stellar Moment) Including brief outline of WHAT was done

_____
_____
_____
_____
_____
_____
_____
_____
_____
_____
_____
_____
_____
_____
_____
_____
_____

CLIENT/COMPANY OBJECTIVE ACHIEVED or PROBLEM SOLVED
WHY it was done

_____
_____
_____
_____
_____
_____
_____
_____
_____
_____

BENEFITS TO COMPANY/CLIENT OF YOUR INTERVENTION
Additional gains from using your ideas/services

_____
_____
_____
_____
_____
_____
_____
_____
_____
_____

APPROPRIATE CV 'SPICE'
Special skills, attainments, qualifications, experience, knowledge or attitudes relevant to this assignment

_____
_____
_____
_____
_____
_____
_____
_____
_____
_____

MINI CASE STUDY
(40 - 50 words)

_____
_____
_____
_____
_____
_____
_____
_____
_____
_____
_____
_____

BROCHURE DEVELOPMENT
PERSONAL OR PROFESSIONAL ACHIEVEMENT (Stellar Moment) Including brief outline of WHAT was done

_____
_____
_____
_____
_____
_____
_____
_____
_____

CLIENT/COMPANY OBJECTIVE ACHIEVED or PROBLEM SOLVED
WHY it was done

_____
_____
_____
_____
_____
_____
_____
_____
_____

BENEFITS TO COMPANY/CLIENT OF YOUR INTERVENTION
Additional gains from using your ideas/services

_____
_____
_____
_____
_____
_____
_____
_____
_____
_____
_____

APPROPRIATE CV 'SPICE'
Special skills, attainments, qualifications, experience, knowledge or attitudes relevant to this assignment

_____
_____
_____
_____
_____
_____
_____

MINI CASE STUDY
(40 - 50 words)

_____
_____
_____
_____
_____
_____
_____
_____
_____
_____
_____
_____
_____
_____

Brochure development

PERSONAL OR PROFESSIONAL ACHIEVEMENT (Stellar Moment)

Including brief outline of WHAT was done

_____

_____

_____

_____

_____

_____

_____

_____

_____

_____

_____

_____

CLIENT/COMPANY OBJECTIVE ACHIEVED or PROBLEM SOLVED

WHY it was done

_____

_____

_____

_____

_____

_____

_____

BENEFITS TO COMPANY/CLIENT OF YOUR INTERVENTION

Additional gains from using your ideas/services

_____

_____

_____

_____

_____

_____

_____

APPROPRIATE CV 'SPICE'
Special skills, attainments, qualifications, experience,
knowledge or attitudes relevant to this assignment

_____
_____
_____
_____
_____
_____
_____

MINI CASE STUDY
(40 - 50 words)

_____
_____
_____
_____
_____
_____

BROCHURE DEVELOPMENT

PERSONAL OR PROFESSIONAL ACHIEVEMENT (Stellar Moment)
Including brief outline of WHAT was done

_____
_____
_____
_____
_____
_____
_____
_____
_____
_____

CLIENT/COMPANY OBJECTIVE ACHIEVED or PROBLEM SOLVED
WHY it was done

_____
_____

_____
_____
_____
_____

BENEFITS TO COMPANY/CLIENT OF YOUR INTERVENTION
Additional gains from using your ideas/services

_____
_____
_____
_____
_____
_____
_____
_____

APPROPRIATE CV 'SPICE'
Special skills, attainments, qualifications, experience, knowledge or attitudes relevant to this assignment

_____
_____
_____
_____
_____
_____
_____

MINI CASE STUDY
(40 - 50 words)

_____
_____
_____
_____
_____
_____
_____

10   Advertising for Professionals

For many years the professions viewed advertising with distaste. It was vulgar - just as charging in pounds, shillings and pence as opposed to guineas was considered to be at one time. It was therefore unprofessional, and for many it was banned .

Today things are different. Lawyers, vets and accountants all vie for the best positions in publications, sometimes with the worst advertisements. Doctors as yet stand aloof, although frequent advertisements for BUPA and private clinics help to promote them. Some NHS practices have video advertising of a range of services and products to provide public information and a source of revenue for the clinic. Whether the growth of 'budget holding' will lead to a medical advertising boom we have yet to see. But it seems that advertising professional services is in, and consultants have been quick to get involved.

Nonetheless I believe that Mr Punch's advice to those about to get married -'don't'- is applicable to those who are considering pouring their money into an advertising campaign.

Advertising is expensive and frequently ineffective, but unfortunately sometimes it is the only way to reach your market. So for those who see no alternative, I will spell out some ways to minimise advertising costs, increase its effectiveness, and reduce the risks.

How not to waste your money

Most consultants, including marketing specialists who ought to know better, base their advertising strategy on two disastrous mistakes. They model their copy on advertisements which they have seen, enjoyed and admired, and they follow the advice of advertising professionals.

I have worked off and on for 30 years with advertising professionals and with few exceptions (David Ogilvie, J Walter Thompson and Patrick Quinn come to mind) I have yet to find more than a heretical few who regard the real purpose of advertising to be that of selling anything. The vast, and very expensive, majority are motivated by the following desires, not necessarily in the order given:

- To show how 'creative' they are.
- To sell the most expensive campaigns regardless of client need or means.
- To win the admiration of their peers.
- To win awards given by their peers.

Advertising is the one field in which 'do it yourself' may be less risky than using professional services. Time and again I have seen 'ordinary' businessmen totally outclass the advertising professional at less cost with just a little general advice.

The philosophy
The small budget advertiser needs to understand that he is not in the same business as the corporation with megabucks to spend. The large company expects its advertising to build image and brand awareness over a lengthy period so that at some unspecified time the buyer with sufficient funds will probably add Product X to his list of possible buys .

Alternatively, the massive spender in fields such as detergents seeks to so inundate the purchaser with a constant stream of advertising that, once in the supermarket, she will grab and pay zombie-like for the brand which is currently being promoted with no more logical reason than that she 'thought she would give it a try'. For Unilever and their competitors everything depends on repetition and shelf position, neither of which have much relevance to us .

I am being a little unfair in the sense that both of the above strategies work if they are repeated often enough over a sufficiently long period. Were you to copy the style of, say, a Mercedes advertisement, it would eventually bring you business because people would eventually come to believe that you are good at what you do. They would know that because you make so much money that you can afford to throw large amounts of it away on daft advertising campaigns.

At worst any advertisement which you place must bring you at least enough extra business to pay for the next advertisement. And that means you must forget about white space.

One day I may meet the individual who tells me that he bought Product X because of the tasteful and informative white space. 'Advertising salespeople' of course love white space, but until I meet the looney of Lymm, clutching Product X in his moist hand and eyes rolling with the aesthetic delights of white space, I am going to continue to believe that it is what you say in an advertisement which will persuade people to buy .

What you write must include the following:

Heading

Your advertisement is aimed at being read by those few among the vast number in the market place who will be interested in buying your services now or in the future. It is competing with the other advertisements and editorial for their limited attention. Make sure that you header says 'read me' loud and clear to the right people.

You need to identify your readers by name, description, profession or shared problem.

For example:

'Are you called Smith?'
'Young men'
'Consultants'
'Short of cash?'

Offer

Once they have started to read, your prime requirement is to ensure that they keep right on reading until they take the desired action. They have to believe that there is something in it for them. So make it clear up front that their wishes will be granted because if you fail to convince them early, you quickly lose them.

'You will learn the secrets of the super rich in one fun-packed day.'
'Solve your money problems the new and exciting way.'

Evidence

Give your readers reason to believe that you can deliver what you promise.

'More than a million delighted users world-wide.'
'A unique, new, but proven approach.'
'Researched and validated by Cambridge University.'

Expand on your offer
If space and budget allow, develop the benefits which buyers of your services will gain. Where possible, create a logical linkage between benefits so that belief in the first guarantees belief in the second which in turn ensures acceptance of the third and so on to the end.

Facilitate action
Tell your readers what they must do to achieve the benefits you offer. Be sure to give them alternatives:

- A tear out coupon to mail.
- The telephone number for those in a hurry.
- Your fax number if you have one.

If you include a mailing coupon, make sure that some way of contacting you is printed elsewhere in the advertisement for those who see the advertisement after the coupon has been cut out.

The eightfold path to enlightened advertising

To determine what you may most effectively say about yourself and to get an idea of what it may cost you to say it take the following seriously.

1 Understand the business environment
- What is the economic, social, legislative and business situation?
- Who are your competitors?
- What are their strengths and weaknesses?
- What are yours?
- What do you have to offer that is unique?
- Is there anything which is being underplayed by your competition, so that if you were to promote it the reader would assume that it is unique to you?

2 Opportunity analysis
- What are the opportunities right now, and in the immediate future?
- Where could you make your biggest gains?

3 Position your business

The least effective advertising is that which says:

'We do anything for anyone and do it cheaper'.

Position your business so that potential clients understand that they are hiring specialist expertise from a company with a defined culture. If you are the consultancy 'which cares and goes on caring', or if you 'do and charge for everything necessary, and nothing extra', or if you offer 'Rolls Royce service at Ford prices,' think how you will communicate the idea clearly in a few, inexpensive words.

4 Write advertising objectives
- Establish the number of responses that you need.
- Calculate the incremental sales which you want the advertising to bring in.
- Identify clearly the market segments which you must reach.
- Determine the key points which readers of your advertisements need to recognise and respond to.

5 Establish your budget

Obtain media packs from those publications which you are considering. Establish precisely what your advertisement will cost in terms of £ per 1,000 target readers reached.

6 Consider an agency

In spite of my views about advertising professionals, a reliable agency can save you much grief. If you are clear about what you want to achieve, who you want to reach and what you want to say, an agency can place your advertisements very advantageously. But be warned, to approach an agency as a means of avoiding having to think for yourself could lead to disaster.

Agencies are paid a commission on the placing of your advertisements by the media who benefit. If you have a large budget they may be willing to handle your account for free. In any case their costs ought to take into account the 10 to 15% commission which they are paid by the publication.

7 Measure the results

Compare the results from different publications, different positions and different days of the week. Consider using a scrapbook to monitor your most and least successful advertisements.Never be afraid to repeat a successful advertisement - you are building business, not seeking prizes for novelty.

8 Determine the risk

What could go wrong with an advertisement?

Incredible as it may seem, two quality national dailies forgot to print my advertisement for my pilot seminar 'how to build and develop your professional practice' in the same week.

From one I got an apology and a replacement advertisement, which they put in by taking out one of their own display advertisements (Daily Telegraph). The other informed me that they give no guarantees of publication, and it is simply 'unfortunate' if that ruins your business (The Times).They did manage to print my advertisement the following week, but nine months and several telephone calls later, I am still waiting for their media pack, or a copy of their terms and conditions. Do not assume that big necessarily means efficient!

Advance trouble-shooting

Consider the following: What could go wrong? Can it be avoided? If so what should I do to avoid or minimise the risk? If problems cannot be avoided, what is the earliest indication that things are going wrong? What contingent action can I take to minimise harm?

When to advertise

As I have said above, the most important reason to advertise is that you know that you cannot reach your target market any other way.

For example, part of my business is conducting seminars for those who are either running their own professional practices, or are thinking about doing so. My market research tells me that there are as many as 300,000 people out there at any time who could benefit from my training. My problem is that they are randomly distributed among the population of 60 million. To reach them by mail, a simple and obvious strategy is open to me: 20 million letters, one to each household in the land.

Twenty million first class stamps, say £5 million. Twenty million envelopes, twenty million inserts. In time alone, stuffing and sealing an envelope every second, day and night without rest it would take almost two years to get a mailing on its way.

What about the indirect methods I have recommended? Good press and public relations, articles, and other seminars are all vital, but they do not make response easy or timely. When I needto be preparing the latest research material for the seminar is just when it would be most useful to appear on television, orgive interviews to the press.

Advertising is, for me, a necessity. I suggest that you too should *advertise only when there is no other way.*

The second consideration is altogether more subtle. All business is seasonal to a greater or lesser degree. If you must advertise, you need to do so when the response is likely to be at its height. There is nothing to be gained by advertising my seminars at Christmas or during July and August for the very simple reason that those who might attend have other priorities during holiday seasons.

Never advertise when business is slack for everyone. The hope of picking up more than your usual share is almost certain to prove unfounded because there are just not enough 'punters' in the market place to justify the expenditure. The cost per enquiry is likely to rise to the point where even getting the business means working at a loss.

The point of advertising is to turn hot prospects into buyers. No hot prospects - no buyers.

If you are a low-budget advertiser you will be depriving yourself of the cash that would enable you to exploit a bonanza opportunity when it comes. Conserve your cash by concentrating on low cost or no cost marketing. Write and place some articles. Give a few well-targeted talks. Confine your spending to food for the family, or keep up the mortgage payments and wait for the upturn.

You can bet your copy of the 'Group Facilitators' Handbook' that others, ignorant of the realities of advertising, will be trying their luck and your advertisement would struggle to be seen among the other products of despair.

The time to advertise is when the market is about to hit a high point. Know your market, analyse the peaks and troughs and advertise to exploit the coming peak. Newspaper proprietors will continue to grow fat from advertising revenues, but by the effective timing of your advertisement you will have a better than sporting chance of adding to your net worth.

The media

Because the majority of consultants who choose to advertise do so through the medium, I have concentrated on print until now. Some readers are likely to be more adventurous and will want to investigate other media. For them a brief overview is appropriate. In order to make an informed choice it is necessary that you:
- Know the types of media.
- Consider the advantages and disadvantages of each.
- Buy the media to your best advantage.

- Understand some of the techniques which add an extra dimension to a medium's effect.

Understanding the media

An advertising medium is defined as being any vehicle which carries your promotional message to the targeted client. Professionals would normally list 10, of which by no means all are relevant to your needs. But for the sake of completeness I list them all.

Newspapers
Dailies (morning and evening editions), weeklies, Sundays and local 'free sheets'.

Magazines
Leisure, hobby, general interest, news, trade and academic journals, county or regional and business. If you name it, whatever 'it' may be, there is an appropriate magazine.

Outdoor advertising
Billboards and painted signs.

Transport advertising
A mobile billboard sometimes used by software houses and IT consultancies, but more commonly the chosen medium, for obvious reasons, for the car trade.

Direct mail
A highly specialised area in spite of its apparent simplicity. The mailing list is the key to its use. If you are offering, say, a specialist seminar to a carefully targeted sector this can be very cost effective.

Radio
There are more than 150 local stations available as I write, and up to 300 planned. More than 50% of the new stations will be commercial. Some recent additions to the commercial network have proved to be far more successful than was anticipated, for example Classic FM with 2.8 million who listen at least once a week.

Television
Thirteen separate areas receive independent television, but cable television and information services are likely to offer more

appropriate media choices for business to business communication. If the BBC's new 'Accountancy Channel' is a success it will open the doors to other specialist business channels.

Cinema
Unlikely to be of interest to consultants, but included for completeness and because professionals other than consultants who draw their clients from a local area have used the medium with considerable success.

Goodwill gifts
Pens, calendars and filofaxes inscribed with the donor name are being seen with increasing frequency in the hands of seminar attendees and businessmen in general. Specialist publications featuring these gifts and the creativity behind their development testify to their success in some applications.

Miscellaneous
Exhibition stands, audio visual displays, newsletters and speculative cold (or even warm) brochure distrbutions are gathered together in this category.

Advantages and disadvantages

Newspapers

Advantages	Disadvantages
1. Good market coverage	1. Circulation pattern may not efficiently cover all prospects
2. Readers are actively seeking information/ideas	2. Publication pattern may not meet your needs
3. Permanency. Ads are torn out for future reference	3. Competition for reader attention
4. High credibility	4. Mass medium, restricts ability to target prospects
5. Position of ad can select readers	
6. Illustration easy and relatively inexpensive	

7. Copy emphasis readily controlled by
   size and style of type, headlines, captions,
   subheads etc.
8. Wide choice of size and therefore cost
9. Geographically as well as
   demographically selective.

Magazines

Advantages	*Disadvantages*
1. Full colour potential	1. Scheduling relatively inflexible - long lead time to publication
2. Prestige	2. Lacks immediacy, can imply lack of urgency for response
3. Effective targeting	3. Quality of artwork required may be difficult/expensive

4. Many more readers than circulation
   figures suggest, 'pass along' readership
5. Can support and be supported by,
   your articles, Press Releases and letters
6. Frequently offer excellent deals to ad
   vertisers for copy close to deadline if
   space still unsold.
7. Some, such as 'Management Today'
   are the official organs of a   professional
   body. (The IM)

Outdoor advertising

This is unlikely to appeal to consultants, but it has been used to win
that massive and difficult account. A major American consultancy
practice was trying to land a multi million dollar account. After
many unsuccessful attempts to make contact with the client, they
bought space on a billboard which they knew that the MAN drove
past every day to reach the office. When they called for the
umpteenth time he saw them because 'I seem to see your name
everywhere I go.....' (Note: MAN is marketing jargon for the person

who has the money, the authority and the need for your services. Man or woman that's the MAN for you.)

Transport advertising

Unless you have a thing about getting your name known on a certain bus route it is difficult to see how this kind of advertising could be applied to building your business. The fact that the advertisement is moving means that the message must be brief and catchy and if you assume that your clients are apt to travel by car they can only see and read the lower rear panel.

Direct mail

Advantages	*Disadvantages*
1. Messages can be directed to a highly selected target group	1. Total dependence on quality of list
2. Messages can be any length	2. Rented lists only usable once
3. Mailing personalised	3. Bought lists need constant updating
4. Timing highly flexible	4. Built in resistance to "junk mail"
5. Continues contact with existing clients leading to potential referral and repeat business	5. Less than 8 seconds attention average
6. Can 'piggy back' with non-competing material	

Contrary to what the lovers of white space will tell you, all of the reliable evidence points to the fact that long copy sells. It is much more important when designing a direct mail piece to design it to provide the detailed information that those who may be interested in your service will want than it is to create something slick and eye-catching that will have those who have no interest in what you have to sell saying 'Wow, that's clever', as they drop it in the bin. The same rules apply for direct mail content as for advertising. The difference is that with a mailing piece you are not limited to 'x' column centimetres. Make the most of it, and tell the already interested what they need to know to become buyers.

Radio

Advantages

1. High frequency at reasonable cost

2. Flexibility. You can change copy right up to transmission
3. Cheap to produce
4. Can be highly creative

5. Relatively low per listener cost

Disadvantages

1. You cannot use visuals to support your message
2. Lacks permanency

3. Very localised
4. Cannot put across detail effectively

Television

Advantages

1. High impact - sight, sound, movement
2. Memorable

3. Convincing demonstrations

4. Scheduling flexibility

5. Closest approximation to face to face communication
6. High credibility: 'saw it on television', or 'as seen on television' have an inexplicable power to attract buyers.

Disadvantages

1. Production costs high
2. Professional help essential to prepare commercials
3. High transmission costs
4. Desirable 'spots' expensive and difficult to acquire

Cinema

Advantages

1. Low overall cost
2. Relatively low production

3. Large screen - colour - sight and sound

4. Relatively attentive audience

Disadvantages

1. Limited exposure
2. Need to check costs carefully types of advertiser you will be associated with
3. Cost per prospect highly dependent on film showing at time of ad.
4. Very difficult to measure results
5. Very local coverage

Goodwill gifts

Advantages	*Disadvantages*
1. Keeps your name in front of client for as long as gift is useful and lasts	1. May be expensive
2. May last many years - eg 'leather' or brass edged document wallets - calculators	2. Much competition
	3. Message limited and static

Pulling it together

Advertising is always expensive, and you cannot afford to let it become a costly failure. Concentrate your attention as far as you can on the no cost/low cost tactics which build your status and reputation.

Use advertising tactically where no effective alternative exists, and use it thoughtfully.

Buy advertising skillfully. Where you have the flexibility, place your advertisements just before press time at bargain prices. You can save 50% or more on the cost of placing an advertisement by taking advantage of the offers which papers and journals are prepared to make when they are faced with the choice of either selling space cheaply, or of reducing the number of pages in the issue.

Measure the effect of each advertisement carefully. Do not rely on the ability of the client to remember where they saw your ad. If you want accurate information provide some inducement for your client to clip and return the advertisement to you. By checking what is printed on the reverse you have a unique and accurate indication of when and where the advertisement appeared.

Do all that you can to predetermine the probable effect of any advertisement before it goes to press. You will still get surprises, but careful checking helps to decrease your chances of missing an important error in style or copy decrease.

Principles for evaluating your advertisements

1. Does the advertisement demand positive attention?
2. Is the headline powerful?
3. Does it offer meaningful benefits for my target audience?

4. Is the message clear?

5. Does it address predetermined needs?

6. Is the layout clear and easy to follow?

7. Is the overall image positive?

8. Is the stimulus for action now likely to be effective?

9. Is it clear how, when and where to respond?

10 Address, telephone number and fax clear and accurate?

11. Does my advertisement indicate why ME, rather than my competition?

12. Would I spend my money in response to this advertisement?

13. How do I rate the overall impression? What will be my readers' gut reaction?

If the answers to each of the first 12 questions is 'yes', and the predicted response in question 13 is positive, *you are in with a chance.*

If your advertising or mailing fails

Symptom
Little response

Possible cause
Message vague
Insufficient frequency of repetition
Advertisement too small
Wrong medium or wrong publication
Wrong placement of ad in publication or wrong timing of transmission
Poor mailing list
Buyers simply aren't there at present.

Symptom
Good response, poor subsequent sales

Possible cause
Poor offer
Inappropriate selling techniques
Lack of sales skills
Economic environment wrong
Wrong stage in purchase cycle
Insufficient promotional material
Style of promotional material inappropriate to offer or potential purchasers

As you can see, there are many potential changes that can be made to improve the situation. Try to discipline yourself to making one change at a time -that way you can accurately identify and resolve problems.

Advertising planning sheet

HEADER; What can I use to capture the attention of my prospective clients?

_____
_____

OFFER; What promise can I make which will get them to go on reading?

_____
_____
_____

EVIDENCE; How can I build confidence that I can deliver?

_____
_____
_____
_____

ACTION; How can I ensure that they take action NOW?

_____
_____
_____

How to contact is clear?   YES___   NO___

WOULD I BUY FROM THIS AD.?

11 Referral Business is Great Business

No-one doubts that referrals are of value. Few seem to realise quite how valuable the referral is.

Research suggests that it costs eight to ten times as much money to win an assignment as a result of your own marketing strategy as it does to gain referral business. If you could reduce 80% of your costs to one eighth of their present level would you make money? You bet you would. You ought to be aiming for 80% referral and repeat business. Those who really take referrals seriously achieve that kind of level of success.

If you want referrals, you need a strategy and you must have personal commitment. Let us look at those strategies which have been proven in the real world. The whole business of asking for referrals is one which is overlaid with strong emotion. Many suggested strategies are met with: 'I wouldn't feel comfortable doing that.'

The answer is simple. If you wouldn't be comfortable, don't do it. I will offer you all the ethical alternatives which I know to be effective. Be selective, and be consistent in your choice.

Sources

A good place to begin is to consider who could, if only they would, provide you with a constant source of referrals.

Current and past clients would head most people's list and a little additional thought would add former employers and colleagues, business acquaintances and possibly old college chums. If pushed, participants on my seminars sometimes include friends and neighbours. If I insist, they might add, very doubtfully, relations.

If you are to be a big winner in the referral game you need to think wider and deeper than that. So who else has an interest in your success?

Four further possible sources of referrals come to mind.

Your friendly bank manager has, or ought to have, a deep and abiding interest in your financial success. What is more, he meets other customers every day who manage their own or other people's business. Many of these would benefit greatly from high quality specialist business advice. So by recommending you the bank manager would serve the interests of at least two clients at the same time.

How close do you keep to your bank manager? Does he understand, in sufficient detail, what you do? Have you kept him advised of your successes and the recognition which they have brought? Have you ever told him how important referrals are to you? Does he receive a copy of your newsletter?

While you reflect on your future relationship with your bank manager, why not throw into your strategic mix two others with similar opportunities and responsibilities.

How much does your accountant or your solicitor know about the detail of what you do? Your status as a consultant who enjoys a reasonable level of profitable business and has not yet been accused of malpractice is insufficient to enable them to refer you to their other clients with confidence. Referrals always include an element of risk: others can never be sure that you are as good as you appear to be. From their point of view, it may be that you look pretty good because they lack the skill to identify your weaknesses. Why not develop a regular way of keeping them informed that clients, who have the necessary knowledge to judge, and your fellow professionals, think very highly of you?

Take away the risk, and the barrier starts to crumble. Let them know how their practices might benefit from access to you and there is a hole that they could drive a client through.

We have three further sources of referral, but I offered four. I am going to suggest that you ought to think seriously about using your competition to provide referral business. In a way that is what you do when you work as a network. Chapter Four of Part One addressed the whole area of networking in detail, but I would like draw your attention to something simpler.

Suppose you were to take one small area of your skills which you believe is of potential value, but is very rare. Suppose further that you practise and promote this skill until you build a reputation as a specialist. Would that be enough to persuade your competition to recommend you when their client has need of your skill? Probably not: there is every likelihood that they would not trust you not to steal their client. But suppose you became known through experience, not protestation, as being totally ethical in all your dealings. What then?

It may be that not only would your competition, who after all are constantly shaking the bushes for business, be promoting you, but if your specialism offered sufficient added value you may be able to charge fees that would enable you to live on that alone. It is a long term strategy, but is it not worth a few moments thought?

Immediate strategy

If you and I do not get enough referral business it is probably because we do not actively seek it. Our clients, delighted as they are with our work, do not refer us for three reasons:

1. It takes effort to write a note, make a call or even respond positively to an enquiry in a conversation. You probably are aware of the times when your well meant offer to 'dig out his address for you' has led to much frustration and a keen understanding of the shortcomings of your filing system.
2. They are never totally sure that the good work that you did for them in the past is typical of a consistently high standard. Maybe your solution to their problem was good, but was it optimal? Are they sufficiently well informed to determine your merit? Unless you have taken proactive steps to keep them appraised of your triumphs on behalf of others, you can perhaps understand their doubts.
3. You have simply not asked them to refer you. If people are to be active in seeking out opportunities to refer you rather than just provide references when you have already unearthed the client, you must make it easy for them. You need to use your skills as a communicator to build their confidence in you.

Consider this case. Bill is an American with a practice which specialises in telesales training. He serves mainly large corporations and financial institutions. He has built his business by the twin strategy of practising what he preaches and encouraging referrals. And when he encourages referrals, he does it wholesale.

The prerequisite for obtaining referrals from a client is that the client is delighted and excited by the work that you have done for them. You must to catch them at the peak of their experience, usually at the completion of an assignment when the good results of your labours are beginning to materialise. Your client is basking in the glory of success and all concerns which he might have had about retaining a consultant have evaporated in the warm glow of experience.

Then is the time to check that some tiny residual concern is not lurking under the general sense of well-being. Identify all the outcomes which were agreed and check off, one by one, that they have been achieved. Ask your client if he feels that anything more ought to be done to ensure that he is delighted with the outcome. If the answer is, as it should be, that he is more than happy right now, it is the time to get those referrals moving.

Explain how important referrals are to you, and ask if he can think of anyone who might benefit from the quality of service that you have provided for him. If he works for a major company, ask specifically which other divisions could use your skills. If the client is below board level in the company, ask which directors ought to be given detailed and personalised information about his achievement and the way he has used your services.

Then make it really easy for him. Offer to write the letters, memoranda or reports. Make it clear that you will be happy to keep on amending anything you write until it represents precisely what he wants to convey. Write on what has been achieved, the benefits, his personal management and control of the project, your supportive role and his delight with the outcome. When he approves, take the responsibility for typing on his headed paper, producing all necessary envelopes and stamp and mail those items which have to be mailed yourself. Leave him nothing to do but sign and smile.

When requests for your services, or appointments to discuss what you have to offer begin to materialise, keep him informed of the results of 'his' labours. When contracts result, a brief note of thanks to your old client will keep him aware that you would appreciate his continued efforts on your behalf. Where interesting and useful new information results from work that you are doing, keep those clients who provide referrals informed whenever doing so does not breach client confidentiality. In short, develop a reinforcement schedule which makes referring you almost a conditioned response.

It takes time, discipline and effort on your part, but that is small inconvenience when compared to the time and effort expended on making sales of your services from the ground up. Remember that when you have been referred to a client, it is only in the minority of cases that any other name is in the frame. You virtually wipe out competition and when you do business you do it on your own terms. That alone must be worth the work involved.

Opportunities to recommend you to others may be more frequent than you expect, but they will not happen every day. The importance of simply keeping in touch with your 'bird dogs' cannot be overstressed.

If you publish a newsletter, every old client should be on your mailing list. If you have no formal newsletter, write an informal note a couple of times a year which lets past clients know what and how you are doing and any good things that have come your way since your last contact.

Be alert for articles of particular interest to your clients which you could clip or photocopy and send. If you write an article pertinent to a client's industry or specialism send a pre-publication draft and ask for any comments.

Divide your personal telephone book into 12 sections and call just to say 'hallo'. Do not continuously badger people for referrals. Once they know how important referrals are to you, the simple fact that they know that you are still there and doing good work will be enough to ensure that when the opportunity arises your name will spring to their their lips.

Much of the marketing section of this book has been dedicated to building your reputation and status as an ethical and effective consultant. There is a way of using referrals to build your status in a unique way. When your name has been passed to a third party, the expectation on all sides is that you will grab the telephone and make speedy contact. To raise your status in their eyes, have your potential client make the first contact instead.

An old client tells you that his good friend Bill Folds is considering putting into place a total quality management approach. Your name has been enthusiastically recommended, and you should get in touch with Bill post haste. For you to do so will make you appear efficient and concerned. You can appear efficient, concerned and important while remaining accessible.

Find something which will be useful and interesting to Bill Folds such as some information – a 'model' or handout, or an article about his problem or opportunity. Give it to your client and suggest that he pass it to Bill with your number, so that Bill can contact you when he is ready for a chat.

When you can do that, and it works, you really have the referral business sown up and you know that your personal reputation will stand any test.

Referral action plan

1. What information can I provide to my professional advisors
which would make it easy for them to recommend my services to
others?

_____
_____
_____
_____
_____
_____
_____
_____
_____
_____
_____
_____
_____
_____
_____
_____
_____
_____

 2. What legitimate concerns might they have about referring me,
and how can I remove them?

_____
_____
_____
_____
_____
_____
_____
_____
_____
_____
_____
_____
_____
_____

3. Which recent or current clients have expressed delight with my
work?

_____

_____

_____

_____

_____

_____

_____

_____

_____

4. How might I most tactfully approach each of them?

_____

_____

_____

_____

_____

_____

_____

5. How will I ensure ongoing contact in the future?   Primary

Method: Newsletter   _____
                   Letter   _____
                   Telephone   _____

Secondary Method:

_____

_____

_____

_____

Make planning for maximising your opportunities for referrals a
basic part of your practice building strategy. When the time
comes that you can say to a prospective client, 'Who is it that is
recommending you to me. I only work for clients who are
referred to me' you can assume that you have made it. Until then,
building your personal group of 'bird dogs' will more than repay
the effort.

Find the approach which sits most comfortably with your
personal style and start today, it really is that important.

12   Selling Your Skills

As the table at the beginning of this Chapter suggests, very few good consultants are good salespeople. Equally, it is an interesting fact that few good salespeople easily become good consultants. There are very deep personality and value considerations which make it difficult for the salesperson using standardised techniques to place the client at the absolute centre of things. It is often at least as difficult for the good consultant to do something which he regards as 'pushy' or manipulative.

The status and reputation building tactics which we have described above are intended to ease the problem by creating a relationship which reduces the 'pressure to pressure'. If you have worked on developing your reputation, your first meeting with the prospective client will be very different from what it would be under less propitious circumstances.

Your client will find himself in the unusual situation of feeling just a little in awe of you. He will have heard of you in circumstances which give you exceptional credibility. You need to be prepared to capitalise on this.

It is important that everything that you do, everything that you say, is consistent with the image that your new client has of you.

First impressions

Approach the meeting without any sense of inferiority. No matter who your client is, your meeting must be a meeting of peers who expect to explore the potential benefits of working together. With the greatest of sincere respect to used vehicle salespeople (some of whom have literally been , over the years, among my best friends), you must be seen as the equivalent of a surgeon rather than a used car or any other kind of salesman. It is not a matter of snobbery, a matter of role, and different roles dictate different behaviours and different levels of sophistication.

You need to make it clear to your client from the beginning that in order to establish whether it would be appropriate to offer your services there are things that you must explore and understand. With that in mind you will avoid wasting your host's valuable time if he could answer a few simple questions. Remember that it is the one who asks the questions, not he who answers them, who controls the conversation.

If your client beats you to the punch by saying, 'tell me what you can do for me,' resist the temptation to start talking about your wonderful services. You will almost certainly say something which gives your client the opportunity to think, 'I don't need that', after which his concentration will be less on what you say, and more on how politely to put off the decision, or reject your offer. Instead say something like:

'We offer a wide range of services, and I will be pleased to tell you in detail those which may be appropriate to your needs. To avoid wasting your time with those which may be least relevant right now, could you tell me what is the major problem affecting your industry?'

This should be followed by: 'How exactly is that affecting you?' Once you have established the expectation that you will conduct the early interview, it is easy to continue. Most people enjoy an opportunity to talk about the things which are important to them, and if you 'sell' them on talking to you, many will talk for hours.

Your questions must not be aimless because there are some things which you absolutely need to know before you can relate your services fully to client needs. We will identify the key questions soon.

When your potential client is talking, listen carefully. Only take notes if you must, and after you have asked permission to do so. Keep notes brief - a mass of written screed is a distraction to the other person who will find it difficult not to keep glancing at what you are writing. We remember by making connections and through repetition. Ask about key points, and mentally connect them so that when you remember one the others come surging back. If Paul Daniels can remember the name of each of 200 or more members of

PRODUCT ANALYSIS - THE CONSULTANT VERSUS THE SALESMAN

PERSONALITY PROFILES OF SUCCESS

CONSULTANT Personality Traits	SALESPERSON Personality Traits
Sense of VOCATION	Desire to WIN
Personal and Organisational DEVELOPMENT	ASSERTIVENESS
AFFILIATION	INFLUENCE
FOCUS on the specific	AFFILIATION
Organisational POWER	DISCIPLINE

KEY CHARACTERISTICS INDICATING SUCCESS

HOW DIFFERENT ARE SALESPEOPLE AND THE PEOPLE THAT THEY SELL?

Figure 12.1

an audience that he has met once briefly as they took their seats, you can remember the key points of a conversation. A poor memory is a mixture of affectation, laziness and sheer bad manners, so learn to use yours.

Show by your body posture that what is being said really interests you. Nod to show understanding. Maintain eye contact, not with a fixed gaze, but with occasional glances. If you find that you are looking at your client's face for a long time, look at a central point on the forehead rather than directly into the eyes.

Ask intelligent questions to clarify your understanding or to direct the client's attention to an area you need to know more about. Avoid creating a sense of an interrogation by injecting your own occasional comments when you have something to contribute which shows that you have done your homework about the industry and the client company. Try to find a reason to sit side by side rather than face to face with the client. Sitting face to face accentuates a sense of being adversarial, while a side by side position suggests mutual problem-solving which justifies in the other's mind almost any exploratory question.

When you have little which is germane to add, punctuate the flow with expressions such as:

'Thank you, that is interesting.'

Reward the other person for answering your questions with smiles, nods and gestures of understanding or concern. Lead the client gently to telling you what you need to know, which is as follows:

Vital questions to be asked every time

What is the client's previous experience of consultants?

Has he used consultants before?

What good results came from the experience?

Were there any problems?

What would they seek to do differently this time?

Do they have any fears or concerns about having consultants in the company now?

Is there anything that they would wish a consultant to be particularly sensitive to at present?

Research shows that any company which has used consultants once is likely to use them again. But they may want things to be very different this time.

What was the nature of the financial arrangement?
Not how much did they pay, but were the consultants paid a fixed fee for the job, or a daily rate, or was the work done on the basis of a performance contract? (If a client goes on to tell you exactly how much they paid, great. You can realistically take that as a buying signal).

What specific outcomes does the client seek from your intervention?
'If I take on an assignment for your company, how will we measure my contribution? How will you and I know that I have done a good job?'
What is the client's ideal outcome?
In a year from today, how will the company be different if the client's wishes are fulfilled?

Regardless of any work you might carry out for this client, what is his most important goal right now?

With many clients you will find that they only have vague answers to the last two questions. My experience is that asking them and helping to clarify their thinking enables me to define measurable outcomes for my intervention, and establish important client goals that I can help to achieve. More importantly, at a time when I am trying to build a relationship, it causes the client to place a very high value on our discussion and creates a proper foundation for the future relationship.

Talking of placing a value on the initial discussion, may I remind you that research suggests that as many as 15% of clients expect to be billed for it. This can lead to an interesting source of conflict.

The potential client, believing that consultants charge for everything, expects to receive an invoice for the marketing call and works hard to get some information or work done by the consultant which will represent value for money. The consultant, sensitive to the fact that clients try sometimes to get something for nothing, is determined to give nothing away. They talk in frustrating and never decreasing circles until the assignment disappears in a game of 'catch as catch can'. If you have the slightest reason to believe that the client misreads the situation, clarify it. Say, for example:

'I have found that some clients expect to be billed for the first exploratory meeting. I like to make it clear that I never raise an invoice unless I have carried out specific work, or have given unique information.'

Professional selling

Professional services must be sold. A great deal can be done to pre-dispose the client toward hiring you, but in the end everything comes down to your ability to demonstrate why your services should be retained today. The contract must be signed. With that in mind I am going to try to explain within the constraints of a short Chapter exactly how, step by step, you can use well-validated techniques to ensure a very high success rate.

First, a little background. Our approach to marketing has involved building your status, and anything we do to make the sale must reflect that. We must never be seen to be using obvious and doubtful sales methods. Our approach must flow naturally from what has gone before, and create a state of maximum comfort both for us and our client.

People love to buy, but they hate to be sold to. If we keep this maxim in mind, we will keep easily and comfortably on track.

A great deal of dedicated research has gone into the analysis of what enables people to buy without feeling that they have been sold to. Research has shown that it is possible to develop a simple and accurate cognitive model of exactly how people think as they go through the buying process.

The salesperson must relate to that process successfully. More than 60 years in-depth analysis of what works in practice enables us to lay out a step-by-step approach. Professionals facilitate that process.

The thought process is presented graphically (Figure 12.2). Each box represents an exact thought pattern for the potential buyer of goods, services or ideas. For each the sequence is precisely the same. Each thought expresses or implies a question. If that question is answered to the satisfaction of the client, the mind moves comfortably to the next. If all questions are answered satisfactorily the decision to 'buy' is only constrained by the ability to proceed.

Selling your services

An approach which will reduce the chances of rejection, demonstrate your professionalism and gain you more assignments is as follows:

1. Plan your presentation from the listener's point of view
• Make your listener feel important by basing your discussion firmly on her objective.

THE PATH TO ASSENT

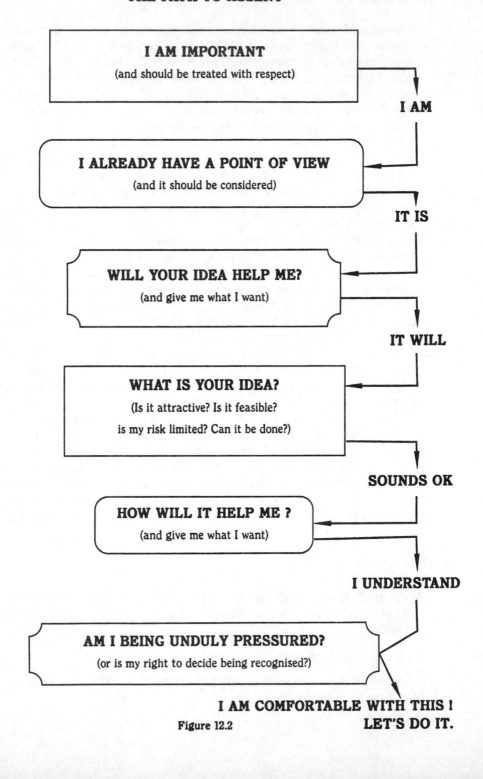

I AM IMPORTANT
(and should be treated with respect)

I AM

I ALREADY HAVE A POINT OF VIEW
(and it should be considered)

IT IS

WILL YOUR IDEA HELP ME?
(and give me what I want)

IT WILL

WHAT IS YOUR IDEA?
(Is it attractive? Is it feasible?
is my risk limited? Can it be done?)

SOUNDS OK

HOW WILL IT HELP ME ?
(and give me what I want)

I UNDERSTAND

AM I BEING UNDULY PRESSURED?
(or is my right to decide being recognised?)

**I AM COMFORTABLE WITH THIS !
LET'S DO IT.**

Figure 12.2

- Test your understanding of the most important issues or problems your listener faces. From their viewpoint NOT YOURS.
- Remember that her present point of view is based on her past success and makes absolute sense to him. To change it will require compelling reasons.
- Match your mood and manner to that of your listener.

2. *Create for the listener an awareness of the need to act - NOW*

- Demonstrate that conditions beyond the control of either of you are changing.
- Show how the changes taking place COULD cause your listener problems in the future.
- Indicate that you have the means to change potential threats to opportunities.

3. *Maintain and build your listener's interest*

- Mention one or two benefits which the listener will gain from using your services before indicating what you will do.
- Make sure the listener regards them as benefits AND APPRECIATES THEIR WORTH.

4. *Tell your listener ALL that he needs to know about your service*

- Explain in sufficient detail:
- What you will do.
- When you will do it.
- Who else will be involved.
- What special skills and knowledge you uniquely offer.
- How she will retain control.
- How she will remain fully informed.
- Who else, that she respects, has already successfully used your services.
- What they say about the experience (if you have their permission to quote them).

Never say how you will do it.

5. Explain the benefits of your services
- Link the benefits logically to prove that if one is achieved the others follow as a consequence.
- Show that the final benefit in your chain of logic is the listener's key objective.

6. If you lose your listener's favourable attention during the discussion.
- Stop talking.
- Wait for your listener to speak.
- Listen actively.
- Show that you have listened by repeating a key idea or feeling in your own words.
- Diffuse the emotion by showing that you understand the right of the listener to react IN ANY WAY HE CHOOSES.
- Deal with his problem.
- Continue when you are convinced that he is satisfied and not before.

7. Ask for the assignment
- No tricks or 'closing techniques' - JUST ASK
- Look for 'buying signals'
  Nods of agreement or approval
  Building on your ideas
  Willingness to give you supportive information or data
  Having asked - stop talking and stay silent until you have a reply.

Figure 12.3 shows in graphic form how this ties in precisely with the client's thought process when facing a decision of whether to buy.

Always start as was indicated at the beginning of this Chapter by asking essential questions. As soon as you have the information which enables you to do it, suggest that it might be useful if you were to summarise the key points as you have understood them. This summary is your sales presentation.

It might go something like this;

'As I understand it your primary concern at the moment is that the reduction of headcount be totally voluntary. Am I right?' (client objective)

'Yes, that's essential.'

'Am I also right in believing that the mess the economy is in has affected managers' confidence and you are finding that there is deep

THE PATH TO ASSENT

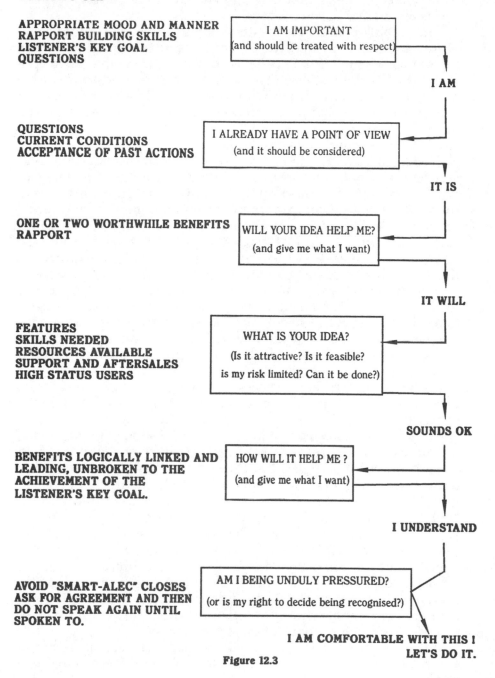

TOOLS TO USE

APPROPRIATE MOOD AND MANNER
RAPPORT BUILDING SKILLS
LISTENER'S KEY GOAL
QUESTIONS

I AM IMPORTANT
(and should be treated with respect)

I AM

QUESTIONS
CURRENT CONDITIONS
ACCEPTANCE OF PAST ACTIONS

I ALREADY HAVE A POINT OF VIEW
(and it should be considered)

IT IS

ONE OR TWO WORTHWHILE BENEFITS
RAPPORT

WILL YOUR IDEA HELP ME?
(and give me what I want)

IT WILL

FEATURES
SKILLS NEEDED
RESOURCES AVAILABLE
SUPPORT AND AFTERSALES
HIGH STATUS USERS

WHAT IS YOUR IDEA?
(Is it attractive? Is it feasible?
is my risk limited? Can it be done?)

SOUNDS OK

BENEFITS LOGICALLY LINKED AND
LEADING, UNBROKEN TO THE
ACHIEVEMENT OF THE
LISTENER'S KEY GOAL.

HOW WILL IT HELP ME ?
(and give me what I want)

I UNDERSTAND

AVOID "SMART-ALEC" CLOSES
ASK FOR AGREEMENT AND THEN
DO NOT SPEAK AGAIN UNTIL
SPOKEN TO.

AM I BEING UNDULY PRESSURED?
(or is my right to decide being recognised?)

I AM COMFORTABLE WITH THIS !
LET'S DO IT.

Figure 12.3

concern over even asking for the facts about voluntary separation?'
(Conditions and losses they cause the client to experience.)

'There certainly is, and it's getting worse.'

'Then I think I have an idea of how I might help you. Your people
would be more inclined to consider accepting your generous
separation package if they believed that they were able to keep a
number of options open. (Throwaway benefit used to maintain
favourable attention). Those who would happily accept the idea of
retirement would have no problem, so if I could focus on the
others?'

'That makes sense.'

'Good. I think that you could give people an increased sense of
security, and confidence in their future if you initiated a series of
workshops which would enable qualified people to prepare
themselves for self employment as management consultants.
(Benefits leading into expression of the key idea). These would
follow the application of a psychometric test which is very
comprehensive and would help people to make an informed
decision whether self-employment would be appropriate for them.
The workshop I have in mind provides participants with strategies
for building a professional practice. Research shows these strategies
to be highly effective in all cultures. We would also prepare them for
the administrative side of running their own business with precise
and detailed information on how to write proposals, develop
contracts and set their fees. Much of the material is transferable to
any kind of high quality business, so those for whom consultancy
does not seem to be the answer would still gain a great deal from the
workshop.'

'What about those who would be looking for another job?'

'Our team includes experts with a proven track record in the field
of recruitment. I suggest that through the use of practical job
hunting workshops we could offer a service to those who prefer to
look for new jobs which would compare very favourably with
"outplacement" at considerably lower cost. By backing this service
with one on one counselling under the supervision of a qualified
psychologist we could make a major contribution to alleviating
stress at this difficult time. Your company could make this service
available to families, whose needs are often overlooked, showing
that you are prepared to do everything possible to continue to
support your people through difficult times. This would have a
positive effect on the morale of those who remain.'

'It does sound interesting.' (Buying signal? Maybe, but not strong
enough to lead to intelligent trial close, Benefits have only been
implied.)

'By approaching the problem this way, you would ensure that your people have the best opportunity to establish themselves quickly in new careers even in these difficult times. That is certain to build their confidence, and by initiating a programme that gives continued support to everyone whatever their career plans, you would be offering a level of service which may well lead to your separation programme being over-subscribed. What do you think?' (Logical flow of benefits, leading to achievement of the client's Objective and followed by a very gentle trial close which will not make the client feel pressured.)

'I think it sounds interesting, but I need to think about it.'

'I understand that, its a major decision. Why don't I let you have a detailed proposal which will give you all the information you need?' (trial close.)

'When could you get it to me?'

'If we can make an appointment now for early next week, I will ensure that it is ready. I could answer any questions that you might have and you would be in the best position to make your decision. As you know, we always work to a formal contract so that you have details of exactly what we undertake to provide, I'll have that drawn up for the same meeting. Is that OK with you?' (trial close.)

'As long as you don't expect me to sign it first and read the proposal afterwards. How about Wednesday? If you could be here for about ten, we could arrange for you to meet the Chairman at noon. I'd like him to know what we're doing. He's very keen on PR and I think I see some spin-off here.' (I think he's bought it!)

Leave aside the inescapably stilted feel of written English in lengthy passages of speech and it is easy to write sales pitches. In real life, however, it seldom goes from start to finish according to plan.

Clients take you off at tangents by raising new ideas as they think of them. Sometimes you inadvertently say something which triggers an unexpected negative response, and you may have no idea why. I would like to give you a little help with both of those problems.

Your client suddenly thinks of something which is of great interest to him, but which does not fit snugly into your flow of argument. For example, in real life the client in my little vignette above was suddenly struck by the PR potential of providing stress counselling for the families of early retirees and started talking at great length and with considerable enthusiasm. What did I do? I listened with keen interest and encouraged him in every way that I could to go on talking.

My interest was keen because;

- The client was selling himself the idea and sales arguments which he developed for himself would have more power than the best that I could devise. (People love to buy, they hate to be sold to.)
- If, in spite of the signs to the contrary, I met some sales resistance later I should be able to build a convincing case around satisfying the chairman's desire for PR.
- If I needed to convince the chairman I could not assume his enthusiasm for PR, but it gave me a foundation for some sensitive probing when we met.
- And in terms of my relationship with my client, I knew that if I could help him to come up with good PR ideas it would enhance his status in the eyes of the chairman. Building my client is an important of the business I am in.

So in spite of my carefully thought out approach I was happy to let him talk on. I lie, it is *because* of my structured approach that I can encourage the client to interupt me and chat away to his heart's content. I have a structure to make it easy for me to remember exactly where I am. I do not have to remember detail, only one key word. My structure is:

- Client's objective
- Conditions he is up against and problems he may face
- Indication that I can help
- Benefits from listening to me
- Detail of my idea
- Logical benefit flow to client's objective
- Ask for action

I have a road map, and by mentally registering a single word as my client takes off, I can return to my route at any time. It does not matter if I repeat a benefit, or part of my idea, the flow will make it seem natural and easy. I can relax and listen and learn. Listening is the key to the next little technique.

The SARAH technique

No matter how careful you are, and regardless of the sensitivity which you show toward others' needs and feelings, there will be times when suddenly and for no obvious reason, your client shows clear signs of being upset. By word or gesture he will indicate that you have done or said something which triggers a negative response.

Many salespeople, seeing the signs, break simultaneously into a sweat and a gallop. They feel that if only they can finish what they are saying all will be well. After all, they have an unanswerable logical case.

Unfortunately, trying to answer emotions with logic does not work. Think about those times when you get upset with little reason. If someone tries to change your mood with logic do you listen to them? If you are anything like me you do not. What I do is to ignore what is being said while I think of all the convincing reasons why I am right to feel as I do. If necessary, I will dredge up wrongs of such distant history that I can remember them only in terms of intense determination to feel ill-used. It works: the more others try to make me feel better with their appeals to logic, the worse I feel, and the more aggressive I become. So what do I do when my client shows signs of anger or distress? Do I panic? No. I relax and enjoy another opportunity to win a brownie point because years ago I was introduced to SARAH. If I use her skills with sensitivity, I will have a grateful and more compliant client.

So when things start to go off the rails, think SARAH. The technique is explained below, and summarised in the following table.

Stop talking

Do not talk faster, in fact do not talk at all. Give your listener the opportunity to express their feelings. No matter how painful the silence seems to you, there is absolutely nothing you can usefully say. If there was, your client would not listen to it anyway. Hold your tongue and within seconds (it will feel like minutes) your listener will break the silence.

Adopt active listening

Listen as if your life depended on understanding how your client feels and what they think. Make no attempts to second guess, always accept what is said as if it were true. Most of all, do not listen as smart-alec salesmen do to customer objections with the intention of hearing something which enables them to think: 'Got you!', followed by an attempt to devastate the listener with their lucidity and grasp of facts.

Feelings are facts, and in this situation it is your client's feelings which are the most salient facts of all. So when he has stopped talking:

HANDLING PROBLEMS
The SARAH Technique

From time to time, even in the best managed conversation, we somehow make a miscalculation and negative emotions are aroused - suddenly, and for no apparent reason.
Such a situation must be managed:-

STOP TALKING

ACTIVE LISTENING

REFLECT CONTENT OR FEELING

AROUSE EMPATHY

HANDLE OBJECTIONS

EMPATHY IS NOT SYMPATHY

I understand you feeling that way - many people do at first.

You have every right to be concerned until I have proved what I can do.

That's a perfectly reasonable point of view.

It can seem like a lot of money until we've fully worked out the savings.

Others have expressed very similar worries.

EMPATHY ALLOWS YOU TO ACCEPT THE REASONABLENESS OF OTHERS' FEELINGS AND STILL CORRECT THEIR UNDERSTANDING.

Figure 12.4

Reflect content or feeling

Paraphrase a key statement your client has made to demonstrate that you really have been listening. Say it musingly to show that you are carefully considering what is being said and not doing parrot-like imitations. If nothing coherent enough has been said then reflect what is clear to you about what the client is feeling.

'You are very upset.'

'You feel that it is unfair?'

If you reflect feeling, wait for a response. The listener will almost certainly now expand on what the problem is and, if you have remained concerned but calm, you will find that the client becomes a little calmer too as he realises that there is no need to try to convince you of the validity of the arguments that he has been rehearsing internally to justify the mood swing.

Act with empathy

Show your acceptance that others have an absolute right to feel any way they please. They may be wrong in fact. They may have completely misunderstood. You may have inadvertently triggered a prejudice of which any right-minded person would be ashamed. Nonetheless, they have an absolute right as individuals to deal with their own problems their own way. But be sure you can tell the difference between 'empathy' and 'sympathy' and take care that you never express sympathy - 'You are absolutely right to feel as you do' - when you intend to convey empathy - 'You have an absolute right to feel as you do'.

The difference allows you, after expressing empathy, to correct their thinking and consequently change their feeling. Once you have shown sympathy you are locked in to their feeling no matter how injurious it is to your case. 'Yes, you're right all consultants are liars and thieves' will not help you to win a sale, or respect. Neither will: 'That's nonsense, and I can prove it.'

Empathy is shown in expressions such as: 'I can understand you feeling that way, many people do.' There are other examples in Figure 12.4.

Handle objections

When your calm, sensitive handling of the situation has made it easy for your client to listen to reason again, deal with any objections raised. Always deal with what your client says. Never try to second guess 'what he really means' - you will almost certainly get it wrong. Even if you get it right, you will destroy the belief that you have been listening carefully and with empathy and understanding.

Research over the last 60 years shows that objections can be classified and the most appropriate tactics for handling each type suggested.

Price

Something appears to cost too much when it seems to offer insufficient benefit for the price to be paid in money or effort. Your service will deliver many benefits which will not fit into the logical flow toward the achievement of your client's key goals. Use them to convince your listener that you are providing exceptional value.

Habit

'We've always done it this way, and it works' is not an invitation for you to focus on why the old way is stupid and your idea is infinitely better. It does give you the opportunity, however, to recognise that you have not shown sufficiently clearly how the changes in the environment in which your client operates are such that major problems may result in the future if steps are not taken now. You will of course need to convince that the steps you are advocating are going to be effective.

Competition

'We have always been happy with Earnest & Elderly' is asking you to expand on what is unique about your offer. Your client is requesting more detail about your idea. But be careful. Be aware at all times that you stick to WHAT you will do, not HOW you will do it. If your potential client has a pal at E&E you may find that they will soon be offering their clients what was once your unique service once you have proudly given away the recipe.

We have covered in this Chapter how you approach the initial meeting with the prospective client: dealing with essential questions to be asked before you start selling; how to structure your sales presentation; and how to deal with outbursts and objections. Before we leave this important area there is one more piece of research which I would like to share with you.

Howard Shenson, who did more to put fact into places occupied by mystique than most, conducted some research in 1990 into what it is that clients fear about hiring consultants. You will be well repaid if you take a little time to think about how to ensure that these fears do not get between you and a profitable assignment.

Remember, fears are not something that we openly talk about in our society. We expect people to portray themselves as confident at all times. The manager who honestly admits to doubts about anything gets short shrift from peers and bosses, so do not expect anyone to admit to these concerns when face to face, or to welcome any clumsy attempt to bring them into the open. What is needed is for you present your service in a way which resolves the concern without embarrassment to the client.

The Shenson survey

The survey covered 600 companies which used, or were actively planning to use, consultants. The fears are presented in order of importance, with the first being regarded as most important by most respondents.

Consultant incompetence
The client considers hiring a consultant because he doubts his own ability in a certain area, or because he lacks the time or internal resources to do the job. It is not surprising if he wonders whether he has enough knowledge to judge the competence of a specialist. By marketing yourself using the methods which I have described you will build client confidence in your ability. By approaching the initial discussion as a surgeon considering whether to operate and by avoiding 'pile 'em high, sell 'em cheap' sales techniques, you will reinforce the client belief that with you at least he need have no concern about consultant competence.

If he feels good about working with you why should he look elsewhere?

Lack of management control
Consultants are often perceived as scuttling about the business, clip-board in hand, answerable to no-one, and finally presenting an hitherto secret report which embarrasses the client who is paying them. I have even known, to the profession's shame, of consultants who, without informing their client, have recommended that he is the source of the problem and should be removed forthwith and without the option.

The person who hires you *is your client* and has an absolute right to your loyalty. When you describe what you will do if assigned, explain precisely how you will keep your client informed of progress and, if appropriate, provide him with information which he can present to his bosses. Your job is to support your client in managing his company and to enhance his standing. It is not to usurp or undermine his position in any way. If your client is doing it all wrong, you find a way to help him to get it right or you withdraw from the assignment. Honesty and honour rule in the profession which you have chosen.

Continued dependency

Respondents suggest that this problem is of equal importance as lack of control. It is not unknown for consultants to put in systems far beyond the capacity of the client company to operate, with the result that the company is faced with buying in specialist knowledge on a permanent or periodic basis. Clients believe that this is a conscious strategy on the part of consultants to ensure a job for life. Conscious malpractice or sheer incompetence, it is unacceptable.

Tell your client what steps you propose to take to ensure growth in the self-reliance and autonomy of his team as part of the work you are doing.

Excessive fees

This book explains in detail how to establish fees which will give you high earning capacity while you offer exceptional value for money.

Be proud of the benefits which your intervention will create and do not assume that the client will value them unless you explain them to him fully. By showing logically that valuable objectives will be achieved you will put a value on your services which will make it unlikely that price will ever be questioned. If it is, follow John Fenton's excellent advice and 'take pride in your price' as an indicator of exceptional value.

Lack of time

Recently there has been an influx into the profession of cut-price consultants who are unable or unwilling to establish sensible fees. Many have tried to make up for the low fees charged by cutting corners, including charging two or more clients for the same rushed work. The result has been unspecific and slipshod. Explain to your client that your fees are set at a level which enables you to resource the job properly and devote adequate time to his needs.

Need for a consultant seen as admission of management failure

Stupidly macho organisations in which idiots like to use foolish Americanisms (which most Americans, being wise, never use) such as 'Didn't know yah couldn't cut the mustard' are found in industry and commerce on both sides of the Atlantic.

Put this concern to rest by emphasising that although the client could probably do what you will do himself if he had time, your position as an outside specialist enables you to concentrate totally on this one small aspect, and use techniques which ensure a positive outcome with least expense.

Fear of disclosing sensitive data

You may need to convince the client of the absolute confidentiality of all information which he may give you. Consider the possibility of even refusing to disclose to anyone who your clients are without their specific permission. When faced with the rare, but occasional request for client references I say that I never disclose even the names of my clients without their permission, but will be happy to ask people for whom I have done similar work to provide any information required.

That is usually enough to put their fears about confidentiality to rest.

Improper diagnosis or needs analysis

It is always easier to market a product than a service, and in the past consultants who peddle off-the-shelf nostrums for all complaints have had more success than they deserve. Because they have only one solution which they cannot amend, they force-fit the client problem to their cure, with disasterous results.

Explain to your client that you develop processes appropriate to the problem, and never use inappropriate methods just because they are easy. Be warned though – never be tempted to show how good you are at diagnosis by attempting something off the cuff at the first meeting. You get paid for identifying and solving problems, and diagnosis is often the hard part of the assignment.

Pushing a product

There is a well-founded concern that some 'consultants' are salespeople in disguise whose main aim is to push a product. Where possible avoid recommending specific products. Your independence is something you should value and promote.

Summary

The approach to sales outlined in this Chapter is one which is appropriate to the role and status of a professional, and which research has consistently shown to be highly successful in many cultures. If you study and practise it you may expect a high percentage of positive outcomes, and you should not expect any rejections.

Although you may not make every sale every time, sensitive use of this material will build respect for your professionalism even when you lose out for some reason. That respect will keep doors open to you. If you want to make every sale, every time, look out for my book, soon to be published, on 'No Fail Sales'.

Consultancy is, or should be, a service rather than a product. As such it is intangible. What is worse it is often by its exploratory nature a particularly ill-defined service. This makes some research completed in the early 1980's by the sociologists George and Myers particularly relevant to the seller of consultancy services.

As you end this Chapter and prepare to put down the book I ask you to consider the following in the light of what you have just read.

Differences in (client) perceptions, attitudes and behaviours when buying services

Consumers' Purchase Perceptions
- Services are less consistent in quality than goods
- Any service purchase is a high risk purchase
- Service purchasing is a less enjoyable activity than buying products (You cannot 'twiddle'the nobs of a consultant')
- Services need to be bought with greater consideration of the seller's reputation

Consumers' Purchase Behaviour
- Consumers make less price comparisons when buying services
- They place heavy reliance on the supplier's reputation and their own and other's experience
- They are less influenced by advertising, and more by personal recommendations

Personal Selling of Services
- Clients seek greater personal involvement in the service activity

- Long term satisfaction is greatly influenced by the salesperson's attitude and personality
- Salespeople may need to spend more time reducing anxiety about the purchase

Does the above help to convince you, if you needed convincing, that the need to market your services on the basis of building your reputation, status and image makes total sense? Does it further help to explain why an approach to selling which makes the client central to the process is essential rather than optional?

Finally, by way of Chapter summary, a brief outline of some recent research into what clients are looking for when a consultant is selling his or her services.

What clients say they want at the selling stage

- Willingness to apply original thinking to our problem - not suggesting the solution to someone else's problem that was supposedly 'the same'.
- Solid agreement on goals, outcomes and scope of work.
- A detailed and realistic commitment of time to undertake the assignment.
- Structured methods but not inflexible packages
- Expertise that really relates to our problem.
- Interest in bottom line improvements or cost reduction.
- Admission of the need to learn first about my business.
- Desire to get going with the project for the project's sake and not the consultant's immediate income needs.
- Looking for a positive win-win relationship.
- Presentation of a range of feasible options.
- A fresh approach, but not an excessively risky approach.
- An impression of competence and energy.
- Doing their homework before and during the visit.
- Spending adequate time defining the problem.
- Knowledge of new developments in our industry, our company, our market and management in general.
- Indication of partnership mentality with in-house brain power.
- Complete confidentiality.
- **Reasonable** prices.

What clients say are the major turn-offs at the selling stage

- The 'dog and pony show approach' that suggests 'stars' sell, donkeys 'do'.
- Dishonesty about credentials of project team.
- Making promises that cannot be met.
- Talking too much and listening too little to learn what is really different about our situation.
- Name dropping and breaching confidentiality.
- Canned rather than customised approaches.
- Trying to 'play it by ear' without any attempt at preparation.
- Asking the same question once it has been answered.
- Tying savings in to cost of fees merely to justify the per diem.
- Talking about other clients and their irrelevant problems.
- Pushing canned solutions.
- Selling as opposed to marketing.
- Trying to sell the package rather than join us in solving problems.
- Seeing all problems as their strong suit.
- Overemphasis on only one solution to our problem.
- Hard sell. Promising savings before knowing enough about our organisation to be confident that they can deliver.
- Telling us that our problem is the same as someone else's problem.
- Too much 'packaging' and too little content.

SALES PRESENTATION PLANNING SHEET

LISTENER'S GOALS	CONDITIONS AND POTENTIAL LOSS	BENEFITS	PRODUCT, IDEA OR SERVICE	BENEFIT LOGIC RUN
List as many as you are confident of.	Actions of people, systems things which are outside your control and that of your listener	Sell the idea of listening to your proposed solution by expressing one or two BENEFITS which are valid, but do not fit your LOGIC RUN	FEATURES	TEST WITH WHICH MEANS
Identify the most important that your product, idea or service can satisfy	Try to identify situations which your listener can accept, but are not threatening in the sense that a prudent person would have already taken action	Look for a positive reaction, and detail your PRODUCT, IDEA OR SERVICE		("which means") ◆ ◆ ◆ ◆ ◆ ◆ ◆ ◆
Mark sub-goals which will be attained en route			RESOURCES	
Cross out any "doubtful" or unspoken goals	Attach only LOSSES which are directly and totally attributable to the CONDITIONS	List ALL BENEFITS which you can deliver		
Re-write key goal below	Connect LOSSES logically ("which means") and show how they threaten achievement of the key GOAL.	Plug all logic gaps ("which means")	SUPPORT	
Propose goals which are indicated by listener's role or previous actions.		Create LOGIC RUN which leads to attainment of KEY KEY OBJECTIVE		
USE PTQ TO CHECK	Connect to BENEFITS with bridging statement: e.g. "To avoid this...."	Attach naturally to definition of PRODUCT, IDEA OR SERVICE.	USERS	
KEY OBJECTIVE				
USE ONE AT A TIME				

Figure 12.5

SALES PRESENTATION PLAN

For:- _____

LISTENER'S GOALS	CONDITIONS POTENTIAL LOSS	BENEFITS	PRODUCT, IDEA OR SERVICE	BENEFIT LOGIC RUN
			FEATURES	TEST WITH WHICH MEANS ◆ ◆ ◆ ◆ ◆ ◆ ◆ ◆
			RESOURCES	
			SUPPORT	
			USERS	
KEY OBJECTIVE				

Figure 12.6

PART THREE:
ADVANCED CONSULTING SKILLS

13   Consultancy Roles

The role which the consultant assumes in any work that is undertaken must be consistent with the client needs, the situation, and the skills, knowledge and experience of the consultant. In any one intervention it is possible that the consultant will assume different roles as the work matures. Effective flexibility is one of the hallmarks of good consultancy.

One can be effective either unconsciously as a result of some fortunate and God-given talent, or consciously as a result of planning, thought and sensitivity to changing need. An actress was once quoted as saying, 'I have been very poor, and I have been rich. Rich is better.' Conscious application of knowledge makes the talented more skilled and gives the less gifted a better than even chance. So when you engage in the practice of consultancy, you will be more effective in direct proportion to your understanding of your role.

Let me see if I can help by clarifying the range of roles which a consultant may be required to perform. They move from being highly prescriptive to being very non-directive. Try to avoid thinking of 'directive' and 'influential' as having the same meaning. The effective consultant is often non-directive, but successful consultants are always influential. It is the form which influence takes which varies.

More directive roles

Advocate

It is possible that, given sufficient expertise, the proper role of the consultant is that of an advocate in its simplest sense. The action which needs to be taken may be clear and unambiguous and the consultant may become the advocate of that action. For example, a skilled engineer may be in a position to identify one and only one solution to the client problem: 'Move that machine to there and the production bottleneck will be eased and one employee can watch both machines.'

In such a case the consultant's role as advocate is clear and appropriate. There are always, however, points to be borne most carefully in mind.

- Problems are usually solved more effectively and stay solved longer if the client plays an active role in reaching the solution. Passive acceptance of someone else's ideas tends to be seen as a form of release from the responsibility for making solutions work.

- Consultants sometimes assume on too little evidence that their first solution is the optimal solution. Too often a situation is seen as being 'just like' a previous experience when in reality it is only 'somewhat like'.

- If a consultant chooses to say 'do this', he had better be sure that he is right. (See my brief thoughts on 'liability' above.)

The advocate role is more frequently assumed by the consultant in the sense of influencing the client to become involved in the problem-solving process, allowing others to become involved, and recognising that in general, the more people are engaged in finding the solution, the better the solution and implementation are likely to be.This is not a plea that should be listened to when over-simplistic trainers coo seductively that consensus cures all ills.

Research shows clearly that consensus is most effective in situations where the problem is one in which not only is the solution not clear, but the situation is so novel that it is not even apparent what information will prove to be relevant. In commoner situations where it is known what information is needed and where it can be found, the decision is best made by the expert after consultation limited to establishing what, if anything, has changed and what feelings need to be taken into account.

An alternative and widely used form of advocacy involves the consultant in seeking to persuade the client that certain changes of value are germane to an effective solution– for example the removal of fear from an organisation which is moving toward a total quality management philosophy, or where the consultant seeks to persuade the organisation to use a particular process in its search for a solution. An interesting example of this must occur from time to time when Charles Hampden-Turner identifies 'laughter' to his clients as a powerful tool for analysing the organisation. When using advocacy in the sense described, it is important that the consultant does not become enmeshed in the coils of advocating a solution rather than a process.

Expert
The traditional role of the consultant is that of a specialist who through the application of unusual skills and knowledge can lead the client to the solution of a problem. It is unlikely that any assignment exists that totally lacks the need for the consultant to act this role. The danger is that the consultant may be dragged into imposing a preferred solution rather than developing the client's ability to solve his own problems. The perception of the consultant as expert can also tend to create the belief that 'there is more to this than appears on the surface'. This can undermine rather than build client confidence, and can lead to ungoing and undesirable client dependency.

I am reminded of my father, who used to run a public house. He spent many hours in the cellar and it was generally believed that this time was spent in doing arcane and wondrous things to improve the beer. Great was my father's reputation locally as a seer of the beer.

While casks were of wood, it was possible to do a certain limited amount to care for the ale by careful attention to temperature, filtering from one barrel to another and so on. But the advent of aluminium barrels should have put a stop to that. They could not be broached, and the only thing to be done with a less than perfect barrel was to return it to the brewery. My dad, however, continued his long vigils in the cellar, much to the satisfaction of his regulars who believed totally in the effectiveness of his interventions. Of course, he now descended the cellar steps carrying a newspaper, some tea and a half pint glass. His chair was already in place.

Trainer and educator
The best consultancy is innovative and developmental. All consultants will find themselves adopting the role of trainer from time to time. The need is, as always, to separate the role of educator from

that of propagandist. The top flight consultant is careful to avoid indoctrination, and seeks instead to build a critical and creative approach to new information in the client organisation. Effective consultants demonstrate skills both as designers of learning experiences and as direct teachers, but always with the aim of leaving the client and his organisation with increased autonomy and self-reliance as a result of the experience.

Less directive roles

Collaborator in problem-solving
Notwithstanding my frequent warnings about seeing one situation as being too much like another, the consultant is employed in part at least because he brings to the situation knowledge and experience of what has worked for others in similar situations. By providing information, stimulating thinking and maintaining objectivity the consultant is able to develop a truly synergistic role in which the client is influenced toward finding for himself a more effective solution than would otherwise be available to him. The information will frequently include processes relevant to different problems which will not respond to a single problem – solving approach.

Identifier of alternatives
The key to effective decision-making is the future attainment of clear and worthwhile objectives. A key role for the consultant in the decision-making process is the identification with the client of a richer set of options than would otherwise be apparent. By establishing a range of possible strategies and their attendant risks, each of which would enable the achievement of the objective, the consultant is performing an important service to the immediate needs of the client organisation and to its future growth.

Fact finder
Fact finding inside and outside the client business is an integral part of the consulting process. Internally it is the vital 'borrowing of the client's watch' in order to tell him the time. Externally it is the objective assessment of information from the market, the customer, the competitor and the supplier about how the company is perceived and experienced. George Feiger, a partner in McKinsey and Company, is often surprised to find that his clients are astounded at the level of understanding he demonstrates of the business in a what they see as an amazingly short time.

He tells them that his approach is simple. He is an unrepentant watch borrower who asks those most likely to know, their employees, their customers, their suppliers and their competitors. He goes on to suggest that in future they may care to do the same. Fact finding is often as simple as that, but you bring the added value that it is easier for you to be objective, you are less likely to hear only what you want to. You will be more probing, and will always follow the receipt of information by asking for the evidence which supports it. Professor Don Thain taught me years ago to always probe by asking: 'Could you give an example please?' or more simply 'What's your evidence for that?'

It is a lesson I have never forgotten and one I commend most heartily to all fact finders who need to be sure that the facts they elicit are real and relevant. I also recommend consultants to avoid a temptation to ignore 'feelings' when searching for the facts. In most human situations the way people feel are facts, and possibly the most important ones.

Internal manager and external consultant

The role which the consultant takes is in part dictated by the sometimes complex interplay between himself and the client management. The expectations of individual members of the client management team can influence the appropriateness of the consultant role at any time, but so do the realities of the situation. Tensions can be created by the differing perspectives of consultant and manager. It is always the consultant's responsibility to be aware of and respond appropriately to the changing needs of the situation. The sources of tension may include:

1. The client manager has a greater investment in the client system as it has developed than the external consultant. Outmoded behaviours will be valued for reasons which are historic and far from obvious to an outsider. Change may be resisted because the manager, not unnaturally, values the experiences and achievements which have been part of his personal development. This is in spite of their irrelevance, or worse, in today's situation.

2. The internal manager, as part of the system, may be part of the problem, and may find the situation threatening.

3. Although the consultant is seen as free to remove himself from the client system, the manager may feel trapped within it and may seek security in unrealistic levels of certainty of outcomes and reduction of risk.

ROLE PLANNING MATRIX

ROLE	STAGE					
	1	2	3	4	5	6
Advocate						
Expert						
Trainer						
Collaborator						
Identifier						
Fact Finder						

STAGES OF INTERVENTION (See Chapter Fourteen for details)

1. PRE-ENTRY

2. INITIAL CONTACT

3. DATA COLLECTION AND PROBLEM ANALYSIS

4. INTERVENTION DESIGN

5. INTERVENTION

6. SEPARATION AND POST ASSIGNMENT

Figure 13.1

4. Additional work or responsibility placed on the manager as a result of the intervention will often fail to attract immediate compensation. The manager who is under an increased work burden may be intensely aware of what he sees as the excessive earnings differential of the external consultant.

5. In the very short term the internal manager is less costly to the organisation than the external consultant and this may reinforce any feelings of 'unfairness'.

6. The internal manager may have made many attempts to promote a solution without success and may see himself in the position of a prophet lacking honour in his own country. He may try to undermine the consultant activity by constant reference to 'That's nothing new, I suggested that years ago.....'

7. The internal manager is unlikely to have the breadth of experience of the consultant and may believe absolutely that the business is so specialised that all knowledge gained elsewhere is meaningless.

8. An internal manager may have been able to 'get by' with less than optimal performance within the system and may see changes to the system as both threatening and unfair.

9. The internal manager may compare his opportunities to exert influence within the business with that of the consultant and may either attempt to play politics to reduce the consultant influence, or try to use the consultant's power to influence to promote 'hidden agendas'.

10. The internal manager will understand the informal hierarchies within the organisation better than the consultant and may seek to mislead the consultant in terms of where power lies in order to enhance his perceived position or to block change.

Whatever the problem it is the consultant's responsibility to identify it, address it and resolve it. It is an unrealistic expectation that the client will have the breadth of knowledge, the sensitivity or the detailed knowledge of a professional advisor. That is why, directive or not, the consultant is always influential. Without influence, the consultant is an expensive waste of space. The only ethical alternative to solving the problem is to withdraw from the assignment, having first introduced and gained client approval of a qualified replacement.

14 Outline Strategies for Each Stage of the Assignment

The consultant will have established a clear overall strategy for completion of the entire assignment. As facts emerge at each stage it will be useful to reassess the strategy in the light of experience and refine the tactical approach for each defined stage of the intervention.

The appropriateness, and thus the effectiveness, of the strategy is subject to the answers to the following questions for each stage in the activity.

Pre-Entry

- Who is the client? What are the clients important products and services? What is the organisation's projected image? Who is the primary contact and what is he like as a person? How was the consultant invited to work with the client?

- What are the consultant's ideas or theories about the client organisation's needs at present? What are the issues and problems facing the client's sector at present? What relevant knowledge or experience has the consultant which may enable him to analyse speedily and accurately the needs of this client?

- What expectations does the consultant have about the probable behaviours of the client? How would the consultant prefer that the initial contact to go? What behaviours on the part of the consultant would facilitate the initial meeting? What additional information should the consultant have at his disposal before the first meeting?

- What could go wrong? Are any foreseen problems avoidable? What should the consultant do to avoid them? What contingency plans should the consultant consider to deal with those problems which are possible and unavoidable?

Initial contact

- What are the objectives of the intervention, and how will the results be measured?

- Is the client clear on his needs and /or problems?

- Why is external help being sought?

- Is the consultant's style appropriate to this client and this organisation? Does it appear that necessary information is, or will be forthcoming?

- What are the important moving and restraining forces in the organisation or department? Are there any recognised 'champions for change'?

- Can the consultant work with this client? (On a personal as well as business basis?) Will taking this assignment affect the consultant's professional image?

- How can the consultant best advance the client/ consultant relationship to the next stage?

Data collection and problem analysis

- What is to be accomplished? What is the likely timeframe? Has the client indicated any constraints which may affect the consultant's ability to perform? Have any 'no go areas' been indicated?

- How is the client business organised? Are there signs of an informal hierarchy? Who is likely to hold critical information? Has the consultant immediate access to the key people?

- What are the key issues and problems? How aware is the client of the issues? Are any issues potentially threatening to the client? What is the actual or likely attitude of employees to having an external consultant on the premises? What are the values and beliefs of the organisation? How ready is the organisation for change, if change is indicated?

Intervention design

- What are the key variables which will determine the success of the intervention?

- What ideas, processes or concepts will the consultant use to ensure a successful intervention? How sophisticated is the client group? How likely is the client to be able to understand and use the process?

- Who within the client organisation will be involved?

- What education or training of the client organisation will be necessary?

Intervention

- What progress toward agreed objectives has been made?

- Are agreed measurement criteria being applied?

- Is agreed feedback system being maintained?

- Are hidden agendas or other unexpected developments emerging?

- Are beliefs, values, behaviours or norms changing? Is the change in the desired direction?

- Is communication accurate, timely and appropriate? Are members of the client team involved, informed and committed?

- Are new and different needs and/or priorities emerging?

- Are the techniques, processes and ideas introduced by the consultant proving to be appropriate to the client organisation in practice?

- Is the client delighted with the results to date?

Separation

- Have expected outcomes been achieved? What specific outcomes have not been achieved? Are they important to the client in the light of present knowledge and goals?

- Is the client organisation capable of managing the changes from now? Has every affected employee had the benefit of any necessary training or development?

- What does the client expect of the consultant in terms of future commitments and follow-up activity? Are those expectations realistic and in line with the real needs of the client organisation?

- Is the client delighted with the outcome?

Exit

- What can the client organisation tell the consultant about the way that the relationship was handled?

- How does the client assess the consultant's impact on the organisation?

- Is the client really delighted?

Introduction

A professional adviser or change agent succeeds in direct proportion to his personal reputation and image. Each is dependent on the level of success which his interventions achieve. This planning guide is designed to assist the professional by drawing attention to key issues which frequently emerge at specific stages in the assignment.

It is a platform for thought and creativity by the practitioner. It is not designed to offer facile and superficial answers, but aims rather at ensuring that the right questions are asked and answered at each stage of the intervention.

The instrument is comprehensive rather than exhaustive, and it is hoped and expected that the user will ask himself other questions specific to the assignment, sometimes triggered by the guide. Use this as a framework rather than a straitjacket and it will provide useful support in that most vital of tasks - economically and consistently bringing TQM to the field of client service.

Consultant planning guide

Stage one; pre-entry
Questions to be considered:
Who is the client?
    Individual_____

Department_____

Organisation_____

What are the client's important products and services?

_____
_____
_____
_____
_____
_____

What is the organisation's projected image?

_____
_____
_____
_____
_____
_____

What is the primary contact like as a person?

_____
_____
_____
_____
_____
_____

What adjustments, if any, to his own behaviour will the consultant need to make to work successfully with him/her?

_____
_____
_____
_____
_____

What are the consultant's ideas, theories or assumptions about the client organisation's needs at present?

_____
_____
_____
_____
_____

What are the the issues and problems facing the client's sector at present?

_____
_____
_____
_____
_____
_____
_____
_____
_____
_____
_____

What relevant knowledge or experience does the consultant have which may enable him to quickly and accurately analyse needs and diagnose problems?

_____
_____
_____
_____
_____
_____
_____
_____
_____
_____

What expectations does the consultant have about the probable behaviours of the client?

_____
_____
_____
_____
_____
_____
_____
_____
_____
_____

What is the evidence which supports these expectations?

_____
_____
_____
_____
_____

What behaviour on the part of the consultant will facilitate the initial meeting?

_____
_____
_____
_____
_____

What outcome(s) does the consultant seek from the initial meeting?

_____
_____
_____
_____
_____

What additional information does the consultant need before the initial meeting?

_____
_____
_____
_____
_____
_____

Where can that information be sourced?

_____
_____
_____
_____
_____
_____
_____
_____

What could go wrong at the initial meeting?

_____
_____
_____
_____
_____
_____
_____

Which anticipated problems are avoidable?

_____
_____
_____
_____

What action should the consultant take to avoid them?

_____
_____
_____
_____
_____
_____

What contingency plans should the consultant consider to deal with those potential problems which are possible and unavoidable?

_____
_____
_____
_____
_____
_____
_____
_____

Stage two: Initial contact

What are the objectives of the intervention?

_____
_____
_____
_____
_____

How will the consultant's performance/results be measured?

_____

_____

_____

_____

_____

_____

Is the client sufficiently aware of his needs/problems?

Yes_____ No_____

_____

_____

_____

_____

_____

Why is external help being sought?

_____

_____

_____

_____

Does the consultant suspect or recognise any political power-play within the client organisation?
Yes_____ No_____

Is the consultant's preferred style appropriate to this organisation?
Yes_____ No_____

What alternative approaches might usefully be considered?

_____

_____

_____

_____

_____

Is it agreed that all necessary client information and resource will be forthcoming?
Yes_____ No_____
What action needs to be taken to ensure availability when required?

_____

_____

_____

_____
_____
_____

What are the important forces for change within the department/organisation/client?

_____
_____
_____
_____
_____
_____
_____

What are the important constraints/restraints?

_____
_____
_____
_____
_____
_____

Are there any identified 'champions for change'?
Yes____ No____
Will the consultant have ready access to them?
Yes____ No____
Who are they?

_____
_____
_____
_____
_____

Can the consultant work with this client?
    Professionally?   Yes____   No____
    Socially?   Yes____   No____

Will taking this assignment affect the consultant's professional image and opportunities?
    Constructively?   Yes____   No____
    Adversely?   Yes____   No____
    Neutral?   Yes____

ALL THINGS CONSIDERED DOES THE CONSULTANT WANT
THIS ASSIGNMENT?
Yes____ No____

If 'YES', how can the consultant advance the client/consultant relationship to the next stage?

_____

_____

_____

_____

_____

_____

_____

_____

Stage three: Data collection and problem diagnosis

What is to be accomplished?

_____

_____

_____

_____

_____

What is the likely time-frame?

_____

_____

_____

_____

_____

_____

_____

Have any constraints been placed on the consultant's ability to
gather information?

_____

_____

_____

_____

_____

Have any specific 'no go' areas been indicated?
Yes____   No____

Can consultant perform adequately in the face of any constraints?
Yes____   No____

What needs to be done?

_____
_____
_____
_____
_____
_____

How is the client business organised?
Highly structured/bureaucratic? Yes_____
Organismic? Yes_____
Flexible/matrix? Yes_____
Boundaryless? Yes_____
Is there an informal hierarchy? Yes_____ No_____
Where does POWER reside in the structure?

_____
_____
_____

Who is likely to hold critical information?

_____
_____
_____
_____
_____

Does the consultant have immediate access to them?
Yes____ No____
Action:

_____
_____
_____
_____
_____
_____
_____
_____

What are the key issues and problems?

_____
_____
_____
_____
_____
_____

How aware is the client of the issues?

_____
_____
_____
_____
_____

Are any issues potentially or actually threatening to the client?
Yes_____ No_____

What is the likely or actual attitude of employees and management to having a consultant on the premises?

_____
_____
_____
_____
_____
_____
_____

What are the key values of the organisation?

_____
_____
_____
_____
_____
_____
_____

Is change indicated?   Yes_____   No_____
Is the organisation ready for change?   Yes_____   No_____

It is strongly recommended that should the consultant consider that change is indicated an appropriate instrument be used to assess readiness for change and to build an outline strategy of how change might most economically and effectively be carried out.

A traditional and satisfactory inventory is 'Harrison'. A more current alternative might be: 'The Organisational Change Readiness Survey', which is available from Management Learning Resources - telephone (0267) 87661.

Stage four: Intervention design

What are the key variables determining the success of the intervention?

_____
_____
_____
_____
_____
_____
_____
_____
_____

What ideas, concepts or processes will the consultant use to ensure a successful intervention?

_____
_____
_____
_____
_____
_____
_____

How sophisticated is the client group?

Highly?   Yes____
Adequately?   Yes____
Less than desirable?   Yes____

What steps need to be taken to ensure the ability of the client to use/understand the process?

_____
_____
_____
_____
_____
_____

Who, within the client's organisation will be involved?

_____
_____

_____
_____
_____
_____

What education/training is necessary?

_____
_____
_____
_____
_____

What is the likely sequence of events?

_____
_____
_____
_____
_____
_____

Are amendments to proposal/time line indicated?
Yes_____ No_____
Client informed?
Date_____

Stage five: Intervention
Date:_____
Key points of progress to date:

_____
_____
_____
_____
_____
_____

Client informed and approved;
Date;_____

Date:_____
Key points of progress to date:

_____
_____
_____
_____

_____
_____
_____

Client informed and approved;
Date;_____

Date:_____
Key points of progress to date:

_____
_____
_____
_____
_____
_____
_____

Client informed and approved;
Date;_____

Date:_____
Key points of progress to date:

_____
_____
_____
_____
_____
_____

Client informed and approved;
Date;_____

Date:_____
Key points of progress to date:

_____
_____
_____
_____
_____
_____

Client informed and approved;
Date;_____

Date:_____
Key points of progress to date:

_____
_____
_____
_____
_____
_____
_____

Client informed and approved;
Date;_____

Date:_____
Key points of progress to date:

_____
_____
_____
_____
_____
_____
_____

Client informed and approved;
Date;_____

Date:_____
Key points of progress to date:

_____
_____
_____
_____
_____
_____

Client informed and approved;
Date;_____

Date:_____
Key points of progress to date:

_____
_____
_____
_____

_____
_____
_____

Client informed and approved;
Date;_____

Date:_____
Key points of progress to date:

_____
_____
_____
_____
_____
_____
_____

Client informed and approved;
Date;_____

ESSENTIAL NOTES TO FILE

_____
_____
_____
_____
_____
_____
_____
_____

Are agreed measurement criteria being applied?
Yes____ No____
Is non-compliance acceptable?
Yes____ No____
Agreed action:

_____
_____
_____
_____
_____
_____
_____

Are 'hidden agendas' or other unexpected developments emerging?
Yes_____ No_____
Action:

_____
_____
_____

Are beliefs, norms, values and behaviours changing?
Beliefs   Yes_____   No_____
Norms   Yes_____   No_____
Values   Yes_____   No_____
Behaviour   Yes_____   No_____

Is change in desired direction?
   Yes_____   No_____
Action:

_____
_____
_____
_____
_____
_____
_____

Is communication accurate, complete, timely and relevant?
   Yes_____   No_____
Are members of the client team involved, informed and committed?
   Yes_____   No_____
Action:

_____
_____
_____
_____
_____
_____
_____
_____

Are new or different needs emerging?
   Yes_____   No_____
Action:

_____
_____
_____

_____
_____
_____
_____

Is the process proving to be appropriate to the client needs in practice?

    Yes____ No____

Action:

_____
_____
_____
_____
_____

IS THE CLIENT DELIGHTED WITH THE PROGRESS TO DATE?

    Yes____ No____

PRIORITY ACTION:

_____
_____
_____
_____
_____
_____
_____

Are agreed measurement criteria being applied?

    Yes____ No____

Is non-compliance acceptable?

    Yes____ No____

Agreed action:

_____
_____
_____
_____
_____

Are 'hidden agendas' or other unexpected developments emerging?

    Yes____ No____

Action:

_____
_____
_____

Are beliefs, norms, values and behaviours changing?

Beliefs   Yes____   No____
Norms   Yes____   No____
Values   Yes____   No____
Behaviour   Yes____   No____

Is change now in desired direction?
Yes____ No____
Action:

_____
_____
_____
_____
_____
_____
_____

Is communication accurate, complete, timely and relevant?
Yes____ No____
Are members of the client team involved, informed and committed?
  Yes____ No____
  Action:

_____
_____
_____
_____
_____
_____
_____
_____

Are new or different needs emerging?
  Yes____ No____
  Action:

_____
_____
_____
_____

Is the process proving to be appropriate to the client needs in practice?

Yes_____ No_____

Action:

IS THE CLIENT DELIGHTED WITH THE PROGRESS TO DATE?

Yes_____ No_____

EMERGENCY ACTION:

_____
_____
_____
_____
_____
_____
_____
_____
_____

Measuring the results

It is useful to hold a specific post-intervention discussion to ensure that all parties have gained the maximum from the work that they have done together. The following questions are offered as the basis for a final assessment of the value of the consultant's work to the client, the consultant and to their ongoing relationship. I strongly urge that such a discussion takes place.

Does the client feel that the desired outcome was achieved?

FINDINGS:_____

_____
_____
_____
_____

Is the client DELIGHTED with the results?

FINDINGS_____

_____
_____
_____
_____

Is there a general feeling in the organisation that it was helped?
FINDINGS:_____
_____
_____
_____
_____

Has the consultant learned anything of value about his own
skills or style?
FINDINGS:_____
_____
_____
_____
_____
_____

Has the consultant been totally successful in avoiding causing other
problems while solving the first?
FINDINGS:_____
_____
_____
_____

ACTION:_____

Does the client feel that the consultant could help in the future in
other ways?
FINDINGS:_____
_____
_____
_____
_____

REFERRALS:_____
_____
_____
_____
_____

Is the consultant likely to be invited back into the organisation?
FINDINGS:_____
_____
_____
_____

STEPS TO BE TAKEN TO MAINTAIN
CONTACT:_____

_____
_____
_____
_____
_____

Does the client organisation have a new look, a new approach or
a new confidence about addressing and solving future
problems?
FINDINGS:_____

_____
_____
_____
_____

Are the client team better able to deal with problems in the
future?
FINDINGS:_____

_____
_____
_____
_____

Do they apply the new skills and knowledge they have in current
day to day activities? (If they do not, what steps are being taken to
ensure that they retain the ability to use learned skills and behaviours when needed?)
FINDINGS:_____

_____
_____
_____

ACTION TO MAINTAIN SKILL
LEVELS:

_____
_____
_____
_____

Does the client organisation now know something about itself that
it did not know before?
EVIDENCE OF KNOWLEDGE AND EFFECT ON
OPERATIONS_____

_____

_____
_____
_____
_____
_____
_____
_____

Is the organisation comfortable with the new knowledge?
FINDINGS:_____
EVIDENCE:_____
_____
_____
_____
_____

CONSULTANT FOLLOW-UP
COMMITMENTS_____
_____
_____
_____
_____

CONSULTANT SELF-DEVELOPMENT
PLANS:_____
_____
_____
_____
_____

15 What Every Consultant Must Know

Accreditation

Four important national markets have either developed legislation to make consultancy a fully certificated profession or are in the process of doing so. International activity is currently focused on ensuring that qualification and recognition is based on a globally accepted 'common body of knowledge'.

Much work remains to be done before the dream of fully qualified consultants operating globally with internationally recognised qualifications and shared core skills and knowledge becomes reality, but it is coming. When the qualification process is fully established it is probable that for a substantial period of time the certificated will operate alongside the uncertificated, but in an increasing number of markets the right to practice will be based on a recognised qualification.

In these relatively early days it might seem perverse to want to accelerate the process, but I feel strongly that such a process can only be in the long term interests of the profession and the client. The consultant will be bound by a Code of Ethics and trained to offer an integrated approach to consultancy. It is the integrated approach which the common body of knowledge, or as we tend to call it in this country, 'Core Competency' will support.

The organisation as organism

Common sense dictates that the business organisation is an integrated system in which change in any part means change, no matter how slight, in every part. The most familiar model of the organisation showing the interdependence of the parts is the Levitt Diamond. (Fig. 15.1)

THE LEVITT DIAMOND

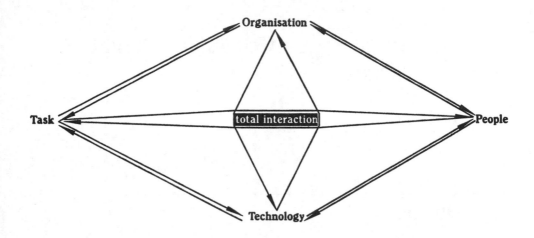

Figure 15.1

Levitt's model can be readily extrapolated to show a similar integration between departments, models of bureaucracy notwithstanding. The growth in recent years through matrix organisations to today's concept of the 'boundaryless firm' and the concurrent growth in the importance of information as a determinant of business success will continue to intensify this interdependent relationship.

Driven by the twin concepts of accreditation based on knowledge and the holistic nature of the commercial organisation, the consultant is seeking to provide a more integrated offering to clients. Such an approach is increasingly seen by the farsighted as good for the client, good for the profession and good for business.

Any effort to encourage a desirable and eventually inescapable tendency in a short chapter of a practical manual is difficult. But convinced that the difficult should always be attempted, I propose to outline how I see developments over the next few months and years.

Crystal ball gazing

There is compelling evidence that professional bodies world wide are seeking to establish a common Ethical Code for consultants.

The Institute of Management Consultants announced in the April 1992 issue of 'Management Consultancy' the formation of 'an ethical guidance panel' to advise members who are faced with ethical uncertainties. Professional bodies in the United States make adherence to their code of conduct a vital precursor to certification processes, believing that the code will evolve in the light of emergent international best practice.

At the same time, the Institute of Management Consultants in London is working to simplify and strengthen its code and encourage its membership to ensure consistency by registering for the quality standard BS 5750. So far so good, but ethics and consistency on their own do not achieve as much as many would wish to ensure professional competence. In the field of competence Canada currently leads the way, with the National Bureau of Professional Consultants to Management of America in hot and enthusiastic pursuit. Canada has established a programme of education, including examinations to lead to certification based on their early estimation of what the common body of knowledge should be.

I believe that in the medium term the realities of the business environment will dictate the knowledge needs of those who seek to serve business, and those realities are still encapsulated in the Levitt Diamond.

Some aspects of a business are so vital to company survival that I believe all consultants need to have a better than working knowledge of each. With the Thatcherite move toward 'the market' showing no signs of abatement under the Major administration, these aspects are of growing importance to what was once called the 'non-profit' sector.

Where and what you practice has limited relevance. To be effective in the client's interest we all need to understand:

The background
• The socio-political-economic environment in which our clients operate.
• Relevant legislation

The organisation
• Organisational structure and design
• The marketing concept
• Management accounting
• Total quality management
• Systems and information theory

Most important of all, we need to know how people behave in organisations

Any attempt to do justice to the range of expertise indicated above would require another book, and a substantial one at that. Readers who wish to enrich their knowledge in a specific area are encouraged to refer to the bibliography and to raid the best library they can find with gusto. In the meantime, an overview of some well-established and current thinking and a small toolkit may be of use.

The macro-world of the total business environment

Before establishing what is feasible for any client, the consultant must have a good grasp of the environment as it is. In a time when the importance of information is beginning to be recognised, misinformation and disinformation by 'interested parties', abounds. I recommend any consultant worthy of the name to seek out the base information and form his own conclusions on the available statistics, rather than taking on board the rhetoric and undue optimism or pessimism of your favoured political party or their media mouthpieces.

If that is too time-consuming I recommend Bob Beckman's important book 'Into the Upwave', (600 hundred or so, pages packed with fact, detailed analysis and prediction). Both Conservatives and Socialists will find much to anger them in the book, but the logic is irrefutable and those predictions which are already testable against experience have an uncanny accuracy which send me back time and again to check when the book was written and to assure myself that this was not a carefully 'updated' revision.

I also expect the consultant to be aware, as an intelligent layman, of the legal constraints surrounding a business. Legal requirements must be met, so the consultant will facilitate meeting them as part of any intervention. From a business-building point of view, the law carries with it opportunities as well as constraints and for client as much as for self the consultant should seek such opportunities. For example, when assisting automotive manufacturers to protect themselves and their distributors by meeting the needs of the product liability legislation it proved possible to motivate the sale and fitting of 'genuine parts' in a market which had become over-competitive and unduly price sensitive, leading to a potentially dangerous drop in standards as the pile 'em high and sell 'em cheap brigade took excessive market share.

The organisation
No consultant should attempt to intervene in an organisation without an understanding of its culture and structure and the relevance

of both to the markets which it serves. This means that in addition to the basic requirement that the business plan is understood, and that the intervention is designed to contribute to that plan, the following are vital areas of knowledge:

The vision
The defined and detailed 'ideal future' of the organisation.

The mission
A challenging, future-oriented statement of why the company is in business, what differentiates it from its competitors and what is believed and encouraged about its attitudes to customers, employees and community.

Values
The 'shoulds', the shared concerns which drive the organisation.

The structure
The reporting relationships, formal and informal, the communication patterns, decision-making and problem-solving practices and the internal reward system.

The climate
The psychological environment, which will include morale, trust, creativity, risk-taking, openness, confrontation, collusion, goal-clarity, goal-sharing, recognition of interdependence, competition, support and authenticity.

Stakeholders
Who are recognised as the 'owners' of the business whose needs must be satisfied? Shareholders? Senior management? The board? All employees? Families of employees? Customers? Suppliers? The community - locally or at large?

Forces
The internal elements which are driving toward or creating barriers to change.

The marketing concept

The greatest disservice which has been done to the organisation by functional models is the alienation of marketing from other activities by placing it in a 'department'. Marketing is or ought to be a philosophy which, like total quality, either drives all of the business

MARKET PLANNING

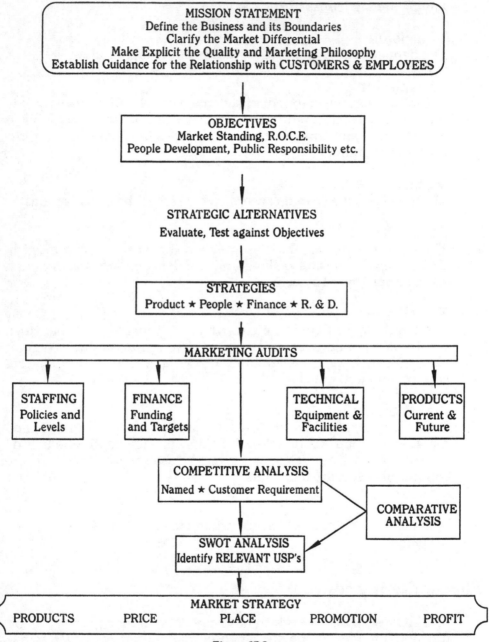

Figure 15.2

or none of it. There are, of course, pure marketing functions, see Fig. 15.2, but marketing is an integrated activity of the total business aimed at creating, identifying and satisfying customer need at a profit. The consultant can do nothing in a firm which genuinely adheres to the concept of marketing without affecting the marketing function. That being so, it is wise to understand at least the concept. Those who sell their services in the field of total quality management, or in the more limited specialism of BS5750, need a detailed understanding of marketing for two main reasons.

Total quality, defined as 'the consistent satisfaction of changing customer need at minimum cost', is little more than a re-vamping of the market concept as promoted by MacKitterick and others more than 70 years ago. It is, if you wish to invest it with a degree of special importance, 'the ultimate marketing strategy', and since marketing techniques are well established and proven by long experience, they should be available to the TQM practitioner.

BS5750 is, contrary to the claims of some consultants, an expensive and time-consuming activity. I believe that the long journey toward accreditation should seldom be undertaken without first establishing what incremental business may reasonably be expected to be won to justify the cost. This information should be as specific, accurate and timely as professional techniques can ensure in a fast changing world. In addition, the move toward BS5750 should be supported by a clear knowledge of what the lack of consistency is currently costing the organisation. To understand this, and the critical role of profitability as a prerequisite of sustained business activity demands knowledge of the following subjects:

Management accounting

It is no more essential for a consultant to be an accountant than it is to be a lawyer in order to serve the best interests of the client. It is necessary, however, to have an understanding of how a business works, and a prerequisite of such an understanding is to feel at home with the role of profit and cash-flow in the firm.

Drucker and others make it clear that the purpose of the firm is:
• To create and keep a customer
• To build shareholder value and competitive advantage
• To grow
• To perpetuate itself

None of these are possible unless profit and positive cash flow are at acceptable levels!

If the consultant intervenes in an organisation without a

satisfactory working knowledge of how the intervention will affect the financial health of the organisation, at best an opportunity will be missed, and at worst the company is facing a potential threat of unknown extent.

Total quality management

Under increasing competitive and legal pressure many thinkers about business, including the author, have belatedly awoken to the fact that the long term security of the enterprise is closely linked to the degree to which it is successful in making the toal quality concept a reality. Like its close relative marketing, TQM is an all or nothing concept and a never ending road of scientifically validated improvement. In short TQM is, as I have said above, the ultimate marketing concept.

TQM is a systematic and scientific approach to ensuring the delight of the customer, all the time and every time. As such it provides a competitive edge which is supreme: more than this, when properly implemented it is a means of achieving the customer satisfaction goal at minimum cost. No consultant can afford to be without a proper understanding of such a powerful business tool in a highly competitive and volatile market.

Consultants need to be conversant with the works of W Edwards Deming, Crosby and Juran. Total quality far transcends BS5750, which provides at best, a framework for consistency and a springboard for quality, and total quality is something which you and I will have to offer to our clients in our own services and not merely as packages for them to implement.

Systems and information theory

The growth in demand for current, accurate information has been outstripped only by its availability - enough to sink the average firm under a welter of facts.

Information is moving from being a mere 'handmaiden of change' to being its catalyst and often its goal. All consultants should seek to build a clear knowledge of the precise information requirements of the client, and should look to building relationships with specialists which are strenthened by the consultant's broad brush. An intelligent appreciation of the subject should be developed which is sufficient to protect constantly the client interest against bias or an excess of zeal.

According to Handy, Drucker and many others we are at the

threshhold of a new era; the information age. Hardware technology is becoming cheaper and simpler, but the essential software appears to keep pace only occasionally. An intelligent, non-specialist understanding of what is desirable and what is possible is becoming inescapable.

Organisational behaviour

Nothing should be done in an organisation unless it meets a clear business need and pays for itself in a reasonable time. Nothing *will* be done unless people address the task with understanding and commitment.

To ensure understanding and commitment, whatever you are doing in their firm:

Help people accept change
- Communicate with them. Listen to them
- Train to meet predetermined measurable objectives. Enable the immediate use of new skills and knowledge
- Recruit and transfer in good time. Consider people's convenience, expectations and needs
- Elicit and handle concerns. Identify and sell benefits

Change can benefit people at work by:
- Enriching and broadening their job
- Increasing the individual's discretion and responsibility
- Providing promotion opportunities
- Offering a change of scene
- Improving rewards
- Enhancing status
- Making work easier and hassle-free
- Increasing job security
- Creating better working conditions
- Developing the quality of work life
- Providing intrapreneurial opportunities

Change can threaten people at work by:
- Deskilling the job
- Impoverishing the work
- Removing perceived significance of contribution
- Removing discretion
- Blocking promotion
- Removing jobs
- Grossly increasing workload

- Devaluing earlier efforts
- Rejecting employee ideas
- Increasing apparent or short term difficulty
- Apparent or actual loss of status

People want from their jobs:
- Interesting work
- Opportunities to use skills
- A reasonable level of challenge
- Some discretion
- Personal and professional growth opportunities
- Significant work
- Some variety
- A worthwhile role
- Recognition by peers and others
- Self satisfaction
- Security
- Confidence in their own ability to handle the job

Job enrichment

For many years trainers and others have been promoting the ideas of Frederick Herzberg, apparently blissfully unaware that the scientific basis for their confidence in the efficacy of their offering was subject to some doubt. There are two problem areas:

1. Job enrichment strategies have not met with invariable success in practice. A situation which has been answered less than satisfactorily by claiming unspecified 'qualitative improvements' where no quantitative improvements are seen to exist.

2. The methodology used by Herzberg to build and test his theories is highly subjective and liable to very idiosyncratic interpretation.

This is not to say that Herzberg is wrong - it is simply that we cannot be reasonably certain that he is right. With this in mind, and still owing much to Herzberg's seminal ideas, two behavioural scientists, Hackman and Oldham developed a carefully designed model which I believe that all consultants can find useful. (Fig. 15.3)

A word or several of explanation and development may be useful, although I suspect that the model does a better job than most of speaking for itself.

Hackman and Oldham assert that the nature of the job itself must provide the following criteria:

Skill variety
This is an inherent opportunity to practise more than one skill in

HACKMAN AND OLDHAM
A New Strategy for Job Enrichment

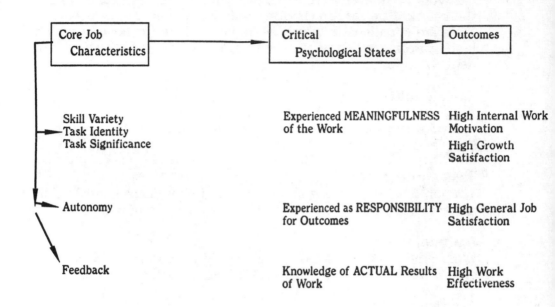

| Core Job Characteristics | Critical Psychological States | Outcomes |

Skill Variety
Task Identity
Task Significance

Experienced MEANINGFULNESS of the Work

High Internal Work Motivation

High Growth Satisfaction

Autonomy

Experienced as RESPONSIBILITY for Outcomes

High General Job Satisfaction

Feedback

Knowledge of ACTUAL Results of Work

High Work Effectiveness

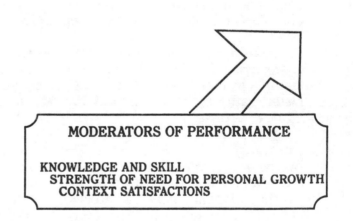

MODERATORS OF PERFORMANCE

KNOWLEDGE AND SKILL
STRENGTH OF NEED FOR PERSONAL GROWTH
CONTEXT SATISFACTIONS

Figure 15.3

execution of work. Where such an opportunity is missing, workers are often seen to make the job unnecessarily difficult by doing such odd things as closing their eyes when performing the task, placing the work at an awkward angle, or doing it with one hand behind their back. Contrary to the idea that we always oppose change, there are situations in which we have a desire for novelty which leads to bizarre behaviours where opportuities for change are denied.

Task identity
As far as possible the job should have a recognisable and complete end product in which the worker may be entitled to take some personal and group pride.

Task significance
The job and its outcome should make a significant contribution either to a shared and valued goal or to a quality product.

Autonomy
Within the job itself the individual should have some sense of ownership and discretion which makes it 'his' job rather than 'the' job.

Feedback
Feedback on performance should be timely, accurate, perceived as objective and relevant. Where possible it should be self-administered.

If jobs are designed or engineered to ensure that they have the characteristics outlined above, they will be effectively completed by teams which are committed to their work and to each other. The fastest path to effctive team building is shared success in a worthwhile enterprise.

Summary
Business is an integrated enterprise. The move toward professional accreditation is in part driven by the professional's need to support his specialised and detailed knowledge with a broad-based and relevant understanding of the totality of the firm, its needs and its environment. The leading professional of the near future will be characterised by an ability to provide holistic solutions to complex problems. This Chapter has been aimed at offering a concise overview of the key elements with an occasional tool which is understandable and accessible to the professional regardless of his or her specialism. A few further tools are available for your adaptation and use in Appendix 2.

16 Avoiding Problems

No book will be perceived as a 'complete guide' without some indication of the problems which may be encountered and some hints on how to avoid or deal with them. Some problems and their solutions have been addressed where relevant in the body of the book. This final Chapter is intended to provide a quick fix guide to many of the remaining problems that professionals meet from time to time.

Overwhelming competition

Occasionally, you will be invited to present a proposal to a new client. On arrival you find yourself awaiting your turn in the company of half a dozen representatives from each of McKinsey and Company, Coopers and Lybrand and P A Consulting. They are laden down with fancy audio visual equipment, and suddenly the hand drawn overhead foils that you were so proud of yesterday seem to shriek of amateurism. You know that the opposition's presentation is guaranteed to be slick and plausible, and possibly exciting and inspirational as well. So what do you do?

The first thing to remember is to play to your strengths. You weren't invited just to make the numbers up, so:

- Consider what it is that you have that caused the client to invite you and centre your thoughts and your presentation on that. (Do you have recent experience of the client problems? The industry?

A high reputation in a specialist field?)

- The competition will almost certainly try for a 'dog and pony show'. Be different. Try to make your approach an informal two way discussion.

- Involve the client from the start and use questions to get guidance about what it is that they want to hear.

- Make it subtly clear, without directly knocking the 'big firms', that unlike your competition with you its a case of WYSIWYG (what you see is what you get).

- Look for the motive behind the client's invitation to the major practices and try to deal with any implied but unspoken concerns. Could they be concerned about continuity? (What will happen if you go under the proverbial bus?) Resources? State of the art knowledge? Are they seeking the sometimes spurious internal reputation that is perceived to come from hiring the big firm? (The consultancy variation on: 'No-one ever got fired for buying IBM'). Is there conflict within the organisation with half the Board championing the large organisation while others are committed to the small?

- Offer personal added value which is unique to you and stress its uniqueness. (Be careful not to give your profit away).

Do not be tempted to cut your fees in an attempt to get the business at a discount. If price was relevant, the big boys wouldn't be there.

Insolvent clients

While working on a contract you have reason to believe that the client may be unable to pay for your services. In that case:

- Breathe a few happy sighs that you are working to a contract and that you have the payment schedule tied up tight. (You have, haven't you?)

- Hold back vital input until you are satisfied that your account is settled.

- Where you can, work on those aspects of the assignment which will be useful to you later and possibly elsewhere.

- If payment is not made on the dot, stop working immediately and tell the client why. Make it clear that you will restart work as soon as his cheque is paid into your account.

- Tell your bank to process the cheque preferentially and let you know when it clears.

- Start to look for, or bring forward a replacement assignment and if two payments are late ask for payment up front or bow out.

Conflict of interest

You are deeply involved in work for a client when you are approached by another prestigious company in the same industry who ask you to undertake an identical job for them.

Politely turn them down, indicating if you can do so without breaching the confidentiality of your first client that there might be a conflict of interest situation and you cannot ethically involve yourself. Do not mention the second approach to your original client. That too would be a breach of confidence.

No matter how prestigious the second client might be, do not seek to duck out of the first job in order to take the second. Your loyalty is entirely to your existing client.Handle this situation professionally, and you will almost certainly be able to add the second name to your client list soon.

Your marketing is ineffective

You have identified what you see as a major market, but you are unable to access it.

- Ask yourself whether you have sectored the market effectively. Do you know in sufficient detail who you prospective clients are and how they may be contacted?

- Identify a specific key player and opinion leader in the sector and target them rather than blast away at the whole sector.

- Try to get some articles printed in the relevant trade magazine, or write letters to the editor.

- Write to the national quality press expressing your views on issues which the industry faces.

- Check your promotional material for appeal and communication.

- Establish a clear and specific goal for yourself. Put a time limit on it and go for it.

- Look for a niche market through which you can enter.

If all else fails raise your fees and make a strong feature of why you are worth more.

Bad business

You are invited to serve a client, but you recognise one or more of the signs of bad business. These are:

Unrealistic client expectations
If the client expects more of you than you can possibly deliver there is only loss for you in taking the assignment.

Either: Teach your client the facts of life and emphasise them in your contract or terms of reference.

Or: Explain to the client politely that you only work to pre-determined outcomes for which you have the time and the resources. Since you cannot expect to complete the job within the time required with the budget and resources at your disposal, you must regretfully decline the assignment. If asked to recommend another consultant politely decline, explaining that since you know that the job cannot be done with these constraints, to give the name of another consultant would be to encourage the client to waste his money.

You lack qualification to perform to your quality standards
If you are unqualified, as a professional you are disqualified from even considering the job. If possible, introduce a qualified member of your network, ensuring that you continue to maintain a high profile with your client as 'project controller'.

Where no member of your network is qualified to meet the client needs, withdraw from the assignment, but only say 'I don't do that', if you really don't and have no intention of doing it in the future. Used as an excuse to get out of the clutches of a bad client it sometimes misfires, as the client appears to be hell bent on telling the world: 'No good going to him with that kind of work, he doesn't do it'.

The client fails to appreciate the value of your services

If the client cannot see the value in hiring you it is unlikely that even a heroic level of performance will have him change his mind. Evoke your constant working to determined outcomes. Set a fair value on what you can achieve and if the client tries to beat you down, withdraw.

Insufficient time available to do the job

Have a member of your network assist,
or;
Check your diary and tell the client when you could give sufficient time to the job
or;
Seek to transfer the job in its entirety to a member of your network
or;
Turn the job down. (If you do this, do not be surprised if the client offers you more money to handle the job at once. If that happens, establish whether you can get help with the other work, and whether that would be acceptable to existing clients. If so, use part of the extra income to ensure exemplary service to ALL your current clients. Keep full and open communication going with each of your clients at all times).

Conflict of interest

Always turn down work the acceptance of which would involve you in a potential conflict of interest. It would be thoroughly unreasonable of any client to expect you to never take work from two clients in the same industry, but it would be inexcusable to do the same job for two competitors at the same time.

Personality clash

I hold totally to the belief that the consultant owes his loyalty and his best efforts to the individual who hires his services. If you find the behaviour of a client is intolerable discuss it openly, focussing on the behaviour, not the personality. If the problem cannot be resolved try to have a qualified member of your team or network complete the assignment.

Mistakes we all make

One of the ironies which the profession finds difficult to live with today is that not one of the major firms, who so confidently sell their crystal gazing facilities to all-comers, predicted the length or depth of the recession. That was left to quirky individuals whose forecasts were patronised or pulverised according to style by the 'big six'. What is worse for some of their ex-employees was that as the recession bit deeper they failed to recognise that the market for consultancy continued to grow. Thus according to a recent report by Key Note Publications an estimated one in ten lost their jobs at a time when they could have been working at full stretch.

I mention this not to crow over the major practices, but simply as an indication that we all make mistakes, and those that consultants make invariably impinge on the lives of others. By recognising and avoiding the most common pitfalls we can do much for our own status and reputation, and a good deal more to protect our clients and their businesses.

Failing to understand that the client does not want change

In recent months there has been a tendency for consultants to concern themselves over what they are called. As salespeople are increasingly referred to as 'consultants', and more early retirers take on part-time jobs (often in their old function), and also call themselves 'consultants', a growing number of those who see themselves at the core of the profession want a new title. A favoured one is 'change agent', and I believe that the simple pleasure the profession is beginning to take in its use is symptomatic of the problem. It is easy to assume that the client wants 'change'. Why else would they bring in, at considerable expense, a change agent?

The simple fact is that not only do clients not necessarily want change in the form in which it would be recognised by the average consultant, their motivation for hiring external expertise is to justify the status quo. Of course, they seldom say that. As a consequence the consultant slips into 'creative mode' and proposes changes so radical that we would only expect someone who is paying for the privilege to even contemplate them.

Meeting resistance the consultant proposes yet more extravagant changes which in turn are rejected or avoided and a crazy game of 'let's waste more money' ensues until either client or consultant succumbs from exhaustion. The consultant should always ask the client at the earliest opportunity:

'In an ideal world, if I could devise a strategy which would enable you to achieve your goals without major change, would you prefer that, or do you really want to see changes in the organisation?'

The client's answer should be probed sensitively probed to ascertain his real feelings as far as possible. Where appropriate, an instrument which measures readiness for change such as Harrison or Huczynski should be used and its results carefully analysed.

Changing a sub-system only

When change is necessary it is almost invariably far-reaching. To change only part of an organisation often means that some other part works a little less well than it did before. The consultant needs to be acutely aware of the effect of his actions and advice. One of the major shortcomings of 'customer care' programmes has been that their sheepdip approach has been highly successful in changing the motivation without addressing the need to change skills. Few things are more destructive of commitment than a passionate desire to achieve without the competence to make necessary and effective changes. Conversely, TQM is successful precisely where it is recognised that it is total or it is nothing.

Every consultant should review his work in the light of its effects throughout the organisation. If one department's pleasure is another's pain we have failed our client and our profession. If we create the dream without giving the means to fulfillment, we are storing up frustration.

A school in the North East has as its motto:'God does not give us a dream unless he also gives us the strength to achieve it'. Consultants are often accused of wishing to play God. This is our opportunity to do so constructively.

Attempting 'bottom-up' change only

It is not true that people always resist change. Many advantageous changes we initiate for ourselves. We get married, we have children and change jobs or careers. But we recognise that all change, no matter how attractive, has its price. What is more, the price is often paid during the process of change. The benefits lie at some time unspecified in the future. We become suspicious therefore when change is apparently promoted as being good for us lesser mortals, but either unnecessary or undesirable for those that sit on high.

Worse, experience tells us that where others prescribe change, but do nothing to change themselves, they are seldom committed to make change work and so they reverse it at the first problem. That being so, we might as well let this go by with as little involvement as possible because, like the buses of my youth, there will be another one along in a minute.

A client sent for me because he had a problem. The TQM system was not working. The history went like this. Initially they had installed quality circles, with the help of consultants. Management had not been convinced of the usefulness of the system and ignored the suggestions of employees. The approach died slowly and quietly. Top management continued to demand quality, so they implemented the Juran approach. Different consultants were engaged: they liked the 'people bits' of Juran's ideas, but were less enamoured by statistical process control. What they did not like they ignored. But 'what cannot be measured cannot be managed', and the system failed.

New consultants were hired to teach SPC, but unfortunately they didn't see it as part of their responsibility to tie in their programme to what was being attempted on the factory floor through the dying Juran system. If Juran doesn't work, Crosby will, decreed top management. Crosby quality workshops were held, management held their breath. Nothing happened. What I now think of as the 'bus syndrome' had set in. Everyone thought: 'Why bother? There'll be another one along...'

I was destined to be that other one. My advice was painful - to me, that is, I was turning away income.

'By now you and your people are probably the world authorities on what causes systems to fail. Capitalise on that. Forget about gurus, don't let a consultant near the place. Start with the MD and the Board, and develop a system which meets your company's needs by cascading workshops down through the organisation. Be sure that the system is owned by those that have to make it work, and let me know how you get on.'

They got on fine. I got no fee.

One other brief point about bottom-up change. If you decide that it is necessary, in the light of changing experience that I change the way I do things, while you do things as you always did, that suggests to me that I got it wrong while you got it right. Fair enough except that all the time I was apparently getting it wrong, nobody told me and from my perspective I seemed to be doing a pretty good job. What the hell were you doing meanwhile? I just don't think its worth bothering.

Unbalanced use of process
'I'm a process consultant, I don't get involved with content.'

True, but process is only useful to the extent that it facilitates achievement of client goals. Too many consultants become so entrenched in process that they forget that the client needs to succeed in the real world today. Process is fine, but only to the extent that it deals with the problems as they are right now.

Agree outcomes and measure your effectiveness against them. A smart process which will be forgotten before it is useful serves no purpose. Consultancy is about outcomes and only, in the final analysis, about outcomes.

Creating change overload
Confirming change to a sub-system is equalled in fatuousness only by attempting to change everything at once, bringing the business

to a halt while everyone plays musical chairs.
Assess with care:
- The overall change strategy
- The key priorities
- Client resources and needs
- Seriousness, urgency and growth potential of any problems.

Then produce a plan which is feasible, attracts the commitment of those who must make it work and has minimal adverse effect on the day to day business of running the business.

Creating change for its own sake
Don't.

Imposing own values
Consultants are, or ought to be, people of strong conviction. That is not an excuse for imposing our beliefs on others. If you cannot live with the values of the organisation in which you are asked to do work and your client is not proactively seeking to redefine those values, you must ask yourself if you are the right man for the job. Consider the following on the question of belief:

> 'A man who has no belief which he would die for has nothing to live for' - Martin Luther King.
> But:
> 'To believe something is to believe that it is true: therefore a reasonable person believes each of his beliefs to be true: yet experience has taught him to expect that some of his beliefs, he knows not which, will turn out to be false. A reasonable person believes, in short, that each of his beliefs are true, and some of them are false. I for one, would expect better of a reasonable person - W V Quine

Beliefs lie at the core of values, an effective consultant seeks to impose neither, but holds the first tentatively and the second courageously.

Inappropriate attachment to client
I have said before that the consultant's first loyalty is to his client - the person within the organisation who has hired him. This does not mean, however, that the consultant must protect the client at all costs. Client and consultant have an overriding responsibility to the organisation which is paying both of them. In the often quoted situation where the consultant establishes that it is the client or the client's behaviour which is the cause of the problem, the consultant's responsibility is, to me at least, obvious.

He must, sensitively and sympathetically, cause the client to confront the problem and his role in it. Then, as joint problem solvers, consultant and client must devise and monitor a plan to change the problematic behaviour. Should the client refuse to face up to his part in the problem the consultant must make it clear to the client that he has no alternative but to face up squarely to both problem and proposed solution in his report and that he must insist, in this situation, that his report be made to the Board.

Failure to be sufficiently candid

Without being obnoxious, it is incumbent on the consultant to provide factual, complete and objective findings to his client.

If the Lords of Appeal choose to interpret product liability legislation as governing the provision of professional services, failure to report the whole story could become a breach of legislation. That would make inappropriate tact a potentially expensive self-indulgence.

Failure to recognise his own resistance to change

I always experience a trace of fellow feeling when I hear Ken Dodd shout:'I have a lot to give, and by God you lot are going to get it.'

It is natural to believe that what has been the foundation of past success will continue to work for us in the future, and if it isn't working this time to keep doing it only harder. John Grinder gives as one of the few 'rules' governing the therapeutic practice of neurolinguistic programming:

'If something is not working do something different. If something is not working it is almost certain that something else, almost anything else, will be better.'

Consultants and other professionals need to be constantly adding to their store of knowledge, and their repertoire of interventions. As a friend, Peter Thomson, says: 'We, more than anyone else, need to commit ourselves to life-long learning.'

That way we will not fear the need to change our approach or style.

Losing professional detachment

A major advantage, sometimes the only obvious advantage which we bring to the client organisation is that we come from outside. We are not part of the problem. If we choose to reject the role of unbiased observer we take on the role of a participant with all the subjectivity and hidden agendas which that implies. We must constantly ask ourselves: 'Am I becoming excessively involved?'

We must care, but we must protect our client's interest by being passionate about outcomes, not routes to achievement.

Not seeking help when out of depth

Sadly, some who perform most happily and ineptly in the game of 'doing just enough' call themselves consultants. I can understand, but not sympathise, with the one man band, who conscious of the need to feed the kids and pay the mortgage decides to 'take a chance'. I have neither understanding nor sympathy for the major consultancy which elects to send into the client premises inexperienced, insufficiently trained 'consultants', who are cheap to employ, expensive to hire, and kept 'on a long leash'.

But at bottom both are equally culpable. Build a network. Ensure equitable rewards for all and always give your client the best service available at any price by bringing in the right level of expertise as it is needed.

Assuming that my particular brand of change is always the answer

Avoid force-fitting client problems to your solutions. Develop your abilities so that you can build solutions specific to needs from the ground up. If you feel that you must have a 'product' to survive in a competitive environment - and there are many who do - try to devise, alone or with colleagues a range of flexible approaches which can be adapted to each situation. And I have to say it again, predetermine and agree outcomes on which you will be judged. That way you will avoid inappropriate process 'just because it's there'.

Conclusion

It may seem to the astute reader that I have at times exceeded my brief of seeking to help the good consultant become a successful consultant, and that I have strayed into trying to turn the good consultant into the better consultant. Mea culpa.

The future of the consultancy profession is bright. The market continues to grow, and the need for professional services will probably far outstrip any forecast yet made. But growth has a drawback. A growing market attracts incomers, and the more opportunities are recognised, the more the competition is attracted. In the end there is only one route to success and that is quality. Quality must be the main characteristic of everything which we do because quality of action builds, in the long term, an unassailable reputation and image.

This book has shared with you the quality secrets of the best and most successful in a profession. Hopefully it has done more, and identified safe and certain short cuts from which you may select your personal route.

If you have gained from this book just one thing to improve your reputation and enhance your personal status, your chances of success are significantly increased. If you have found several, your success is certain.

Here's to success!

PART FOUR:
THE CONSULTANT'S TOOLKIT

Appendix 1: Building Your Practice: a Key Point Summary

Proven Tactics to Build a Practice

Marketing

1. The so-called 'window of opportunity' is open only briefly as an organisation's priorities change. When they recognise the need for the services which you supply, yours must be the name which they know. You marketing therefore must be consistent and in direct. Aimed specifically at making you well known to ALL your prospective clients.

2. Indirect methods of marketing bring clients to you, clamouring for you to serve them. Indirect methods include:
>   Public speaking engagements to suitable audiences.
>   Writing books and/or articles for the trade journals.
>   Publishing your own newsletter.
>   Writing 'letters to the editor'.
>   Being listed in directories.
>   Being prominent in professional or trade associations.
>   Developing and delivering seminars.
>   Using the press effectively to promote you.

3. Your overall marketing strategy should be aimed at becoming well-known in your field.

4. The tactics which you select must be consistent with building your image and reputation and must be comfortable for you to perform.

5. Marketing must be regular and consistent. When you are 'fat, dumb and happy', still discipline yourself to market a minimum of 15% to 20% of your time.

6. Consistent and effective marketing is the only way to smooth the peaks and troughs of business.

7. Mailing brochures to potential clients 'cold' seldom brings a response and is prohibitively expensive. Only mail to those for whom you have identified a need which your services can meet.

8. Watch and read the news specifically as a market development exercise. Look consistently for opportunities to serve.

9. Avoid using a CV to promote your services to business. Personnel Departments have become the 'bin' into which unsolicited CV's are automatically dropped by directors and line management. If your offer is not specific to the personnel function you have little hope of attracting business. Worse, the use of a CV says 'please give me a job', and that is not the image for a professional to convey.

10. If you elect to advertise, do so only when there are many buyers in the market. Advertising professional services is difficult and if you choose to use it to stimulate a flagging market it is ruinously expensive and ineffective. Advertising must turn prospects into buyers. No prospects, no buyers.

11. If you advertise try to do so through a 'knowledge product' which may also bring you some revenue – something like a booklet, or the subtle advertising of a paid for newsletter.

12. When speaking before groups of potential clients be sure to give each person something which they will take away and to which they will refer and so keep. This excludes brochures almost by definition. Some information from a survey you have completed, a brief note on some new legislation, a list of sources of information or a little psychometric self test are the kinds of things audiences keep.

13. Make sure that your contact details are clear on all pieces you

hand out, and format them to easily go into handbags or pockets.

14. If you promote an information product through advertising always charge for it. People with no real interest in your services will send for 'freebies', a small charge produces qualified leads.

15. When you see an item in print which you believe is of interest to a potential client photocopy it and send it with a handwritten note. To make most effective use of time write the notes when watching TV or travelling by train or air. This will keep those who could use your services, or refer you to others thinking of you and a little indebted to you.

16. Regard lifelong learning as a critical part of your marketing strategy. The more knowledgeable you are the more ideas you have to exploit and the easier it is for you to find material for articles and talks.

17. Don't be afraid of becoming a guru. Comment on trends and happenings in your chosen field to the press. Once they start to use your written pieces or calls there is a snowball effect as they begin to turn to you for comment.

18. Ally yourself in the public mind with the decision-makers in the field that you serve. Comment on what important people are saying or doing and you will rapidly become seen as one of the 'makers and shakers'.

19. Demand of yourself that each day you will think of three ideas to promote your practice. They may not all be viable, but your enthusiasm and energy will remain high and the exercise is good for the brain.

20. Always be prepared to walk away from bad business. Bad business includes those who do not pay you on time (or ever), those who fail to appreciate your services and those who will damage rather than enhance your image if you are associated with them.

21. So that you can afford to walk away when client business is lean, build static income. Charge for your newsletter having tested its value. Franchise your successful seminars.

22. If small and impoverished clients come to you, serve them by encouraging them to build a little consortium who by sharing the cost and rewards of your services can afford you.

23. When you write a sales letter or brochure concentrate on communicating not impressing. Check everything for readability. If an intelligent nine year old would have difficulty understanding, most clients will.

24. Add a handwritten PS to letters. In spite of its overuse by the direct mail pro's, it still gets read.

25. Use your PS to direct your reader back into the main text. 'PS John Harley of Megabucks estimates savings of one zillion in the first year using this approach.'

26. If you decide to offer seminars to existing or potential clients approach them as an entrepreneur rather than an educator. Select your subject as one which you could do off the top of your head while standing on it. Keep costs and handouts to a minimum. You can always develop fancy materials when you know that it is worthwhile from a healthy and potentially profitable response.

27. Always have available two or three short talks which you could give to audiences of prospective clients at the drop of a hat. Association secretaries who can turn to you in an emergency are friends indeed.

28. Consider holding free of charge client meetings or clinics a couple of times a year and invite existing or prospective clients. Take a theme which relates to your field, eg 'The avoidance of litigation', 'New technologies and how they affect your profit potential', 'Current thinking in total quality circles' or simply run profit improvement clinics.
   Bringing people together to discuss matters which are important to them under your leadership will enable you to identify the major problems and issues, show something of what you can do and build your reputation at a stroke. It will also enable those who have used your services to tell each other and interested prospects how good you always are.

29. Schedule half a day each month to call prospects. Don't try any hard sell. Just say hallo and pass on some piece of information which may be of interest. Ask what the important issues are at present by way of natural conversation. Ring off earlier rather than later, they will call you or stop you ringing off if they see a need for your services right now. Its an easy way to keep in touch without pressure and to be the name that they think of when the need arises to buy in your expertise.

30. When awards, unusual or prestigeous assignments or honours come your way let people know. Write a short press release and mail a handwritten note to existing and old clients. Send a slightly more formal note to prospective clients to let them know what they are missing until they hire you. People like to tag on to success. Your successes make you valuable to know, and from a fee perspective just plain valuable.

31. If your business needs dictate that you must do some cold calling on prospective clients avoid being seen as 'another salesperson'. Ask for the interview to get information for an article that you are writing. Write the article. Send a pre-publication copy to your prospect and ask for his comments and approval of any quotes. When the article is printed send, if possible, 20 generous photocopies that your prospect may send to his friends and business contacts. His desire to have his name seen in print can interest influential others in your article and your services.

32. Don't go overboard on the cost and quality of your marketing and promotional bumf. Try to match where possible the quality in general use by your clients. They will feel comfortable with that.

33. When making a speech or presenting a proposal to a senior group prepare a short introduction for your host or the chairperson which which provides relevant information. They may not use it, but if they do not only are you in control, but someone else is doing some subtle selling on your behalf and that adds credibility. Some professional speakers are prepared to live with the waffling introduction they often get, but they write and insist on the script for thanking them at the end of their presentation. How's that for practical cheek?

34. Always accompany press releases with a photograph. It is estimated that the attachment of a good photograph increases the chances of publication by up to 30%.

35. If you use a photograph have an 'executive portrait' taken by a good professional. This is one of those areas where economy will not pay.

36. Market your services as highly specialised added value to your competitors. Find a niche where they are weak. Fill it and have them knock on doors for you as part of their offering. Most successful professionals' sub-contract and associate work counts for almost 16% of the business.

37. If you have difficulty finding the time for all activities never reduce the time spent marketing. Subcontract if you must some of your fee-earning activities, but do your marketing. It is that important.

38. By way of research survey past and current clients to assess their future needs and establish the services which you should be planning to provide. In your survey determine the value that they would put on any new service and re-consider your fee structure if they value it particularly highly.

39. Use surveys as the basis of press releases and consider selling them to business or commerce.

Networking

1. Networking, if done effectively ensures an adequate flow of business and a quality service to the client because the professional is not forced to accept business which others are better qualified to fulfil.

2. To network effectively only work with those who you trust, respect and who share your values.

3. Make it worthwhile for others to pass business to you. Pay at least 25% to the 'finder' of the business.

4. The client remains the client of the finder. With 25% of the fee she can afford to spend one day in four looking after the client, ensuring that satisfaction is maintained and identifying further opportunities to serve.

5. Position yourself as the leader of the network and lay down the ground rules.

6. Don't spend time in unproductive networking. If business flows only one way, or not at all, leave them to it. Spend your time marketing yourself, build your reputation and be choosy when selecting from those who clamour to work with you.

7. When working with associates or sub-contractors always have a written agreement and include a non-competing clause stopping them from soliciting further business direct from your clients. (And vice versa of course.)

Sales

1. When you meet your client for the first time it is important that you understand and project the appropriate relationship. If he is to buy your expertise it is essential that you should be in all things but your specialism his peer. In your specialism you are his superior.

2. Approach the sales meeting as being your assessment of whether you are able and willing to serve this client. You are a surgeon, not a salesman.

3. Make sure that your client understands and accepts from the start that your purpose is to identify whether you are able to help. To do that effectively means that you have a number of questions which you need to ask.

4. Control the conversation by asking questions and listening carefully to the answers. An effective salesperson spends better than 60% of the time in a sales visit listening rather than talking.

5. Listen to understand what the client thinks and most important what he feels.

6. Use questions intelligently. Open questions first and most to help the client to talk freely. Closed questions next and less to clarify your understanding. Leading questions with subtlety and least to build agreement. Progress questions frequently during your presentation of your proposal to ensure that the client accepts and understands what you are offering. Closing question preferably only once to agree to the assignment.

7. If you are constantly asked for references assume that your sales techniques need improving.

8. Communicate to your prospective clients very clearly that you only take assignments to which you can be totally committed. They really will want you all the more if they think that you are not begging for the job, and your insistence on work worthy of your total concentration will set at rest any concerns they may have about the standard of service which you will provide if you take the work.

9. Make it clear by the way that you get down to business that your time is valuable and you don't waste it. Remember that in due course the client will be paying for it.

10. Concentrate your attention on the client's problem and what

you can do to resolve it. Avoid giving a long and unnecesssary history of your firm. If the client wants to know he will ask.

11. When making an appointment to see a client steer a middle path between being too available and too busy. Too available and they will try to take advantage of your hunger for business. Too busy and they will suspect that you will give inadequate time to their problem.

12. Plan your response to any request for references. I would prefer to hear a professional say: 'I will be happy to ask one of my existing clients to contact you after our discussion. I never reveal anything about my client's business, not even their names to a third party without their specific permission so I must check with them first.' Above all, don't get flustered and don't offer the name of anyone who has not given you recent permission to use it. And remember if you are asked for references most of the time you ought to consider how persuasive your sales approach is.

13. When talking of your past successes do not try to impress by mentioning clients by name. Clients worry about what consultants say about them to others. Put their minds at rest by avoiding the tendency to drop names which so easily becomes a tendency to gossip.

14. Ask some prospects if you may record your discussion with them. Not only will it provide a perfect form of note-taking, but it will teach you a lot about your sales skills.

15. If you take notes, do so only after getting permission and keep them short. If you write pages it will be a distraction to the client from the important content of your discussion.

16. If you feel at the first meeting that you will have a personality conflict with this client turn down the assignment.

17. Never exagerate and oversell. Be specific about what you can achieve and tell the client what they must provide in order that you may be successful.

18. Make sure that you always explain to the client why they can be confident that the following will not happen. Research shows that clients fear that the consultant will:
   Prove to be incompetent
   Overcharge
   Spend too little time on the job

Operate beyond of managements' control
Make the organisation dependent on the consultant for the future
Disclose sensitive and confidential information
Force fit the problem to the consultant's standard solution
Diagnose the problem inadequately
Overestimate needs
Assume that this problem is 'exactly like' others
TALK TOO MUCH AND FAIL TO LISTEN

19. Clients are tired of being sold to by angels and served by donkeys. That is they are sick of those major consultancies which use subject experts to sell and then send in inexperienced people wearing 'L' plates to do the job. They are beginning to demand WYSIWYG (What you see is what you get).

20. Avoid at all costs running down your competition. If the client is in danger of using 'Barrelmaker and Juvenile' and you believe that they would make a dog's breakfast of it don't say so. Explain how your service offers unique advantages.

21. Each client believes that their problem is unique. Always talk of your experience with 'somewhat similar problems'. If you find yourself about to say 'exactly like'; bite your tongue.

22. Even if their problem is 'exactly like', it isn't to them.

23. Before spending time with a prospect be sure that you are talking to the M A N - one who has:
    MONEY to pay for your services
    AUTHORITY to sign the contract
    NEED for what you have to offer

24. Follow up on sales calls, but don't create a feeling of pressure. Provide some extra information as the reason for your call.

25. If by mischance your first contact is not with a decision-maker don't be hesitant about insisting that you talk to the M A N yourself. The chances of anyone, no matter how well-intentioned selling your services as well you can is remote.

26. If you are selling to a committee try to talk to individuals separately and establish each decision-maker's needs and expectations.

27. If the decision is to be made by the board of directors make yourself available for the board meeting at which your proposal

will be discussed. If they have questions they will prefer to get their answers from you direct.

28. When building information only ask questions which are relevant and to which you do not already have the answer. If you know the answer and seek to show off your knowledge ask: 'Is it still true that.........' Better yet, don't waste time.

29. Never leave without agreeing the prospect's next action. It may be to sign the contract; it may be to acquire some information. Never walk away from a vacuum.

30. Take responsibility for contact. If your next conversation is to be by telephone, make sure it is you that does the calling.

31. Much is said about dress. It is generally accepted that the best form of dress for a salesperson is that which the customer is comfortable with. If your client is formal you should mirror his formality. If in doubt, dress up just a little.

32. Research shows that when a client is being sold to, his mind follows a specific route. If you can satisfy the questions implicit in each step of the thought process you will help the client buy rather than have to sell and that is more comfortable for both of you.

33. The questions are:
• Does this person recognise that it is my situation which is important?
• Does he understand that I already have a point of view and I value it, although I may be persuaded to change it?
• Is he making it clear to me how I will benefit?
• Is he really making clear what he offers?
• Will the idea give me what I want?
• Is he avoiding undue pressure?

34. If you are able to convince your client step-by-step that the answer to each question is 'yes' they will buy.

35. Avoid smart-alec closing techniques. If you want the assignment and you have demonstrated your ability to meet the client's needs you are entitled to the contract. Just ask for it - and then shut up until the client says 'yes' or raises an objection.

36. Welcome client objections. When they express a concern to you they are still interested in what you have to say. They are inviting you to convince them.

37. Before closing be satisfied that you have made it absolutely clear to the client: How they will benefit from your services   Why they personally will gain from working with you   How much they will benefit   When they may expect to enjoy the first results.

Client care
1. Look for ways to provide unusual added value.

2. Tape your conversations with clients and give them the tape. They will have something tangible and if you have helped them to look at their business more analytically or in unusual depth they will appreciate having the full information.

3. Spend about 30 minutes per client per week identifying good ideas in their interest and send them a note or mini proposal.

4. Keep in touch with clients and supply them with clippings and other pieces of information which may be of value to them whenever the opportunity occurs.

5. Sometimes, rather than accept an assignment from a client, show them how they could achieve the results they seek by using their own resources.

Fees
1. Establish your fees professionally:
   Decide on your value as a salaried employee
   Add your best estimate of your overheads including 'perks' and your salary on days you will not be billing direct to clients
   Add a suitable profit margin to enable you to invest in the growth of your business.

2. Always be prepared set your fees on the value of services provided rather than just time expended. Do not under-estimate your salary value.

3. Assume the risk and profit opportunity by expressing your fees as a fixed price to solve the problem rather than an open-ended daily rate. You will attract more business and if you are effective you will be more profitable.

4. Never cut your fees to win business. It gives the impression that you are 'flying a kite' and invites clients to see how far they can beat you down.
5. Where possible protect your cashflow by having travel expense,

hotels etc billed direct to the client.

6. Some clients prefer that you 'lose' expenses in a daily allowance which is added to your per diem charge. As long as you are properly re-imbursed it matters little how.

7. Avoid billing pennies for small items like telephone calls and the odd photocopy or postage stamp. Clients can be irritated by what they see as a penny-pinching avarice. Add these to your overheads, and thus into your per diem rate.

8. Some clients expect to be charged for the first meeting. If you propose to charge make this clear from the outset, give value for money and use the opportunity to clarify your terms and conditions.

9. If the client cannot afford your total costs look with her for those parts of the assignment which they could do themselves. You will find more often than not that they suddenly find some 'flexibility' in the budget if they really have been sold on using you and you will usually do the complete job on your terms.

10. The old car salesmen claim that it is not good policy to quote a neatly rounded figure as your fixed price fee. Their experience leads them to believe that £30,000 say, is best received by the client when rounded up: £31,623 is seen as precise and accurate costing with all the fat trimmed.

11. Charge for all services, particularly diagnosis or need analysis. Clients may try to persuade the unwary that it is in their interest to do the diagnosis for free to get a fat contract thereafter. Diagnosis is usually the part that requires the maximum skill, do that for free and the client can usually manage the rest himself.

12. Resist all blandishments to 'do this at a cut price to show what you can do, and charge your full fee for future work'. Not only may there not be future work, but even if there is the client will expect their 'usual discount'.

13. Don't price products like services. If your work for one client produces products which you can sell to many others, it is unacceptable greed to charge your development costs anew every time.

14. Do not leave it too long in an inflationary economy to raise fees. Too big a jump in costs could kill your business. Better to raise fees

a little somewhat more often.

15. When you have to raise fees use it as a marketing ploy. Advise existing clients early and offer the old fee rate for new jobs started within a given time of your announcement.

16. Ask for retainers where it is obvious that the client has long term need of your services.

17. When you have retainers or long-term contracts build in a cost of living clause so that your income retains its value.

18. Ask for up front payments. You will be surprised how ready some clients are to fund the early stages of your work if they value your services.

19. Take a pride in your prices, let them properly reflect the value of your services and products.

20. When faced with the price objection:'Doolittle and Drink are cheaper!'the renowned sales consultant John Fenton used to reply; 'Well they're an excellent company and I have no doubt that they have worked out to the penny what their service is worth. What I'm offering is............' I don't think John lost much business.

Brochures and proposals
1. Delay using a brochure until the pressure of time forces it on you. For as long as possible write an individual letter for each client showing how you are uniquely qualified to solve his problem.

2. When you write one make it factual, not sales bumf.

3. Say what you have achieved in a range of situations; the special skills and knowledge that you brought to bear and the benefits to your clients, (quantified where possible) of using your services.

4. Spice lightly with those details from your CV that you cannot bear the world to remain ignorant of and you're there.

5. If desirable write a separate brochure for each sector or client group that you serve, using cases relevant to their forecast needs.

6. Use nine year olds to test for readability as usual.

7. A good brochure makes the potential client want to talk to you.

That means it must raise as many questions as it answers, but they have to be the right questions.

8. Provide some useful information but never quite enough.

9. Always write a proposal, even when the client does not ask for one.

10. A good proposal is essential to accurate costing and it helps you to clarify the job in your mind.

11. Proposals are intended to sell your services, if you have been employed in an organisation where proposals are designed to primarily to satisfy a senior partner's view of what is 'proper' you may need to rethink your proposal writing skills or lose business.

12. If you are an engineer or scientist think carefully about writing proposals which sell rather than inform.

13. A proposal should state:
   What you will do, but not how you will do it.
   Unique skills or knowledge which you will apply.
   The benefits which the client will gain.
   When you will complete each part of the assignment.
   How much your intervention will cost.
   Your terms and conditions of doing business.

The rest is padding.

14. Be careful to write proposals not recipes. Recipes can be too easily handed to another to cook.

15. Do not include the contract or letter of agreement in your proposal. Clients dislike anything which indicates that you are taking them for granted.

16. If you are invited to present your proposal verbally prepare as carefully as you would for an important speech. Check the room and equipment as a matter of course and find out all that you can about your audience.

17. When by mischance a good proposal fails to get you the business recycle it. Take out of it all references to the would have been client and send it to the CEO's of the other major players in the industry with a letter which reads: ' I have recently conducted research into some of the major issues which your industry is currently facing. The enclosed briefly covers some of my conclusions

and recommendations. I would welcome an opportunity to discuss them........'

Contracts

1. Always work to a contract.

2. Regard a contract less as a legal document and more as a method of communication.

3. Contracts may be a short letter or a long legal document.

4. All contracts should include the following:
   What you will do
   What your client will provide
   When and how you will be paid
   Who owns the rights to the outcome of your work, particularly intellectual rights to 'products'
   Circumstances under which you can bring in 'sub-contractors'
   Circumstances under which the client can re-assign the contract.

5. The contract should only be re-assignable in the event of your death.

6. Do not try to limit your liability through the contract. It looks bad, and it won't wash in court anyway.

7. You should write the contract. If your client has a legal department and insists that they write it expect them to try to tie you in to some totally unrealistic outcome. Get it put right before you sign.

8. Spell out your payment terms in the contract. Don't assume that because you provided a copy of your standard terms with the proposal the matter is settled. Clients have their standard terms too and they may be at variance.

9. Use the contract as a marketing tool. 'We seem to be agreed, shall I draw up a draft contract?' is a beautiful trial close.

10. Make your clients aware that you always insist on a contract. It raises your credibility and gives them a sense of security.

Process and administration

1. Client employees will either see you as a threat or a potential saviour. Remove the threat by having your client introduce you fully to staff explaining your role.
2. Remove any threat which your client may feel by explaining up

front how you will work for and through him while you are in the organisation.

3. Ensure that you and your client meet frequently to discuss progress and invite early and open expression of any concerns which he may have.

4. Never let your relationship with the client become adversarial. Your role is to serve the client first and only. If you cannot do that either sort your problems or walk.

5. If you elect to walk, ensure that a competent colleague or associate is available to take your place. Never leave the client dangling.

6. Respond to all correspondence within seven days. If it takes you that long to provide a detailed answer, acknowledge receipt of the letter in the interim.

7. Always return telephone calls within 24 hours wherever you are, and what ever you are doing. Maintain daily contact with your office and home.

8. In addition to using libraries for self-development and research spend half a day at least twice a year wandering around a good university library and just see what is available. You will add greatly to your process skills with a little imagination.

9. Be aware that you will need to play different roles at different stages of an assignment. (Facilitator, problem solver, developer, catalyst etc.)

10. Plan your withdrawal from an assignment with as much care as you planned your entry. How will you ensure the client ability to carry on your work?

11. Collect your fees at the agreed time or stop work until you are paid. It is not a matter of 'trust' but of business. You can only reasonably trust those who live up to their promises.

12. To turn down work without complications simply say that it would create a conflict of interest. By definition to discuss your reasons further would be a conflict of interest, so you can leave with dignity whatever the reason.

13. Always ensure that the client accepts ownership of the problem and does not pass that ownership to you. They must continue to

implement the solution after you have gone.

14. Try always to provide your client with more alternatives than were initially apparent. The quality of implementation of solutions often hinges on the attractiveness of the solution to the client.

15. *Always be open to new forms of process. Professionalism is, or should be, a matter of personal growth for professional and client.*

APPENDIX 2 Consultant Models

Introduction

'They may be of wider use than I think'

Questions, of the 'could you suggest' variety, which I am frequently asked even by experienced consultants, suggest that from time to time everyone welcomes a new model to work from, or an old one in a different format.

Space and time dictate that it is impossible to provide a comprehensive range. For such a range see the entry under Marshfield Publications below where you can read how to acquire, at very modest cost Brian Cawthray's classic collection of management tools.

This Appendix contains a few basic and wide ranging models which, if not classics in their own right, at least ring the changes a little on the classics themselves. You are welcome to use them, and the information which supports them.

My intention is mainly to provide the specialist with a range of accessible, simple to use tools which will enable a more holistic approach to the practice of consulting and will give a mild flavour of the areas which are considered essential to the common body of professional knowledge. I have omitted three important categories from the CBK, and included no financial models because these would require at least a working knowledge of the balance sheet, profit and loss account, shareholder value, budgeting and, above all perhaps, cash flow planning. If you have that knowledge you have little need of the models. Without the basic understanding implied by the above, the models would be of little use.

Total quality management models are omitted because they are limited to things like 'The Fourteen Points' of Deming and similar 'rules' developed by Juran, Crosby, Taguchi, Ishikawa et al. These are fully described in the recommended book 'Implementing Total Quality Management' by Lesley and Malcolm Munro-Faure (see bibliography)

IT is, of itself a whole cadre of models and consists of styles of modelling which are not in a format conducive to inclusion.

This leaves us with three key areas:

> Business planning and development
>
> Marketing and market strategy
>
> Organisational and individual behaviour

plus   Generic consultancy models

I suspect even the specialist in these areas will find something to his taste in what is included.

Business planning and development

Modified Beckhardt

This is one of the most versatile and useful models ever designed. As modified, I have used it successfully in situations as varied as: board meetings, corporate planning workshops, management training programmes, team building and conflict reduction groups, marketing planning and organisational development. Its value lies in its almost unique ability to define a desired future, analyse the present and develop a bridge between the two which has the support of all.

It is best built up in steps as shown.

Step one:
This is an ideal future for the organisation without regard for feasibility – a mixture, if you will, of creative dreaming and wishful thinking. In popular parlance the first step in the use of the model defines the vision.

The short flow chart of planning actities serves as a reminder of the total planning process of defining the goal, assessing the present internal and external situation, identifying alternatives, choosing and designing the action plan, implementing, reviewing and modifying against a changing reality.

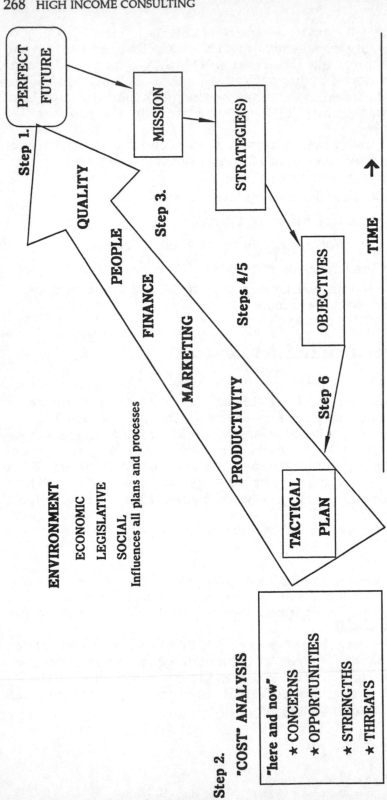

THE CORPORATE PLANNING PROCESS

Figure 2.1

THE PLANNING ACTIVITIES

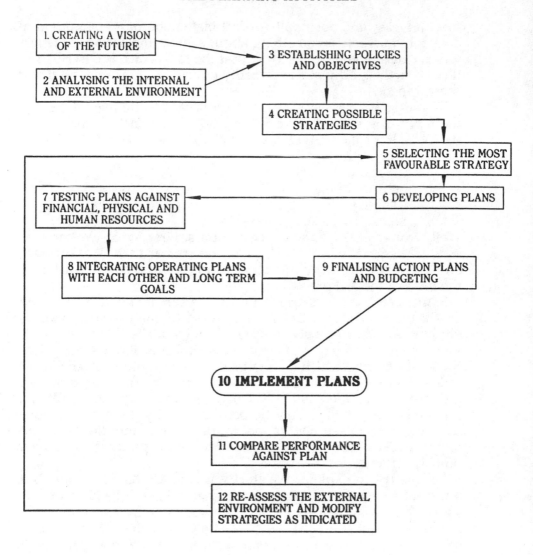

Figure 2.2

Step two:

It is both easy and potentially unfortunate to become enamoured of an acronym. There is something about some combinations of letters which cause us to take the view that the tool which is described is, if not exactly cuddly, at least worthy of being put on a pedestal and worshipped.

That is a pity because such an attitude can lead to the potential of the tool being wasted. Take for example everyone's friend SWOT Analysis. It is called 'SWOT', and that's how we use it:

Strengths
Weaknesses
Opportunities
Threats
....Right?

Well wrong actually, and on two counts. First, what we know as 'SWOT' began life as 'SOFT', ('Failures' rather than 'Weaknesses', and the order distinctly different.) And it is that order that lies at the heart of the real problem.

Some research was carried out a few years ago which indicated that if most business plans are subjected to analysis there is little obvious relationship between the findings of the SWOT Analysis and the final plan which emerges. It is almost as if the SWOT identifies information which people tacitly agree should be ignored or at least underplayed. Further research suggests that this is indeed the case. We complete the SWOT because we always do the SWOT, but we ignore the SWOT partly because it is by no means obvious from the model itself how to incorporate it fully into the plan, and partly because the SWOT causes emotional pain which is best quickly forgotten.

Let me try to explain. We start with 'STRENGTHS'. Fine, but often we also with a group of people who have little clear understanding of what is relevant and a tendency to excessive modesty based on: 'Well everyone has/does that don't they? Leave it off,' or 'That's pretty trivial, we don't want to include that!' The result can be a very short list of 'strengths'.

When it comes to 'WEAKNESSES' we are getting the hang of it. Confidence is increasing. Out come the 'war stories', trivial or not, and the 'hidden agendas' emerge. We may not have done too well on 'strengths', but our 'weaknesses' are enough to place any organisation belly-up. We are moving from positive to negative and negative is coming out better. While those who have not had the deep spiritual pleasure which comes from sliding a knife neatly between ribs are feeling totally depressed, we look for 'OPPORTUNITIES'. Happily there are apparently few. With weaknesses like ours what would we do with opportunities?

Finally we address 'THREATS', and not a moment too soon, if anyone is in danger we are. We list them as if we love them. Threats appear to be coming at us every which way and we have little or nothing to fend them off with. The most immediate threat however, is the absent boss. He is a rhinoceros. He believes that if you believe you can, you can. He also believes that those who fail to believe that they can, at all times and in all conditions, have no place in his organisation. Confidence is the order of the day, and optimism must shine like a beacon through everything we do. So what do we do? We clamber off the switchback which took us from mild positive to deep negative, from weak optimism to despair, and produce a positive plan.

We treat SWOT as 'an exercise' and write our plan as if the analysis never existed. But SWOT isn't an exercise its a tool, and tools do the job they were designed for if they are used properly. SWOT is a good tool. Don't be tempted to throw away the baby with the disposable nappy. If you are using it with a group try this:

Address 'WEAKNESSES' first. Ask for evidence that what is claimed to happen, happens most of the time. Identify those things that could lose business because they go directly against what the customer wants, prioritise them and start planning at once to resolve or mitigate them.

Look for 'OPPORTUNITIES'. Have every team member an 'intrapreneur'. Decide what can be exploited, and actively plan to resource every profitable opportunity. If everyone is a rhinoceros, the boss could yet be right.

Really go for 'STRENGTHS'. Get them all down. Identify those which could be offered to the market as unique selling points. Remember that if competition is not promoting a strength which you have, and which is relevant to market need, as far a client is concerned it is unique to you when you tell the world about it. Build realistic confidence and enthusiasm.

Deal fully with 'THREATS', but plan to overcome them from the start. If a threat can be avoided, get down on paper the steps which will keep it off your back. If something is unavoidable, plan to ensure that the earliest possible signs of it happening are recognised and timely action is taken to minimise the harm.

The following forms are designed to ensure the fullest possible use of SWOT Analysis. You are welcome to photocopy them and use them freely. Better yet, improve on them and send me a copy of yours.............

Perhaps the ultimate action which I can take is to invent a new acronym so that users are inclined to apply the tool in what is psychologically and practically the preferred sequence. I suggest therefore 'COST ANALYSIS';

- CONCERNS rather than WEAKNESSES completed FIRST (to develop meaningful weaknesses relevant to the customer and the situation and backed by evidence)
- OPPORTUNITIES as at present but completed NEXT (to clarify where we can and ought to plan to go)
- STRENGTHS completed THIRD (to identify specific tools to exploit opportunity)
- THREATS completed LAST (to specify only 'what could go wrong' and form the basis for realistic contingency planning)

Step three
Write a mission statement which is an unambiguous and challenging guide to management behaviour and the way in which customers, suppliers, employees and the community are, or will be, treated. Make it clear what makes this organisation different from its competition. Why employees are proud to work here and why customers are proud to buy and use the offered products and services.

Steps four and five
Identify all the strategic possibilities which could move the firm from where it is to where it needs to go. Select the best, the most exciting, feasible and likely to succeed and incorporate it into a strategic plan with a 'planning horizon' of between five and fifteen years.

Step six
Develop corporate goals which are 'SMART'.
- SPECIFIC - Precisely what is to be achieved.
- MEASURABLE–Put numbers including 'all' and 'one hundred percent'to everything.
- ACHIEVABLE
- REALISTIC – Achievable with existing or possible resources.
- TIME SPECIFIC – When, precisely each goal needs to be attained to ensure the success of the overall strategy.

COMPANY CONCERNS

DESCRIPTION OF WEAKNESS (AND EVIDENCE THAT IT OCCURS PERIODICALLY)	PRIORITY			ACTION
	S	U	G	

To Prioritise: Score 0 (Low) to 5 (High)

For: Seriousness – Effect on ability to give customer service
      Urgency – Degree to which weakness affects ability to
                meet needs of current Business Plan
      Growth – Tendency of problem to worsen if not addressed.

Figure 2.3

OPPORTUNITY ANALYSIS

DESCRIPTION OF OPPORTUNITIES	Resources to Exploit ?		Exploit?		
	Yes	No	Now	Future	No
OUTLINE STRATEGY TO ACQUIRE RESOURCE(S):-					

Figure 2.4

COMPANY STRENGTHS

DESCRIPTION OF STRENGTH	Marketable ?		Possible USP?		ACTION
	Yes	No	Yes	No	

Figure 2.5

THREAT ANALYSIS

WHAT COULD GO WRONG	AVOIDANCE PLAN	CONTINGENT PLAN

Figure 2.6

Step seven:
Develop individual tactical plans, operational objectives and
budgets for each operational unit.

Making it happen - the tactical plan

Imagine if you would the organisational strategy in the form
of a large sheet of paper. Imagine further that the sheet can be
effectively torn into strips in such a way that relevant pieces
could be given to each operational area and that each operation simply makes its appropriate contribution to the goals
which it receives, resulting in the full attainment of every
organisational objective.

A model which facilitates this is 'RAISE'. Departmental/
divisional goals are defined in terms of the organisational
goals to which they make a significant and worthwhile contribution. The acronym RAISE covers:

'Responsibility'

A line manager or director is personally responsible for
achievement of the objective within the specified timeframe.
On the planning form which follows the designated individual should ideally write her signature in the column provided. The application of a signature rather than the entry of a
name emphasises ownership of the project and personal
responsibility for the outcome.

'Authority'

If the application of organisational resources toward the
achievement of the objective requires authorisation at a higher organisational level the signature of the authorising execu-
tive/director should appear in this column. A signature in the
column indicates:
- The signatory confirms the sigificance of the goal
- The signatory commits his support to the manager
  responsible for achieving the goal should this prove
  necessary
- Authority to take all necessary action in pursuit of the goal
  is delegated to the responsible manager.

'Informed'

Any changes which result from the pursuit of a new goal are
liable to affect the work of other departments and individuals
who are not directly involved. This column permits the man-

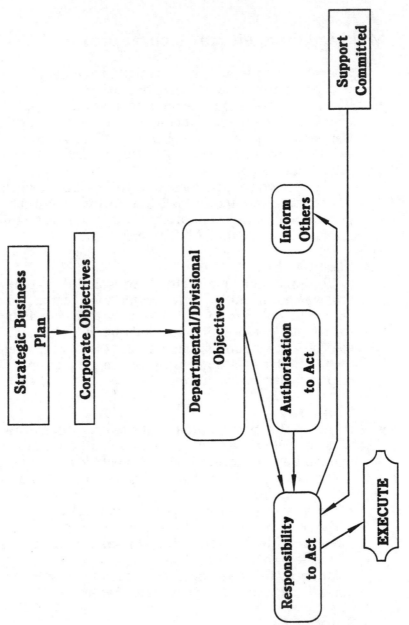

RAISE

Strategic Business Plan

Corporate Objectives

Departmental/Divisional Objectives

Inform Others

Authorisation to Act

Support Committed

Responsibility to Act

EXECUTE

Figure 2.7

ager or employee responsible for the attainment of the objective to ensure that disturbance is minimised by proactive communication.

'Support'
Should the objective to be achieved be one where success is dependent on the provision of data or other support by other individuals or departments this column enables the provider of support to commit to timely provision, again by signature.

'Execution'
This column enables the person responsible for action to note any ideas relevant to getting the job done which may expand the entries in other columns. For example, as the activity matures it may become clear that there is a necessity to INFORM a wider range of co-workers of emergent or imminent changes.

When used in a planning workshop, ALL signatures should be negotiated and appended before the group disperses.

Step eight

Potential problem identification

Two different types of problem can scuttle a plan and because they are different they must be handled in a different way.

Analyse all of the potential problems which could arise in implementing the plan. Separate the avoidable from the unavoidable.

Avoidance planning
Having identified the avoidable potential problems build into the plan specific steps to be taken to ensure that they do not arise.

Contingency planning
Establish the first indicators that are likely to suggest that an unavoidable problem is emerging or about to emerge.

Consider at what stage in the implementation of the plan it is most likely to emerge and who is will be most quickly aware of the problem.

Outline a contingency strategy which can be speedily put into effect if the problem arises and which will resolve or mitigate the losses. Allocate, if practical, responsibility for timely implementation of the contingency plan.

RAISE

Organisational Objective ; _____

Departmental Objective : _____

Commence (Date)	Complete (Date)	Responsibility Accepted (Signature)	Authorised by: (Signature)	To Be Informed (By Name and Department)	Support Committed Signature(s)

Execution: Notes and Comments

Figure 2.8

RAISE 2

Departmental Objective : _____

Responsible Department : _____
Responsible Executive requesting support : _____

Nature of Support/Information Required	Required By: (Date)	Received By: (Date)

Figure 2.9

POTENTIAL PROBLEM WORKSHEET

WHAT COULD GO WRONG ? - Assess THREATS - Analyse RISKS inherent in PLAN(S)	WHAT PREVENTIVE ACTION (S) WILL REMOVE RISK ?	WHAT CONTINGENCY ACTION(S) WILL MINIMISE LOSSES ?	TRIGGERS To Implement Plan

Figure 2.10

Step nine

Communication strategy

Experience in conducting many hundreds of Organisational Development workshops and top team business planning sessions confirms the obvious. Planned communication is the essential prerequisite to effective and committed implementation of a strategy.

Where the organisational top team have, perhaps untypically, removed themselves to an off-site location to develop the plan strong interest in, and concern about what has been happening is natural in those left 'minding the store'. Gossip and rumour, often unconstructive is a frequent possibility.

It is therefore almost mandatory that communication of the outcome should be speedy, consistent and complete.

The following guidelines have been forged and tested by experience and have been found useful:

1. The communication strategy should be designed and agreed by all as part of the planning process.
2. Briefings of ALL those affected should take place at the earliest possible opportunity before the 'scuttlebut' has had time to be effective. For example, it is always helpful if planning workshops are held during weekends with the briefing sessions completed early on Monday morning. This has the added advantage of beginning something new at the start of a week.
3. Either a single briefing to all concerned, or simultaneous briefings should be held to avoid any 'watering down' or distortion of the messsage as a result of peers 'reporting back' after their session.
4. Where a number of briefings are unavoidable, it has been found useful to script these to ensure consistency.
5. A video, audio or simple written message to all from the Chief Executive emphasising key points is often helpful.

The above may seem like a great deal of effort, but this must be evaluated against the fact that the long-term strategic plan will drive the organisation for anything between five and 15 years. Time invested in getting it right first time will pay abundant dividends.
Note: Although, because of the relative complexity, it has been necessary to emphasise the use of planning tools in a group setting, all of the tools and models suggested are equally suitable for individual managerial use.

STRATEGIC PLANNING
A Summary

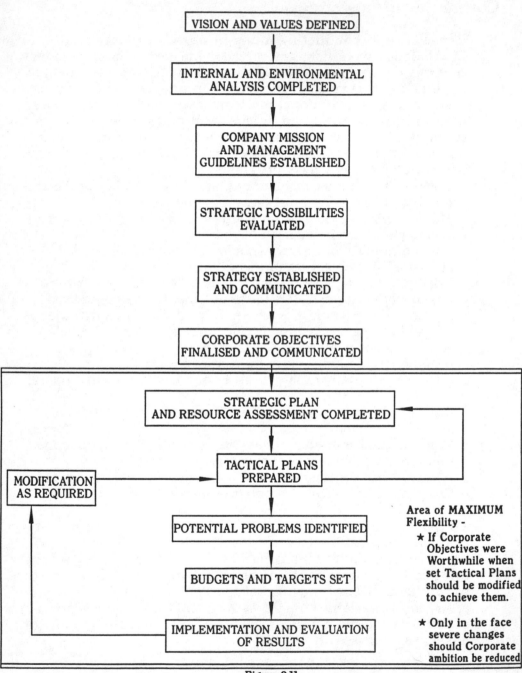

Figure 2.11

Potential pitfalls of strategic planning
Corporate planning often fails when:

- The chief executive dominates the decision making process.
- The culture, leadership style, products and services of the organisation are perceived as being unchangeable.
- Change is introduced for the sake of novelty rather than in response to a new vision or internal or external forces.
- Time cannot be found to fully develop strategies and develop a comprehensive written plan.
- 'Hidden agendas' and company politics are allowed to motivate contributions.
- The people involved are not committed to ensure that the organisation does measurably better as a result of planning than it has ever done before.
- The plan is not communicated to all those whose efforts and commitment will be needed to make it work quickly and in simple concrete language.
- Reasonable aspirations of employees, management, share holders and other stakeholders are ignored.
- The establishment of objectives is rushed and goals are vague.
- The company is so close to going 'belly up' that long term planning is irrelevant to survival. The chief executive does not believe in the planning process and senior management are not committed.
- The top management team do not proactively and daily demonstrate their commitment through their consistent behaviour. To use an Americanism which puts it succinctly: 'management must walk like they talk' for strategic planning to succeed.
- I have developed this example of the use of the model and its supporting documentation against a background of strategic or corporate planning because this is an area of complexity. Other and more simple uses of this versatile tool are limited only by the imagination of the professional.

Market planning
Continuing the theme, this flowchart is included to underline thecomprehensive nature of the marketing concept. Marketing is notsimply a matter of advertising, sales promotion and personal selling, it is a total business philosophy.

The definition:

'An integrated effort by every unit of the organisation to create, identify and satisfy customer need at a profit' shows how comprehensive the marketing function is. As I have said elsewhere, 'it is all, or it is nothing.' This model is a potent and useful reminder to the non-specialist of what is involved.

Competitive analysis

This simple tool is of enormous value to the professional advisorand to any business. It enables you to evaluate, on a single piece of paper and with very little effort:

Your customer/client needs and expectations

The relative strength/importance of each need from the customer perpective

The organisation's ability to meet key customer requirements

Competitors (by name) ability to do so

Your, or your client's unique selling proposition(s).

This is a potent tool which I have presented as relating to your practice. you will find it useful for the service of your clients, you may find it critical to the success of your own business.

MARKET PLANNING

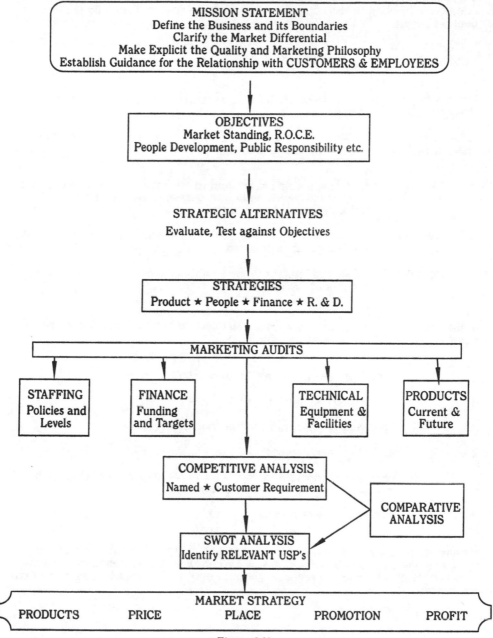

Figure 2.12

COMPETITIVE ANALYSIS

This model enables you on a single page to check your Practice Image and relate your offering to the competitive environment in a realistic and client-centred manner.

INSTRUCTIONS

List the key needs of the major sectors of the market which your practice serves down the left side of page two.

In the "Importance" column rank each, from your perception of the client point of view, using the following simple coding.

H (high) Of considerable importance to my potential and actual clients right now. Symptomatic of a critical issue which the industry/sector faces today.

M (medium) Desirable to my present or future clients, but not as yet in the forefront of their thinking.

L (low) Of limited interest to my client's at present, but potentially an area of recognised need in the future.

In the "Your Practice" column rank your capability to service each identified need using the following numerical gradings.

5 Excellent, exemplary ability to handle

4 Good, markedly better than average

3 Satisfactory, somewhat better than average

2 No better than average

1 Poor, not acceptable (if important to clients must develop ability or re-consider my Marketing Strategy)

★ Unsure at present - will research if important to clients.

Having assessed your own practice, assess and compare competitors (identified by name) using the same marking system. Where you lack information, consider how important it is to your practice right now, and ACT to acquire any and all critical information.

COMPETITIVE ANALYSIS WORKSHEET

CUSTOMER NEED	IMPORTANCE	MY CLIENT SCORE	COMPETITOR(S)									

Professional negotiating
This is adapted from Roger Fisher and William Ury's brilliant best seller 'Getting to Yes'. The concepts in this summary are very much those which I have been teaching professionals to use for more than 20 years.

I have added the sub-title 'Beyond WIN-WIN' because I know that these tactics, properly applied build relationships and change other's behaviour in a way which leads to long term and frequently repeated win/win situations.

Organisational diagnosis
A model and checklist of some of the key determinants of the organisational culture and the relevance of its structures and systems to the achievement of its goals.

Motivation
It would be difficult to find a businessman today without some understanding of the various theories of motivation. Hackman and Oldham's approach to job enrichment is featured in the main text and the two models here enable the probable level of motivation in the organisation to be assessed and a specific individualised motivation strategy to be developed.

The astute profession will consider the benefits, tangible and intangible, which motivate different individuals when considering her own sales presentations.

Personal relationships
The personal relationships model reduces the complex determinants of human interaction to manageable proportions. The key to conflict is almost invariably found by examining the values of the people involved.

The concept of the self-fulfilling prophecy is a vital one to management. My knowledge of the world is the result of my experience. My attitude to individuals and groups is a function of my knowledge and drives the specifics of my behaviour toward them. Frequently the behaviour of others is a direct reaction to the way in which I behave toward them which in turn re-inforces my world view, my attitudes and my behaviour. Thus circles become ever more vicious. Experience cannot be negated or forgotten, attitudes are firmly entrenched, if you want to make a change aim to change behaviour, even if reluctantly and only as an experiment. Thus, sometimes, vicious circles are broken.

Examination of the relative strength of values is often highly productive. The standard approach is Kelly's Repertory Grid. The grid however is cumbersome and time consuming to use. Much easier is the little value hierarchy matrix which follows.

Leadership style

The preferred style of leadership exercised in any organisation can have a critical effect on the organisation's ability to achieve goals.

Certainly the most successful approach to leadership so far this century is the situational leadership model of Hersey and Blanchard as all the 'One Minute .....' books testify.

Hersey and Blanchard's work was developed on the firm foundation provided by Tannenbaum and Schmidt. These two little models bring together the key concepts and facilitate practical analysis of the prevalent leadership style and its relevance to the total work environment.

Those in need of a more detailed and individual rather than cultural assessment will find Hersey and Blanchard's 'Leadership Adaptability and Style Inventory', also called 'LEAD' extremely useful and reliable. As a potent alternative instrument, 'Fleischman' is easy to use and has considerable face credibility.

A new and compelling concept is that of 'SuperLeadership'. Developed by Sims and Manz this approach enables the leader to become an 'empowerer' who releases the talents of others. If Handy is right and the future of business is to be in the hands of key 'knowledge workers', 'telecommuters' and 'intrapreneurs' this will be the key concept of the coming century. Details and materials are available in the United Kingdom through Management Learning Resources Ltd (see Addresses Section of these appendices.)

PROFESSIONAL NEGOTIATING - BEYOND WIN-WIN

SOFT	TOUGH	PROFESSIONAL
RELATIONSHIP TACTICS		
Participants are "friends"	Participants are adversaries	Participants are problem solvers
The goal is avoidance of tension and easy agreement	The goal is VICTORY	Goal is an outcome reached efficiently and amicably separate the people from the problem
The relationship is cultivated through concessions	Concessions demanded as price of continuance	
Soft on the people and the problem	Hard on the problem and the peolple	Soft on people Hard on the problem
High real or simulated trust	Major distrust	Proceed independent of trust
Easy position changes	Dig in and tough it out	Focus on solutions not positions Interests explored
Offers made	Threats made	
RATIONAL TACTICS		
Bottom line disclosed	Mislead as to bottom line	Avoid having bottom line
One-sided losses accepted to ensure agreement	One-sided gains demanded as price of agreement	INVENT OPTIONS FOR MUTUAL GAIN
THE SINGLE ANSWER sought (the one THEY will accept)	THE SINGLE OUTCOME sought - MINE	Develop MULTIPLE OPTION and explore
Insistence only on agreement	Insistence on MY position	INSIST ON OBJECTIVE CRITERIA
Any contest of will avoided	The contest of will is to be WON	Reason, and be open to reason. Yield to LOGIC never to pressure
EMOTIONAL TACTICS		
Response to pressure to yield and make easy promises	Pressure applied and maintained	
Emotions high and positive unless threatened	Show of emotions perceived as weakness	Candid discussion of emotions
Conflicting promises made to competing claimants - many will not be kept	Promises will be enforced - guarantees demanded	Promises will, when carried out, be of benefit to all parties
BASED ON WEAKNESS	**BASED ON POWER**	**BASED ON PROFESSIONALISM**

Figure 2.13

THE PATH TO ASSENT

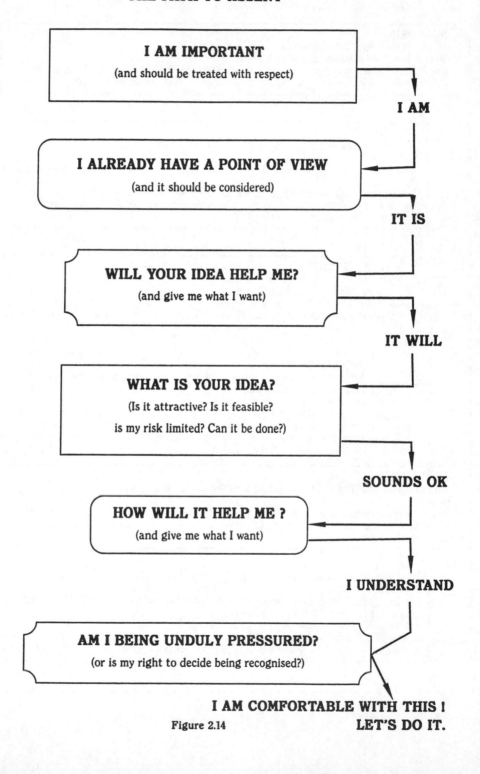

Figure 2.14

ORGANISATIONAL DIAGNOSIS

PURPOSE
Is the Long-Term PURPOSE of the organisation clear?
Does it have the commitment of all?
Does Management and employee behaviour reflect the PURPOSE - at all times?
Is the PURPOSE relevant in today's and tomorrow's business environment?

STRUCTURE
Does the formal Organisation Chart reflect "who does what"?
Is there a Status Hierarchy?
Does the existence of an informal hierarchy support or threaten the achievement of objectives?
Do any important responsibilities fall outside everyone's mandate?
Are such responsibilities seen as an "optional extra", or are they picked up by senior management by default?

RELATIONSHIPS
Who needs to interact with whom?
Who actually interacts with whom?
What is the effect of any discrepancy?
Does the organisation recognise the concept of the "Internal Customer"?

REWARDS
Are salaries, wages, bonuses and incentives related to the specific contribution of individuals and groups to achievement of objectives?
What is actually rewarded and what is punished?
Does the REWARD/SANCTION system make sense against the goals?
Are there appropriate psychological rewards to re-inforce desired behaviours?

LEADERSHIP
Is the LEADERSHIP STYLE consistent with the goals, values, and PURPOSE of the organisation?
Does the prevalent style offer an appropriate role model for junior management?
Is the style congruent with the maturity, skills, knowledge and expectations of the workforce?

SYSTEMS
Are Budgeting, Planning, Management Information and other SYSTEMS consistent with goals and values of the organisation?
Are any SYSTEMS subverted for other purposes?
Are any SYSTEMS not used at all?
Are formal COMMUNICATION SYSTEMS in place and effective?

Figure 2.16

GROUP MOTIVATION TEST

LAMBERT - BASED ON LAWLER AND PORTER

1. If a group see either no reward in the task for them, or see rewards limited to a level which they do not value, they will not be motivated. Rewards which others think that they "oughta want" do not motivate.

MOTIVATION IS DEFINED AS THE DRIVE TO ACHIEVE REWARDS - NO REWARD = NO DRIVE = NO MOTIVATION.

2. If a group values the potential reward, but believes that they will fail to achieve it - they will not try to achieve. It is believed to be better to not try than to fail. (cf. Idiosyncracy balance)

Only if the reward is perceived as so vast that success would equate to winning the treble chance by picking the entries with a pin will any meaningful attempt be made? Such an attempt is likely to collapse at the first set-back.

3. If the effort to achieve the reward is out of balance with the value placed on the reward, the result will be low motivation.
Too much effort for too little reward will not motivate. Conversely if the effort is seen as being so slight that "any fool could do it" there is little motivation even though the perceived value of the reward may be seen as relatively high.

4. Motivation is high when;

> rewards are apparent and valued
>
> targets are challenging but achievable
>
> the effort required is seen as reasonable when compared with the perceived value of the reward.

Figure 2.17

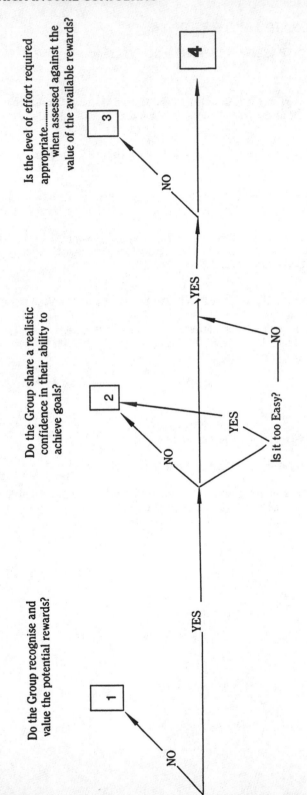

GROUP MOTIVATION TEST

Do the Group recognise and value the potential rewards?

Do the Group share a realistic confidence in their ability to achieve goals?

Is the level of effort required appropriate......... when assessed against the value of the available rewards?

1

2

3

4

NO

YES

NO

YES

Is it too Easy?

YES

NO

NO

YES

Figure 2.18

PERSONAL RELATIONSHIPS

ME AND MY;

Motives
Values
Beliefs
Expectations
Tolerance of Ambiguity
Dependence/Autonomy
Deviance/Conformity
Attitudes
Concerns
Fears

NORMS
Standards of Interpersonal
Behaviour
(Rules)

VALUES
Principles We Believe In
(Oughts)

SHARED VALUES AND NORMS = COHESION

DISPARATE VALUES AND NORMS = CONFLICT

KNOWLEDGE → BEHAVIOURS

ATTITUDES

(Self-fulfilling Prophecy)

REWARDS
SANCTIONS

YOU AND YOUR

Motives
Values
Beliefs
Expectations
Tolerance of Ambiguity
Dependence/Autonomy
Deviance/Conformity
Attitudes
Concerns
Fears

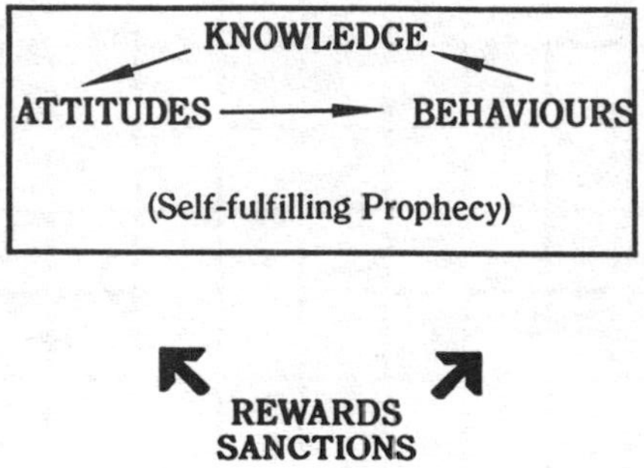

Any relationship will be maintained only as long as the rewards of membership are greater than the cost of maintenance

Figure 2.20

VALUE HIERARCHIES

Values are the concepts which you believe everyone should honour and practise. e.g. HONESTY JUSTICE, COURAGE, LIBERTY, HUMOUR (yes HUMOUR) etc.

Put the initial letter of the value which you believe is the more important of each

pair into the square.

COUNT THE NUMBER OF ENTRIES FOR EACH VALUE.
THE HIGHER THE NUMBER - THE MORE IMPORTANT

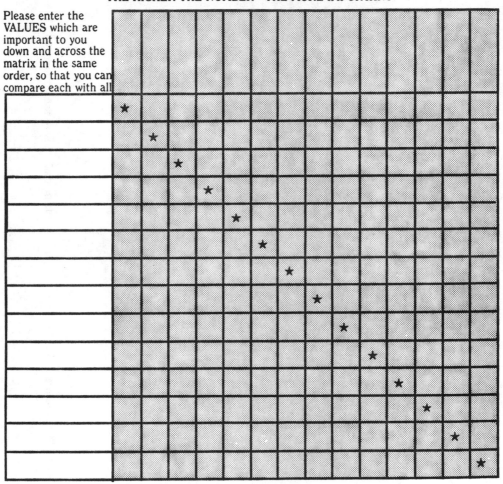

Please enter the VALUES which are important to you down and across the matrix in the same order, so that you can compare each with all

BUSINESS ORGANISATIONS HAVE VALUES - WHAT IF THOSE OF THE ORGANISATION AND ITS EMPLOYEES CONFLICT?

WHAT ARE THAT ORGANISATION'S CHANCES OF ACHIEVING GOALS?

THINK ABOUT IMPORTANT PERSONAL RELATIONSHIPS - WHAT IF THE PEOPLE FOR WHOM YOU CARE MOST HAVE TOTALLY DIFFERENT VALUES?

Figure 2.21

SITUATIONAL LEADERSHIP
Based on the Theories of;
Tannenbaum and Schmidt
and
Hersey and Blanchard

Low ─── High

GROUP MATURITY
LEADER MATURITY AND GROUP SUCCESS

TELL	SELL	TEST	CONSULT	JOIN	DELEGATE/PLAN
What to do When to do it Where to do it How to do it To what standard	What When Where How Why Standards	Line of least potential resistance	Identifying and exploiting group and individual skills knowledge and commitment	Joint problem - solving	Delegating and Trusting

Results Orientation			Development/Growth Orientation		Future Orientation

KEY LEADER SKILL:

INSTRUCTING SETTING AND COMMUNICATING OBJECTIVES AND TARGETS	PERSUASION INFLUENCE	SHARING COACHING	DEVELOPING TRAINING	CHALLENGING DEVELOPING TEAM BUILDING	EMPOWERING

KEY LEADER TRAITS:

AUTHORITY PROFESSIONAL COMPETENCE	INFLUENCE SELF- CONFIDENCE	CLARITY	OPENNESS FLEXIBILITY	CONFIDENCE MATURITY	TRUST VISION

FORCES DICTATING/INFLUENCING STYLE

SITUATION
Task
Market
Goals
Economy

MANAGER
Skills
Track Record
Comfort Zone

WORK TEAM
Competence
Task Maturity
Relationships
Confidence

Figure 2.22

LEADERSHIP STYLE CONGRUENCE

OUR SUPERORDINATE GOAL (The Present Most Important Reason for this GROUP'S Existence):

IN THIS ORGANISATION AT PRESENT :			The TASK Requires:	
WE **TELL** PEOPLE WHAT TO DO			a)	Creative and committed input from all involved:
			b)	Simple routine work only
MANAGEMENT DECIDES AND **SELLS** THEIR IDEA			a)	Self-sacrifice of time, autonomy or earnings capacity by those involved
			a)	Tangible rewards are high and valued by the group
WE ASK FOR OPINIONS AND **CONSULT** BEFORE TAKING ANY ACTION			The PEOPLE involved are:	
			a)	Competent and self-confident
WE **JOIN** AS A TEAM TO MAKE KEY DECISIONS			b)	Over-confident and inexperienced
			a)	A mature group used to working together
			b)	A new group, or under new management
KEY DECISIONS ARE **DELEGATED** TO THE LOWEST LEVEL FULLY COMPETENT TO DECIDE			a)	Used to success as a team
			b)	Used to near misses or failure
			MANAGEMENT are:	
			a)	Flexible and fully trained
			b)	Rigid and bureaucratic

Each (a) ticked indicates the usefulness of a **MORE PARTICIPATIVE STYLE**

Each (b) ticked suggests: **A MORE CONTROLLING STYLE**

Figure 2.23

Organisational change questionnaire: twenty questions for change agents

1 Does the organisation know where it wants to go?
    Mission established?
    Goals defined?

2 Are the goals meaningful in today's market/business environment?
    Are key issues recognised?
    Opportunity analysis complete and current?
    Strengths related to customer/client need?
    Weaknesses prioritised in terms of barrier to quality of customer/client service?
    Are risks known, quantified and understood?

3 What resources exist?
    People?
    Finance?
    Materials?
    Plant?
    Equipment?

4 What is the structure of the organisation?
    Formal structure?
    Hierarchical?
    Matrix?
    Boundaryless?
    Is there an in informal 'status hierarchy'?
    On what is it based?
    By whom is it valued?
    What specific effects does it have on the effectiveness of the organisation?
    What is the evidence which separates fact and scuttlebut.

5 What are the required interactions?
    Who is required to communicate with whom?
    Who initiates work for whom?

6 What are the actual interactions?

7 What is the reward and sanctions process?
   -   What is actually rewarded?

What is really punished?
Is the existing economic and psychological environ
ment appropriate to the desired outcome?

8 Is the culture characterised by dependence on the
hierarchy, or flexible use of the skill pool?

9 Are flexible and appropriate problem solving strategies
generally understood and applied?
Rational approaches (For deviations from norm)?
Creative approaches? (For attractive, feasible and
novel solutions)?
Morphological approaches (For developments from
current or past success)?

10 Are feedback systems timely, objective and accurate?
Is feedback driven by: problem solving?
blame fixing?
Is the past treated as unchangeable?

11 Do goals take precedence over 'rules'?

12 What is the general psychological climate? Is the
organisation:
People oriented?
Product oriented?
Market driven?
Is the orientation appropriate to the desired outcome?

13 What are the sources of power within the organisation?
Hierarchy?
Function?
Expertise?
Informal status?
Control of rewards?
Control of sanctions?

14 What is the limit of the power to act of the client?

15 Do 'champions for change' exist?
Who are they by name?

_____
_____
_____
_____

What is their level of organisational power?

What is their degree of organisational influence?

16 Who wields power within the organisation?

17 Who are the opinion formers within the organisation?

18 How specifically can you influence the infuential and the powerful?

19 What lines of communication do you need to establish to ensure that you achieve the required outcomes?

20 What, if anything must you do to facilitate working with and through your client?

When to start work

A danger which I and others experience is that of becoming so enamoured of research that it is difficult to stop amassing information and start working. This little tool will help with the decision of when to stop investigating and start grafting.

WHAT INFORMATION DO I LACK? _____

_____

WHAT ARE THE RISKS OF PROCEEDING WITHOUT IT?

_____

PROCEED NOW?   YES___   NO___

IF I MUST HAVE INFORMATION, HOW DO I FIND IT?

_____

_____

_____

_____

_____

_____

_____

_____

_____

RESOURCES TO HAND

_____

_____

_____

_____

_____

_____

RESOURCES NEEDED

_____

_____

_____

_____

_____

SOURCE (S)

_____

_____

_____

_____

_____

_____

Appendix 3: Simple Newsletter

September 1993
Vol.3 No. 9

The Professional

THE OFFICIAL NEWSLETTER OF THE NATIONAL INSTITUTE OF CONSULTANCY
AND TRAINING

Published by: Beaumont Lambert International , 51 Mill Lane , Greenfield , Beds. MK45 5DG

MARKET STRATEGIES

THE MOST RECENT (JULY 1993) INSTITUTE RESEARCH INTO MARKETING STRATEGIES EMPLOYED BY THE PROFESSION WAS ANSWERED BY 1021 PROFESSIONALS 63% OF WHOM ARE MEMBERS OF THE NATIONAL INSTITUTE.
THE FINDINGS CONTINUE TO RE-INFORCE THE EMPHASIS PLACED ON STRATEGIES WHICH ENHANCE PERSONAL REPUTATION AND STATUS BY HIGH EARNERS. A SUMMARY OF KEY FINDINGS IS AS FOLLOWS:

MARKETING STRATEGY	UPPER QUARTILE	LOWER QUARTILE	TOTAL (% Sample)
Cold personal calls	14.4%	70.7%	58.5%
Direct mail brochures/ letters to cold list	20.8	71.3	70.6
No charge diagnostic services to pre-qualified leads	19.8	58.1	42.7
Promotion to referrals or names obtained by clients	71.6	22.9	60.5
Lectures to trade and professional audiences	40.1	9.6	17.8
Writing articles/books	37.6	8.3	15.2
Publishing newsletters (free)	21.7	5.7	10.6
Publishing Newsletters (paid)	24.7	0.8	8.2

Upper Quartile Average personal earnings £72,402 per annum

Follow-up interviews were conducted in which a majority of lower income professionals reported that direct marketing strategies were relatively ineffective in promoting their practices.. Asked why they continued to use strategies they knew to be ineffective, the reason given by most was that they knew of no alternatives.

TIME MANAGEMENT TIP

When needing to compare prices, use your fax. A client, needing new stationery, wrote up a single page "Request for Price Quote" with specifications. Having identified potential suppliers he faxed to them in one burst. Replies were in next morning.
BENEFITS:
The process which enabled prices to be obtained from 25 printers took a little over 10 minutes. No need for conversations, callbacks etc. Quotes were all in writing with no chance of error regarding paper, inks, deadlines, sizes, quantities etc.

Page 2. "It pays to explain your billing policy"
Page 3. "Consultant Chief hits out at Price War"
Page 4. Cash Flow tips......Changes to VAT rules...........Face to face selling......and more.

CPCM
CERTIFIED
TRAINER
CERTIFIED PROFESSIONAL CONSULTANT AND TRAINER

APPENDIX 4: A Short Bibliography

A brief and somewhat idiosyncratic selection based on the use I have got from them over the years.

First, read anything and everything by Charles Handy and the great old man, W Edwards Deming, if you have not already done so. Then:

BELBIN R Meredith 'Management Teams, Why They Succeed or Fail', Butterworth Heinemann 1991

COURTIS John 'Marketing Services', Kogan Page 1988

CRAWLEY John 'Constructive Conflict Management', Nicholas Brealey 1992

D'ARCY, MASIUS, BENTON AND BOWLES 'Marketing - Communicating with the Customer', CBI Books 1990

DRENNAN David 'Transforming Company Culture', McGraw Hill 1992

DRUCKER PETER 'The Practice of Management', Heinemann Professional Publications 1955

FOSTER Timothy R V '101 Ways to Generate Great Ideas', Kogan Page 1991

HACKMAN Richard and OLDHAM 'Work Redesign', Addison Wesley 1980

HACKMAN Richard 'Groups That Work and Those That Don't - Creating Conditions for Effective Teamwork', Jossey-Bass 1990

HUNT John W 'Managing People at Work', McGraw Hill 1992 (3rd Ed)

LEAVITT Harold J 'Managerial Psychology', University of Chicago

Press 1978 (Like the Drucker and some of the Handy books, possibly the oldest, certainly among the best.)
LIDSTONE John 'Face the Press', Nicholas Brealey 1992
MANN Nancy R 'The Keys to Excellence', Prestwick Books 1987
MOLE John 'Mind Your Manners', Nicholas Brealey 1992
MUNRO-FAURE Lesley and Malcolm 'Implementing TQM', Pitman Publishing 1992
P A CONSULTING GROUP 'Information Technology - The Catalyst for Change', CBI Books 1990
PENN Bill 'Be Your Own PR Expert', Piatkus 1992
PRICE Frank 'Right Every Time', Gower 1990
ROBBINS Anthony 'Unlimited Power', Simon and Schuster 1986
ROWE Christopher 'People and Chips', Blackwell Scientific 1990
THUROW Lester 'Head to Head', Nicholas Brealey 1993
TURNER Charles Hampden 'Charting the Corporate Mind From Dilemma to Strategy', Blackwell 1990
TURNER Charles Hampden 'Corporate Culture - From Vicious to Virtuous Circles', The Economist Books 1990
URY William 'Getting Past No', Business Books 1991

APPENDIX 5: Essential Resources and Useful Addresses

Essential addresses

You are in the information business so I will not inundate you at this stage. There are, however some contact points that are of such enormous value that I am prepared to risk your response of 'I know that' to ensure that those who do not are not put to inconvenience and possible loss of income.

Resources:

Management Learning Resources Ltd, PO Box 28, Carmarthen, Dyfed SA31 1DT: Tel (0267) 87661
An essential resource for the HRD professional or trainers in any field. The most comprehensive range of psychological instruments and training and workshop resource available in the U.K.

Marshfield Publications Ltd. (see last entry)
The late, and very much missed Brian Cawthray's brilliant and copyright-free 'Outlines' on almost any managerial topic, suitable as workshop notes, handouts or revision guides are now available from MLR above.

Pinnacle Training Ltd, 'Avonside', Grange Road, Bidford on Avon, Warwickshire B50 4BY: Tel (0789) 778299 Skills and motivational audio tapes based on practical success rather than theory. Peter Thomson concentrates on describing the specific tactics that he used to build his first business and retire in his early forties (until boredom pulled him into consultancy and training.)

Saville and Holdsworth Ltd., The Old Post House, 81 High Street, Esher, Surrey KT10 9Q
A psychometric tests for administration by certificated users.

Hunter Clark Associates, 93 Wardour Street, London W1V 3TE: Tel (071) 287 0033
Detailed reports on best business banking practice and cost reduction strategies.

Wyvern Business Library, Wyvern House, 6 The Business Park, Ely, Cambridgeshire CB7 4JW: Tel (0353) 665522
Superb, by post, business books service including ten days to consider before payment. (And I'm a quick reader!)

Numerous participants on my training seminars ask who handles my press coverage. For their benefit and that of others who are looking for a professional service:

Chameleon Ltd, 63 St Pauls Road, Islington, London N1 2LT: Tel (071) 359 7831 (Lizzie Deane Director)

Institutes and professional bodies

Institute of Management Consultants, 5th Floor, 32/33 Hatton Garden, London EC1N 8DL: Tel (071) 242 2140

National Bureau of Professional Consultants to Management (United Kingdom), 51 Mill Lane, Greenfield, Bedfordshire Mk45 5DG: (0525) 713503

The Strategic Planning Society, 17 Portland Place, London W1N 3AF: (071) 636 7737

Institute of Directors, 116 Pall Mall, London SW1Y 5ED: Tel (071) 839 1233

Information sources

The amount of information readily and freely available from your local library is both astounding and worth a fortune to the professional. Almost all libraries of any size now subscribe to Extel Company Services and offer access to a range of on-line information.

The number of written reports and directories is so vast that to all intents and purposes it might as well be infinite. What follows therefore is not a comprehensive listing, but a very idiosyncratic selection of those publications which I tend to find most useful in day to day situations.

I urge you to get to know your way around your library if you do not already make full use of its services. You will save many days of work and since you are in the information business, while many are either too lazy or too ignorant to use their libraries fully, you are in the happy position of selling from another's stock. In an age in which the dependence of business on information is growing logarithmically, that is good business.

CODLIN - 'THE ASLIB DIRECTORY OF INFORMATION SOURCES IN THE UNITED KINGDOM' The Association for Information Management, 20-24 Old Street, London EC1V 9AP Almost six thousand entries with effective cross referencing.

'ULRICH'S INTERNATIONAL PERIODICALS DIRECTORY'
Three volumes of international source information organised in a similar way to the well-known and well thumbed KOMPASS Directories.

'THE CLOVER NEWSPAPER INDEX' - Clover Publications.
Read something vital in the newspaper? Cannot remember quite when or where? You will find it listed in Clover and your library will have the paper in hard copy or microfiche. What makes this a marvelous source is that many of the microfiche readers take photocopies at the press of a button.

'CURRENT BRITISH DIRECTORIES' - CBD Research Publications.
If you are not sure where to look, this will help like you would never believe possible; and in case you need more.....

'THE TOP THREE THOUSAND DIRECTORIES AND ANNUALS' - Dawson (UK) Reading , Berks. Provides answers to unusual questions such as: 'Did the IM produce a National Management Salary Survey this year?' 'Can I get at a list of the world's wealthiest individuals?'

HENDERSON - 'CURRENT EUROPEAN DIRECTORIES' - CBD Research Ltd, Beckenham Kent.
Another detailed listing of directories and their contents.

SMITH - 'BUSINESS INFORMATION WORKBOOK' - Headland Press, Cleveland.
Who owns what, up to date information on mergers, acquisitions, market intelligence and a great deal more.

'THE CONFERENCE BLUE BOOK' Spectrum Communications Ltd, London W3 7QS
Detailed information on conference and seminar venues throughout the U.K. with the detail going all the way from room size and lighting arrangements to the location of telephone points.

'DIRECT MAIL DATA BOOK' - Gower Publishing
If you want to rent a list, find a broker or an advertising agency, this is a good place to start looking.

'KEY NOTE REPORTS' - Keynote Publications Limited.
Individual dated reports on industry sectors from 'Adhesives' to 'Womens' Magazines', (or possibly by now 'Zoos!'). A recent report (July 1992) on the major consultancy firms.

And finally, my number one best friend in marketing:-

'BRAD (BRITISH RATES AND DATA)'
Up to the minute, well, up to the month, information on magazines, journals, periodicals and papers - national, regional, local and free. All you need to direct your Press Release or article straight into the right person's hands.

APPENDIX 6:Public Seminars and Courses for Professionals

Seminars and workshops

Tom Lambert offers a range of research driven, practical and intensive workshops for professionals both as public programmes and in-house for corporate clients.

All programmes are aimed at the immediate and total transfer of learning to the work environment and are fully integrated with the Common Body of Knowledge for Certified Consultancy Practice. Through these programmes professionals of all disciplines can make fast-track progress in building the practice and delighting the client.

Where possible it is recommended that participants attend with a colleague mutually committed to support each other in the implementation of learning. Research shows that through the use of of an appropriate 'buddy' or 'mentor' system transfer of skills and knowledge is increased from the average of 5% - 13% to a sustained level in excess of 95% (Maryland 1984 and ongoing). Participants who elect to attend alone are encouraged to team up with a learning partner from among the seminar attendees.

Seminars include:
ENTREPRENEURIAL SUCCESS AND STYLE :   1 day
This seminar is based on the use of proven instruments and individual counselling. It enables the participant to produce a personal successs strategy by meeting the following OBJECTIVES:
On completion of the seminar the participant will understand the

following and will implement a personally congruent strategy:-
* How to plan for entrepreneurial success
* How to be a successful intrapreneur
* Assessing entrepreneurial style and success factors
* How to manage behaviour to build exceptional client relationships
* Exploiting entrepreneurial strengths

BUILD AND DEVELOP THE PROFESSIONAL PRACTICE: 2 days

(this programme can be expanded to three days by incorporating the Entrepreneurial style and success Inventory as above.)

This is a fully Europeanised version of the world's leading seminar for strategic growth of a professional practice. With close to 200,000 enthusiastic alumni worldwide it provides an unequalled route map to professional success.

Objectives:

On completion of the seminar the participant will understand the following, select those proven strategies which are congruent with his desired professional image and preferred personal behaviors and implement them effectively.
* How to price services for maximum profit and income
* How to build your image and have clients come to you
* How to avoid giving away your services for free
* How to generate 'static' income
* When to use and how to write contracts
* 9 Low cost\no cost ways to win professional exposure
* The 5 key factors of consulting success
* How to flourish in all economic circumstances
* How to get more and better referral business
* Professional liability and what to do about it
* How to turn the first client meeting into a contract
* How to write business winning proposals
* Advertising and direct mail strategies
* Using the press and the media
* How to make networking pay
* How to get advanced payments and retainers
* Collecting your fees

SELLING PROFESSIONAL SERVICES AND HIGH VALUE PRODUCTS: 3-5 days

This seminar is based on a total of more than 130 years research into techniques of influence and sales success strategies. Parts of the programme have been mandated at top level in major conglomerates, but this is the first time that these proven concepts have been brought together to enable specialists to easily and successfully apply subtle and effective sales techniques which are fully consistent with their need to project an image of professional competence and behaviour. THE SKILLS ARE EQUALLY RELEVANT TO SELLING THE 'SOLUTIONS' AS TO SELLING THE SERVICE.

Objectives

On completion of the seminar the professional will:
- Sell her services in a manner appropriate to the role and status of a professional adviser
- Identify the client's principle objectives and relate her services directly to the achievement of client goals
- Overcome totally and for all time any fear of failure or rejection
- Manage 'difficult' clients positively and build a uniquely con structive client relationship.

PROCESS CONSULTANCY SKILLS: 1 day

This seminar provides the consultant with proven process skills. It also gives a clear framework in which to identify and adopt the appropriate consultant roles along with the tools of the profession.

Objectives:

On completion the consultant will:
- Identify each stage of the consultancy assignment, clearly establish and fulfill the critical information needs and implement an economic and effective strategy.
- Facilitate comprehensive cultural and organisational changes which 'sticks'.
- Build ownership and commitment to her ideas.
- Analyse the degree of transferability of personal experience to the client environment and use proven process to bridge the credibility gap.
- Understand and adopt key role strategies to facilitate any assignment.

HOW TO SELECT, MANAGE AND CONTROL CONSULTANTS AND OTHER PROFESSIONALS: 1-2 days

Aimed directly at the needs of the manager or director who needsto make an informed choice;Whether to engage the services of a professional adviser and if so;
- How to select the best available at the most reasonable cost
- How to manage and control the intervention

This programme has been proven in practice to be an invaluable key to ensuring the economic use of professional advice and protecting the client, his investment and his organisation.

Objectives:
On completion of this workshop the client will:
- Establish when to use and when not to use external advisers.
- Identify the right professional adviser at the right price.
- Ensure effective control of the assignment is maintained at every stage.
- Ensure an appropriate and speedy return on the investment in professional services.

To offer flexibility to meet needs and enable clients to choose between an intensive information packed presentation, or a participative workshop environment all seminars are offered in-house in concise or full-length versions tailored to analysed need.

For more complete information you can talk to Tom or Trish Lambert on (0525) 713503 or write to
Beaumont Lambert International
51 Mill Lane
Greenfield
Bedfordshire
MK45 5DG